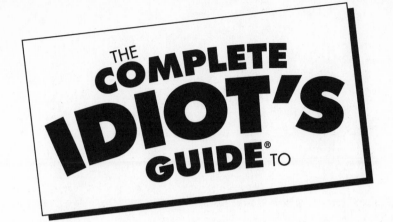

THE
COMPLETE
IDIOT'S
GUIDE® TO

Being
Vegetarian

Third Edition

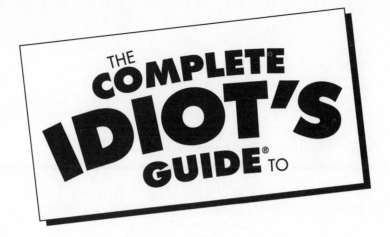

THE COMPLETE IDIOT'S GUIDE® TO

Being Vegetarian

Third Edition

by Frankie Avalon Wolfe, M.H., Ph.D.

ALPHA

A member of Penguin Group (USA) Inc.

ALPHA BOOKS

Published by the Penguin Group

Penguin Group (USA) Inc., 375 Hudson Street, New York, New York 10014, USA

Penguin Group (Canada), 90 Eglinton Avenue East, Suite 700, Toronto, Ontario M4P 2Y3, Canada (a division of Pearson Penguin Canada Inc.)

Penguin Books Ltd., 80 Strand, London WC2R 0RL, England

Penguin Ireland, 25 St. Stephen's Green, Dublin 2, Ireland (a division of Penguin Books Ltd.)

Penguin Group (Australia), 250 Camberwell Road, Camberwell, Victoria 3124, Australia (a division of Pearson Australia Group Pty. Ltd.)

Penguin Books India Pvt. Ltd., 11 Community Centre, Panchsheel Park, New Delhi—110 017, India

Penguin Group (NZ), 67 Apollo Drive, Rosedale, North Shore, Auckland 1311, New Zealand (a division of Pearson New Zealand Ltd.)

Penguin Books (South Africa) (Pty.) Ltd., 24 Sturdee Avenue, Rosebank, Johannesburg 2196, South Africa

Penguin Books Ltd., Registered Offices: 80 Strand, London WC2R 0RL, England

International Standard Book Number: 978-1-59257-682-1
Library of Congress Catalog Card Number: 2007930856

09   08   07   8   7   6   5   4   3   2   1

Interpretation of the printing code: The rightmost number of the first series of numbers is the year of the book's printing; the rightmost number of the second series of numbers is the number of the book's printing. For example, a printing code of 07-1 shows that the first printing occurred in 2007.

Printed in the United States of America

Note: This publication contains the opinions and ideas of its author. It is intended to provide helpful and informative material on the subject matter covered. It is sold with the understanding that the author and publisher are not engaged in rendering professional services in the book. If the reader requires personal assistance or advice, a competent professional should be consulted.

The author and publisher specifically disclaim any responsibility for any liability, loss, or risk, personal or otherwise, which is incurred as a consequence, directly or indirectly, of the use and application of any of the contents of this book.

Most Alpha books are available at special quantity discounts for bulk purchases for sales promotions, premiums, fundraising, or educational use. Special books, or book excerpts, can also be created to fit specific needs.

For details, write: Special Markets, Alpha Books, 375 Hudson Street, New York, NY 10014.

Publisher: *Marie Butler-Knight*
Editorial Director: *Mike Sanders*
Managing Editor: *Billy Fields*
Executive Editor: *Randy Ladenheim-Gil*
Senior Development Editor: *Christy Wagner*
Production Editor: *Megan Douglass*
Copy Editor: *Krista Hansing Editorial Services, Inc.*

Cartoonist: *Dan Rosandich*
Cover Designer: *Becky Harmon*
Book Designer: *Trina Wurst*
Indexer: *Johnna Vanhoose Dinse*
Layout: *Ayanna Lacey*
Proofreader: *John Etchison*

Contents at a Glance

Contents

Introduction

It doesn't take much *not* to eat meat, but it does takes a little creativity to have a satisfying meal without the use of meat—until you get into the swing of it, of course. This updated and expanded third edition of *The Complete Idiot's Guide to Being Vegetarian* not only serves to strengthen your desire to cut meat from your diet, but also gives you some satisfying, delicious, and nutritionally dense alternatives to try.

This book will not only help you eat less meat, it will make your transition simple, nutritious, and exciting for your taste buds—and hopefully present you with a few ideas you might not have thought about before. Whether you're interested in going completely vegan or choosing somewhere in the middle of the vegetarian diet scale, this book will get you cooking and experimenting with new flavors, and serve as your guide along the vegetarian path.

How This Book Is Organized

I've divided this book into six parts:

Part 1, "The Beef About Going Meatless," covers the benefits of giving up meat and gives you a framework on which to hang your vegetarian hat. This part is basically a condensed version of the entire second edition, and it's here that I pack all the basics on nutrition and weight management and provide a plan on how to go meatless when traveling or dining out. I also include a chapter on the animal and environmental impacts of why most vegetarians choose a gentler diet.

Part 2, "What's for Breakfast?" focuses on the importance of breakfast in the morning and how when and what types of foods you eat in the morning can affect the rest of your day. I also provide plenty of information on the foods generally considered breakfast foods: eggs, their pros and cons, eggless meals, and egg substitutes; nutrition-packed smoothies; and big breakfasts. And my editor's favorite part about this new edition: Part 2 is where the recipes begin!

Part 3, "What's for Lunch?" covers lunch foods of all kinds—sandwiches, salads, soups, and chowders. It also contains a chapter on kid-friendly foods, along with tips on nutrition for mothers-to-be, babies, and growing kids. Many yummy recipes are included at the end of each chapter—just be sure to save room for dinner in Part 4!

Part 4, "What's for Dinner?" gives you information on the many benefits of some of the main staples in a vegetarian's diet. Each chapter focuses on a different category, such as beans, grains, dark leafy greens, cruciferous veggies, and special, delicious main entrées that feature each. It also contains a chapter on comfort foods, for when you're craving that warm-fuzzy feeling inside.

In **Part 5, "International Main Dishes,"** you rediscover ethnic foods. I have included not only wonderful recipes, but also a little bit of "flavor" and tidbits from each of the areas covered, including Italy, the Mediterranean, India, Mexico, and Asia.

And finally, in **Part 6, "Holidays and Entertaining,"** I wrap up with all the tips, tricks, and yummy foods you can prepare for picnics, barbecues, parties, and even holiday dinners.

Extras

Throughout these pages, you'll see some boxes that give you even more information. Here's what to look for:

Veggie Soup for the Soul

Veggie Soup for the Soul boxes include statistical info or personal anecdotes I think you might find interesting.

Steer Clear

Steer Clear boxes are warnings that give you some information to watch out for or be aware of so you can make better choices.

Sprouts of Info

Sprouts of Info boxes include practical tips, tidbits, and miscellaneous pieces of information you can use to make your veggie life easier. When these are placed with a recipe, be sure to read them before shopping for or cooking that recipe because they can contain vital tips.

Lettuce Explain

Lettuce Explain boxes contain definitions for the terms that might not be familiar to a new vegetarian. (A full glossary of all these terms can be found in Appendix A.)

About the Recipes

In an attempt to make all the recipe ingredients read more uniform, I've left out repeating some things over and over (such as putting organic in front of every single ingredient). However, there are several important things I'd like all you veggie cooks to know. Please read this section before you shop or cook, as this information may answer some questions that could arise.

cooking oils   For the majority of the recipes, you'll see olive oil listed. One of my favorite discoveries is olive oil in a spray! You use less and it's so easy to grease a pan. But there are *many* different kinds of oils to use for cooking—all with their benefits and drawbacks. Please see Chapter 22 for different oils so you can choose to equip your kitchen with your faves. Feel free to substitute the cooking oil I have listed for the recipe with any of your favorite cooking oil(s).

dairy   When a recipe calls for any dairy product, please go *organic and hormone free* whenever possible. Many vegan cheese products are available made from soy, rice, and nuts for you to discover and experiment with. And for butter, I usually go for the unsalted.

eggs   I don't eat eggs, so all my recipes are eggless, and I list Ener-G Egg Replacer as the standard egg replacement product. There are several different types of egg replacers to try, so use your favorite. See Chapter 8 for more on egg replacements.

mayonnaise   My favorite eggless mayo is Vegenaise by Follow Your Heart made from grape seeds. See Chapter 10 for more on condiment choices.

herbs and spices   Use fresh whenever you like for herbs and spices. I mostly list dried unless specified fresh, because of the ease, except when used as a topping, of course. Use this general conversion as a general rule of thumb: 1 tablespoon fresh = 1 teaspoon dried.

produce   *Always* use *organic*, fresh produce when possible. This goes for frozen veggies, too. See Chapter 3 for more on produce.

peeling   The skins of most fruits and veggies contain extra nutrients, so I like to leave them. However, if you'd rather peel them, feel free! Also, use a good fruit/veggie wash when cleaning your fresh produce and wash them before cutting them to avoid contamination.

onions   Yellow, white, red—I usually specify only if the recipe calls for a red (purple) onion where it would make a bigger difference in the flavor. Yellow onions are sweeter, and whites tend to be hotter.

scallions/green onions   When cooking with scallions and green onions, use the white part only. I tend to use the subtle onion flavor of scallion greens as a topping, but I never use the leek greens. If you like more onion flavor in your foods, use the white parts *only* and save the greens as topping.

salt   When I add salt to a recipe, I generally use sea salt because it's natural and contains more nutrients than the processed table salt. You can also use dried kelp powder as a salt substitute, which is also rich in iodine.

tofu   Regular tofu is slightly different from silken in texture, and in my recipes I call for regular tofu without specifying "regular." Regular tofu is generally found in the chilled produce section, and is packed in water or sometimes vacuum packed and has a relatively short expiration date. Silken tofu is generally found on the inner aisles of the grocery store, many times with Asian foods, is not water packed, and has a long shelf life. Silken may be better for baking and smoothies or egg recipes.

canned goods   Some cans of broth or beans are 15 ounces, some are 14.25 ounces, and some are 14.5 ounces. For clarity, I've called for a standard 15-ounce can. And I made all small can sizes equal 6 ounces. These would be the small cans that hold diced green chilies, tomato paste, or sliced water chestnuts. Sometimes you'll find these in 4- to 7-ounce cans, depending on brand and what your store carries; those are fine to use in the recipes. The same goes for the 15-ounce cans. A few ounces here and there, for my recipes anyway, won't make a difference!

Acknowledgments

No book is written without a number of people who make contributions, either emotionally to the author or in some other aspect by adding their time, opinions, or words of wisdom. Thank you, Townsend, for all your unselfish support with this and all my books, including your photography skills, your cooking and kitchen input, and your bravery for sampling a few of my recipes that contain ingredients I know you don't like! Your tastes have come a long way, and I look forward to enjoying veggie meals with you for the rest of my life.

Special thanks to Executive Editor Randy Ladenheim-Gil at Alpha for your continued support and confidence. Because of your input on the wants and needs of the target audience for this book, you helped me make this a greatly improved version. Christy Wagner, as always, you are the queen of editing!

To my long-time forever friend, Glenn Beckmann in Alaska, your artistic talents continue on in this book—thank you! And thank you, Sherry Trenkle, for sharing some great recipes I modified for this book, and for all the great meals you've made and served in the past. You showed me how cooking for others is about love.

And as always, love and thanks to my very bestest friends, who I consider family, for always being there to help me keep the balance between work and play. And my grandma Fran, who I am so grateful for; and Connie and Bob, who are unconditional in their love …. I need and appreciate all of you. Your love, graciousness, and communication give me comfort and strength to keep producing. I hope I give back to you just a fraction of what you give me. (Although you *still* have to keep buying my books!)

Special Thanks to the Technical Reviewer

The recipes in *The Complete Idiot's Guide to Being Vegetarian, Third Edition*, were reviewed by an expert who double-checked the accuracy of what you'll learn here, to help us ensure that they give you everything you need to know about making delicious vegetarian food at home. Special thanks are extended to Ellen Brown.

Ellen is the founding food editor of *USA Today* and the author of more than a baker's dozen cookbooks, including the IACP–winning *Gourmet Gazelle Cookbook* and six *Complete Idiot's Guides*, including *The Complete Idiot's Guide to Slow Cooker Cooking, Second Edition*, and *The Complete Idiot's Guide to Cooking Substitutions*.

Trademarks

All terms mentioned in this book that are known to be or are suspected of being trademarks or service marks have been appropriately capitalized. Alpha Books and Penguin Group (USA) Inc. cannot attest to the accuracy of this information. Use of a term in this book should not be regarded as affecting the validity of any trademark or service mark.

Part 1

The Beef About
Going Meatless

The reasons why folks go vegetarian are as varied as the people themselves, but in Part 1, I share some common rationale people cite for omitting meat from their diets. Along the way, I give you tips on nutrition and ideas on transitioning to and staying with a vegetarian diet and lifestyle. I also give you a tour of the health food store, help you stock your vegetarian kitchen, introduce you to a variety of meat substitutes, warn you about some dining-out traps, and share tips on weight management.

Also in these pages, you learn about the positive impact your food choices make on the animals, the earth, and the world. Overall, Part 1 should make you feel good about eating your veggies.

Nutrition and the Meatless Diet

In This Chapter

◆ Just because it's meatless doesn't mean it's tasteless

◆ Busting the protein myths

◆ Understanding why some fats are essential

◆ Do you know what your body is made of?

◆ The general benefits of vegetarian fare

> A human can be healthy without killing animals for food. Therefore if he eats meat he participates in taking animal life merely for the sake of his appetite.
>
> —Leo Tolstoy

Vegetarians have different reasons for why they reached the decision to go meatless. For some, it's health reasons. For others, it's compassion for animals. And just as some people don't understand vegetarians' reasoning for eliminating meat, just as many proclaim that a vegetarian diet isn't a healthful diet. The fact is, it has been proven, undeniably, that vegetarians enjoy better health than their meat-eating counterparts. You *can* sustain your convictions for a lifetime in a sound, fit, nutritionally healthy body *and* be able to enjoy a variety of delicious, satisfying foods. And who better than you to serve as an example that vegetarians are conscious, intelligent people, concerned enough about themselves, the plight of animals, and the planet that they choose a diet that is deliberate, informed, balanced, delicious, and healthful? Eliminating meat can help you on your way to new, positive changes in your life, your health, your outlook, and your purpose.

This chapter gives you the lowdown on the nutritional main topics new vegetarians should know and shows you just how interesting—and delicious—your new diet can be!

Defining *Meatless*

I recently heard a comedian say, "My girlfriend calls herself a vegetarian, but she eats chicken sometimes and eggs and cheese and fish … I don't call that a vegetarian— I call that a liar!" Well, maybe not a liar, but folks define *vegetarian* in many different ways. As a loose interpretation, *vegetarian* defines someone whose primary diet is based on vegetation. Anything you add to the diet can be added to the term *vegetarian*, such as *lacto* (for dairy) vegetarian.

The following table outlines the many variations of a mostly plant-based diet so you can "find yourself" in the vegetarian spectrum. (Even if you're not a vegetarian, this table might come in handy if you need to cook for one. Be sure to find out what type of vegetarian you'll be serving so you can understand what *not* to cook.)

Sprouts of Info _____

I'm a lacto vegetarian, so the recipes I share in this book (starting in Chapter 7) are all meat, fish, foul, and egg free, but not all are dairy free. Strict vegetarians can substitute dairy-free products in most of my lacto vegetarian recipes, and vegans can use substitutes such as stevia, molasses, or maple syrup for any recipes containing honey or sugar.

Specialized Diets

Type of Diet	What They *Don't* Eat	What They *Do* Eat
Lacto ovo vegetarian	animal flesh or seafood	eggs, dairy, and plant foods
Ovo vegetarian	animal flesh, dairy	eggs and plant foods
Lacto vegetarian	animal flesh, eggs	dairy and plant foods
Pollo vegetarian	seafood, animal flesh	chicken and plant foods
Pesco pollo vegetarian	animal flesh	fish, poultry, and plant foods
Pseudo vegetarian or semivegetarian	reduced meat consumption	mostly plant foods, dairy, eggs, and occasional meats
Pescatarian or pesco vegetarian	animal flesh, fowl	fish and plant foods, eggs, dairy
Strict vegetarian	animal flesh, seafood, dairy, eggs	plant foods, honey
Fruitarian	animal flesh, seafood, dairy, eggs	fruits and vegetables that do not kill the plant when they're harvested, such as apples
Vegan	animal flesh, seafood, dairy, eggs, honey, any product derived from an animal, such as leather, wool, silk, gelatin, or lanolin	plant foods
Macrobiotic diet	any denatured product (processed food, refined flour, sugar), microwaved food, foods cooked on electric stoves, most animal flesh	whole grains, lightly steamed vegetables, some fresh seafood
Breatharian	food	air

Now let's look at the benefits of plant-based foods, and later you'll see the vegetarian food pyramid to see how you'll get all your nutrition.

Meatless Doesn't Mean "Tasteless"

Lasagna, spaghetti, burritos, enchiladas, casseroles, stews, chili, burgers, pizza, nachos, stir-fries, sandwiches, soups, salads, and pot pies … does this sound like what a vegetarian eats? You betcha! As you'll see, *meatless* does not mean "tasteless," nor will you starve on a diet that doesn't include meat.

> **Veggie Soup for the Soul**
>
> The Vegetarian Resource Group estimates that in 2006, more than 4.7 million adults in the United States were vegetarians. And that figure doesn't include those adults who choose vegetarian fare at least some of the time, estimated to be about 30 to 40 percent of the population.

Because of the increasing demand for more healthful food choices, including meatless items, big food corporations have been buying up the smaller health food manufacturers and making these items more readily available. Thanks to this trend, you'll also see the more mainstream restaurant chains offering more veggie choices. Even if you can't find ready-made vegetarian dishes, almost any dish you can think of that contains meat can be made to be just as tasty with the meat removed. Even restaurant owners are finding value in the fact that they can serve meatless dishes without purchasing any new ingredients.

For example, think about a taco salad. Most taco salads contain ground beef, but as long as the restaurant serves vegetarian beans, all you have to do is ask for no meat and extra beans, and you have a satisfying taco salad with corn chips, beans, cheese, lettuce, salsa, sour cream, guacamole, jalapeños, tomatoes, and onions. With all those ingredients, you probably won't even miss the beef! Plus, a veggie taco salad gives you plenty of protein, carbohydrates, essential fats, and fiber and can fill you up for the rest of the day. The salsa and tomatoes provide vitamin C, which also helps you to absorb the natural iron content in the meal. And you'll be getting servings of grains, legumes, dairy products, and vegetables all in one entrée!

So no doubt about it, *meatless* doesn't mean "tasteless," nor does it mean "bland," "nutritionally imbalanced," or "unhealthful."

If I've already whetted your appetite for food, you can turn to the index of recipes in the back of the book and look up something good to whip up tonight. If you're practicing restraint and sticking with me here, next we dig into the specifics of nutrition for the meatless eater.

The Power of Protein

Most of us connect *protein* with "strength," "muscle," "stamina," and, of course, "meat." That's largely because of the programming we received early in school and on TV that told us that meat is the only source of protein. But vegetarians can and do get enough protein to survive and even to grow up big and strong. In fact, some of the world's most powerful animals—gorillas, elephants, and some types of whale—are strict vegetarians. See? You don't need protein from animal sources to build a strong, healthy body!

How Much Protein Do You Need?

The U.S. Department of Agriculture's (USDA) recommended daily allowances (RDAs) for protein are listed in the following table.

The USDAs RDAs for Protein

Age and/or Gender	Grams Protein Daily
Infants (0 to 6 months)	13
Infants (6 months to 1 year)	14
Toddlers (1 to 3 years)	16
Children (4 to 6 years)	24
Children (7 to 10 years)	28
Preteen male (11 to 14 years)	45
Preteen female (11 to 14 years)	46
Female teenager (15 to 18 years)	44
Male teenager (15 to 18 years)	59
Female adult, healthy, average size (19 to 50+ years)	46 to 50
Female, pregnant	60
Female, nursing	62 to 65
Male adult, healthy, average size (19 to 50+ years)	58 to 63

Remember, though, that there's really no such thing as "average," or one right amount for everyone, because, biochemically, we are all individuals whose needs depend on a variety of factors. These figures give you some general guidelines to follow, but you'll want to adjust them for your lifestyle, activity level, and state of health.

Adult protein needs can be calculated as .8 grams per kilogram or .36 grams per pound body weight. So for example, if you are 140 pounds, you would need about 50 grams protein each day. Requirements are much lower for infants, of course, and higher for pregnant women.

You Complete Me

You may have heard that vegetarians get only *incomplete proteins* because they don't eat meat. An incomplete protein lacks one or more of the *essential amino acids*. Incomplete proteins mostly come from plant sources; however, not all plants are lacking in all the essential aminos, and all plant foods vary in which aminos they do have present. Any diet that contains a mixture or variety of foods completes your proteins. The only way you wouldn't get enough protein is if you ate a mono-diet (one type of food, such as rice, over a long period of time).

Lettuce Explain

An **incomplete protein** is a protein that lacks one or more of the essential amino acids. A *complete protein* contains all the essential amino acids and is found in some plant foods, such as soybeans, and in animal products. **Essential amino acids** are amino acids that cannot be manufactured by the body and need to be supplied in the diet. They are lysine, isolecine, leucine, methionine, phenylalanine, thereonine, tryptophan, valine, and histidine.

Here's a short list of some vegan foods, along with their protein content in grams (g):

1 cup cooked black beans	13 g
1 medium-size potato	4 g
8 oz. firm tofu	22 g
1 cup tempeh	41 g
1 bagel	9 g
½ cup sunflower seeds	12 g

But you weren't created with a calculator in one hand to measure the food value of every item going into your body, so you shouldn't expect to have to make eating every meal fit into an algebraic equation. There really are only two rules you need to remember to get what you need from your meatless diet:

♦ Eat enough.

♦ Eat a variety of foods.

That's all there is to it! Now that the protein myth has been laid to rest, let's talk about some other nutrients essential to your good health.

Sprouts of Info

A peanut butter and jelly sandwich on whole-wheat bread provides a nutritionally complete protein combination. However, you don't need to eat these two together in one meal for your body to complete the protein. If you eat a handful of peanuts in the afternoon and a piece of whole-wheat toast later, your body will figure it out.

What Your Body Is Made Of

Your body is made up of various minerals and vitamins, and your organs favor certain nutrients for health. When there's a dietary deficiency of any of these nutrients, the body picks up what it needs from your organs. This is an important factor in staying conscious of nutrition; by learning what your major organs are made of, you better understand what type of nutrients you need to keep them healthy.

The following table lists some of the elements that comprise your body—that big mineral and vitamin warehouse, made of the same items found in nature.

What the Body Is Made Of

Element	Major Organ	Plant Source (Examples)
Calcium	bones, teeth	sesame seeds
Chlorine	digestive tract	pineapple
Fluorine	teeth, bones	brussels sprouts
Iodine	thyroid gland	seaweed
Iron	liver, blood, bone marrow	black cherries
Lecithin	semen, nervous system	soybeans
Magnesium	muscles (relaxer)	wheat germ

continues

What the Body Is Made Of   (continued)

Element	Major Organ	Plant Source (Examples)
Phosphorus	bones, brain, nerves	almonds
Potassium	muscles (heart)	blackberries
Silicon	skin, nails, hair, glands, nerves	barley
Sodium	joints, stomach lining	celery
Sulfur	brain, nerves, bowel, liver	garlic
Zinc	eyes, prostate, thyroid, pancreas, liver, kidneys, skin, hair, nails	pumpkin seeds

Pyramid Schemes

Now let's take a look at the food pyramids for strict vegetarians, or those who eat no animal products, and nonstrict vegetarians, or those who occasionally consume some dairy and sometimes egg—also called a lacto (dairy) or ovo (egg) vegetarian.

The strict vegetarian pyramid doesn't contain optional items such as alcohol, and it excludes dairy and eggs. Still, you have to admit it looks pretty fulfilling.

The basic food pyramid a strict vegetarian or a vegan lives by.

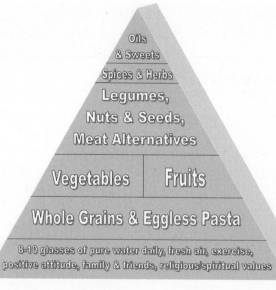

Oils
& Sweets

Spices & Herbs

Legumes,
Nuts & Seeds,
Meat Alternatives

Vegetables   Fruits

Whole Grains & Eggless Pasta

8-10 glasses of pure water daily, fresh air, exercise,
positive attitude, family & friends, religious/spiritual values

The pyramid for nonstrict vegetarians allows optional eggs and dairy. Here's what the lacto ovo vegetarian food pyramid looks like, following the ADA guidelines:

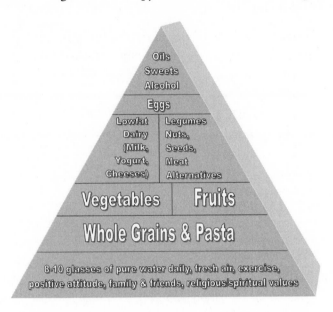

A food pyramid with options for the not-so-strict, or lacto ovo, vegetarian. Keeping a balance is the key.

How much of all these good foods are you supposed to eat for nutritional balance and health? The following table helps orient you on what makes up a serving size and how many of these servings you should be getting each day.

Daily Food Guide for Vegetarians

Food Group	Serving Size	What Makes Up a Serving?
Whole grains, bread, cereals, pasta	6 or more	1 ounce ready-to-eat cereal; 1 cup dry cereal; 1 slice of bread; $1/_2$ bagel, bun, or muffin; $1/_2$ cup cooked pasta or grain
Vegetables	4 or more	1 cup raw or $1/_2$ cup cooked vegetables
Legumes, nuts, seeds, meat alternatives (like tofu)	2 to 3	4 ounces tofu or tempeh; $1/_2$ cup cooked beans; 8 ounces soy milk; 2 tablespoons nut butter
Fruit	3 or more	1 piece fresh fruit; $3/_4$ cup fruit juice

continues

Daily Food Guide for Vegetarians   (continued)

Food Group	Serving Size	What Makes Up a Serving?
Dairy (optional)	up to 3	low-fat dairy is suggested; 1 cup skim milk; 1 cup yogurt; 1½ ounces cheese
Eggs (optional)	up to 3 to 4 per week	1 egg or 2 egg whites
Fats, oils, sweets, salt, and alcohol	use very sparingly	

Essential Nutrition

Everyone is born with various genetic weaknesses, we all live very different lifestyles, and everyone's body has different requirements for differing nutrients. For instance, your body uses up more of the B complex vitamins when you are under stress. Today, even those who eat the most healthful foods still require some form of nutritional supplementation either on a regular basis or for additional aid during occasional health challenges.

How much and what types of supplements you use are as individual as you are. Please work with a guide trained in nutrition, herbs, and natural health to come up with a game plan for your specific supplementation program.

Let's take a look at meatless sources, for both food and supplements, that help you get all the nutrients you need.

Essential Fats

These days, it's all about cutting out fat from the diet. But what you might not realize is that some dietary fats are good for you. At least two of them are essential to your health—in fact, that's what they're called: *essential fatty acids* (*EFAs*). Your body cannot produce EFAs on its own, so they must be provided in the diet. The good news is that these fatty acids are found in a variety of nuts, seeds, fruits, and vegetables, as well as in vegetarian supplements.

Lettuce Explain

Essential fatty acids (EFAs) are fatty acids that are not manufactured by the body but are essential to its proper functioning. Essential fatty acids are the building blocks for hormones, cell membranes, and various chemical messengers.

You really only need to concern yourself with getting two of these fatty acids: alpha linolenic acid, an omega-3 fatty acid, and linoleic acid, an omega-6 fatty acid. When you supply both of these to your body, it can then synthesize the other *conditionally essential* fatty acids on its own. (Isn't the body amazing?) If either of these two EFAs is missing in the diet, their by-products may then become conditionally essential in the diet. This means that sometimes the body cannot make enough for your needs.

Veggie Soup for the Soul

Omega-3s and omega-6s include groups of essential fatty acids with differing chemical makeup. If you supplement with essential fatty acids, be sure you provide a balance. Not all supplements tell you which is which, so here's the breakdown: the omega-3 group contains alpha-linolenic acid (LNA; essential), eicosapentaenoic acid (EPA), and docosahexaenoic acid (DHA). The omega-6 group includes linoleic acid (essential), gamma-linolenic acid (GLA), and arachidonic acid. Get some of each.

Essential fatty acids provide the following general health benefits:

◆ Support the immune system

◆ Balance body chemistry

◆ Improve blood circulation and vascular dilation

◆ Protect against heart disease

◆ Balance hormones and eicosanoid (EPA) production

◆ Regulate cholesterol levels

◆ Regulate blood clotting, blood pressure, and heart rate

The essential and conditionally essential fatty acids have been used therapeutically for overcoming some of these problems:

◆ Allergies

◆ Arthritis

◆ Asthma

◆ Cancer

◆ Eczema

◆ Glaucoma

◆ Hair health

◆ Headaches

◆ Heart disease

◆ High blood pressure

- Hyperactivity
- Infertility
- Inflammation
- Low infant IQ
- Lupus

- Menstrual difficulty
- Migraines
- Premenstrual syndrome
- Skin health

> **Sprouts of Info**
>
> Monounsaturated fatty acids, or omega-9 fatty acids, are also very important and are good for the skin and circulatory system. They're even used to help prevent cancer. Good sources include olive oil, peanut oil, nuts, and avocados.

See? We do need fats after all! However, do be wary of one very bad fat known as *trans fat*, seen on fried food, commercial snack, and most margarine labels as *hydrogenated* or *partially hydrogenated* oils. These oils can be found in all deep-fried foods, as heating oils to high temperatures causes this chemical change. Trans fats are not found in significant amounts in nature except in meat and dairy products. The body can't use them properly, and they interfere with production of good fatty acids, cell membranes, and even brain development. Pregnant women should avoid trans fats.

The following table shows how you, as a non-meat-eater, can get the fatty acids you need. If you're supplementing with omega-3 fatty acids, be sure to balance them with supplements or foods containing omega-6s.

Meat-Free Essential Fatty Acid Sources

Source	Rich In
Almonds and their oil	omega-6s
Black current oil	omega-6s
Borage oil	omega-6s
Canola oil	omega-3s and 6s
Cod liver oil	omega-3s
Corn oil	omega-6s
Dark-fleshed fish	omega-3s
Egg yolks	omega-3s
Evening primrose oil	omega-6s

Source	Rich In
Fish oil lipids	omega-3s
Flaxseed oil	omega-3s
Peanuts and their oil	omega-6s
Safflower oil	omega-6s
Soybeans and their oil	omega-3s and 6s
Sunflower seeds and their oil	omega-6s
Walnuts and their oil	omega-3s and 6s
Wheat germ oil	omega-3s and 6s

Veggie Soup for the Soul

Lecithin (from soybeans), although often mistakenly thought of as an essential fatty acid, is manufactured in the body and is therefore not called "essential." However, it is essential in the sense of being necessary to the health of your nervous and circulatory systems. Lecithin is a well-known brain food and is used as a supplement along with extra fiber in the diet to help lower cholesterol. It even helps emulsify dietary fat.

B_{12} and Be a Vegetarian

Vitamin B_{12}, one of the many B vitamins, is critical for the metabolism of every cell in the body, especially the bone marrow, GI tract, and nervous tissue. B_{12} is created in the intestinal system but also must be supplied in the diet. B_{12} may eliminate fatigue, prevent Alzheimer's, and support memory and thinking … now what was I saying?

Oh, right, if you don't receive enough B_{12}, you can eventually use up your body's supplies, which can lead to health problems, including headaches, bruising, depression, fatigue, anemia, and irritability. You can go several years without ingesting any B_{12} before deficiency symptoms show up.

B_{12} (cobalamin) is used therapeutically to reduce or reverse the following:

◆ Fatigue

◆ Nervous irritability

◆ Pernicious anemia

Sprouts of Info

All B vitamins are important, especially for the brain. Do you remember your dreams? Insomniacs and those with no dream recall are commonly deficient in vitamin B_6 and/or zinc. If you choose to supplement, keep in mind that too much zinc or B_6 is not better than too little. Always follow the recommended dose or work with a practitioner who can guide you.

- Insomnia
- Stress
- Mental illness
- Multiple sclerosis
- Poor memory
- Neuritis
- And many other nervous system ailments

All the B vitamins work together, and all are important. For example, B_9 (also called folate or folic acid), works with B_{12} to help prevent heart disease and stroke by lowering homocystine levels. B_6 can help you sleep. B_{10} would complete my bingo card and I'd win $500! But seriously, a B-complex vitamin can be a helpful supplement to almost all diets.

B_{12} is produced by bacteria and is naturally found in animal products as well as some cooked sea vegetables. However, this doesn't necessarily mean that a deficiency is strictly a vegetarian problem. Most reported B_{12} deficiencies occur because of the digestive system's inability to absorb the vitamin or a lack of a carrier protein called *intrinsic factor.* Sometimes antacids or laxatives can inhibit the absorption of the vitamin. If you are unable to absorb B_{12}, it can be taken by intramuscular injection or through sublingual (under the tongue) supplementation. See your nutritionally oriented practitioner for guidance.

Nature's Garden

These strictly vegetarian foods from nature's garden have been shown to contain vitamin B_{12} and should be included in any diet:

- Alfalfa, with more in fresh than dried
- Algae, usually sold in nutritional supplements such as spirulina and green drinks
- Bee pollen

◆ Legume sprouts such as mung beans and lentils

◆ Nutritional yeast (check labels)

◆ Rice polishings

◆ Sea vegetables such as kelp, nori, and kombu

Bee pollen and nutritional yeast are naturally occurring sources of B_{12} for many vegetarians, although these are unacceptable sources for some vegans.

Veggie Soup for the Soul

Cyanocobalamin is the usable part of the B_{12} vitamin. Other forms of B_{12} are called analogs, and scientists believe that the analogs could interfere with the useful cyanocobalamin, leading to a deficiency. Even if your blood results show normal levels of B_{12}, you still could have an absorption problem. If you really think it could be a problem, you can ask your doctor for a methylmalonic acid (MMA) blood or urine test. Methylmalonic acid test is the most specific test for B_{12} status because B_{12} is the only necessary co-enzyme needed to keep MMA levels low. If they are high, B_{12} status is poor. At that point you can work with your doctor to help your absorption improve or consider injections.

The Well-Nourished Vegetarian

Most vegetarians are pretty well nourished due to the variety of fresh foods they eat, but strict vegetarians especially can benefit from herbal supplementation, if only for a little extra nutrition boost to ensure their diets are well rounded.

The following table gives you a list of the most common elements missing in the average American diet, along with herbal sources of B_{12} and iron, which tend to be a concern for those on strict vegetarian or vegan diets.

Common Elements Lacking in Most American Diets

Element	Herbal Source	Vegetarian Food Source	Things That Deplete This Element	Purpose
Calcium	alfalfa, buchu, chamomile, dandelion,	cashews, seeds, carrots, carrot juice, broccoli, chickweed, yogurt, horsetail, oatstraw, parsley, sprouts	coffee, salt, sugar, high animal protein diet, sesame seeds, soda, excessive phosphorus, oxalic acid	bones, structural system; teeth; bone and skin mending joints; stomach acid; buffer
Silicon	horsetail, alfalfa, dandelion, yucca, barley juice, cornsilk, skullcap, gotu kola, chlorophyll	asparagus, leaf lettuce, cauliflower, apricots, apples, wild rice, barley, nuts, seeds	fats, starches, sugar	hair luster and strength; more youthful-looking skin; prevents cracking skin and nails
Iodine	kelp, dulse, black walnut, spirulina	seaweed, sea fish (whitefish with fins and scales), garlic, onions, eggplant, mushrooms, potatoes	radiation from tv, x-rays, power lines, stimulants such as caffeine and ephedra	feeds thyroid gland, which controls weight, metabolism, energy levels
Sodium	hydrangea, alfalfa, safflower, rosehips, peppermint, parsley, licorice	celery, cucumbers, strawberries, goat milk and whey, okra, dandelion, sesame seeds, swiss and roquefort cheeses, raisins, red cabbage, black mission figs, watercress	salt, antacids, prescription diuretics	can prevent stomach disturbance or joint distress; dissolves hard calcium build-up in the body; adds flexibility

Element	Herbal Source	Vegetarian Food Source	Things That Deplete This Element	Purpose
Potassium	kelp, parsley, irish moss, ginger, peach bark, licorice, horsetail, capsicum	bananas, raisins, potato peel broth, parsley tea, bitter greens, almonds, whole grains	red meat, coffee, alcohol, laxatives, diuretics, salt, sugar	helps regulate water retention; muscle cramps, or spasms; muscular fatigue; hypertension; hardening of the arteries
Iron	yellow dock, capsicum, butcher's broom, kelp, red beet root, red raspberry leaves, chickweed, nettle, mullein leaves, dong quai	black cherries, blackberries, dried fruits, strawberry juice, dark leafy greens, spinach, black strap molasses	food additives, coffee, black tea, excessive phosphorous, food preservatives	necessary for hemoglobin production; a remedy for anemia; improves protein assimilation; mental vitality; circulation; liver and kidney functions; promotes vitality
B_{12}	alfalfa, ginseng, bee pollen, comfrey, spirulina, dandelion	sea vegetables, nutritional yeast, miso	junk food	essential for healthy gastrointestinal tract; formation of blood cells; supports nervous system; healthy skin and mucus membranes

Now that you know how well nourished and fulfilled vegetarians are, in the next chapter, I help you set up a plan for going meatless!

The Least You Need to Know

◆ Meatless choices are becoming more available to everyone.

◆ Vegetarians tend to eat a variety of foods, which makes for a flavorful, nutritious, and interesting diet.

◆ Vegetarians who eat a variety of foods get all the protein they need to maintain good health.

◆ B_{12} is most commonly found in animal products. It can be supplied in trace amounts in the vegan diet by alfalfa and other herbs, but a synthetic vitamin supplement is generally the best insurance against deficiency.

◆ It is important to eat foods rich in healthful essential fatty acids and avoid trans-fatty acids.

Chapter 2

The First Bite—
Where's the Beef?

In This Chapter

◆ Create your own plan to go meatless

◆ Implement your replacement diet

◆ Trick your household into enjoying a vegetarian meal!

◆ Change your taste buds

◆ Turn vegetables into meat look-alikes

You've got this new vegetarian diet, new foods to try, and old foods to replace in your diet. Trying to come up with a plan for moving forward can get overwhelming. Relax. You've come to the right place, because this is the chapter where I show you how to implement your new veggie diet. Parts of this chapter are abstract; I share ideas and give you thoughts to ponder to help you find yourself in the garden of sprouting vegetarianism. Changing your diet to meatless is going to be like anything else you do—you have to do it *your* way. But we have some fun discussing some different ways to approach it.

For those who desire a concrete, systematic way of making the transition to meatless, I outline a plan and we walk through it together. Then I sum it up in a reference table at the end of the chapter so you have a handy place to go for support. I also provide some ideas about making your new diet more fun—not only for you, but for those around you. Let's take a look at how to make this all work.

One Bite at a Time

How do you eat a 2,000-pound tofu "cow"? One bite at a time, of course! And for many people, including you perhaps, this is the best way to approach any big change in your life. Going slowly helps make any change permanent.

Sprouts of Info

You can make more of a psychological impact if you make your elimination of animal flesh a memorable celebration. This celebration makes your choice seem more significant, and really, to you, going meatless is significant because it can mean a longer, healthier life.

The first question you might want to ask yourself is, what would make the biggest impact on your diet if you eliminated it? Do you eat a lot of red meat? What about chicken, fish, cheese, lamb, or eggs? It wouldn't, for instance, make much difference to most people if they decided to put their foot down and give up rhino nuggets. Think about what you eat most of the time. If you draw a blank, you need to get more in touch with your diet. I suggest you keep a food diary for a while to see what you eat most often. When you can pinpoint a certain animal product as being a big part of your diet, eliminate that one first.

Celebrate for Impact!

Food poisoning from eating undercooked chicken or "bad fish" is a strong motivator for many people to give up a certain animal after it has made them sick. But you don't have to wait for food poisioning! Instead, make a positive emotional impact on yourself by doing something outrageous with the commencement of your new diet. Following are some examples of what you could do to celebrate ending the consumption of a certain animal:

- Start a fund for farm animal abuse specifically for the animal you discontinue eating.

- Post cute, fluffy, doe-eyed close-up photos of the baby animal on your refrigerator and circle it with the "no" symbol.

◆ Do a little dancing ritual around a statue of the animal while singing "Old MacDonald had a farm, E.I.E.I.O.," giving special attention to the sounds of the animal you're giving up eating. (You might want to keep the shades drawn while you perform this one!)

◆ The next time you get invited to a costume party or Halloween rolls around, dress up as your animal.

◆ Give a lecture, write an article or a book, or build a website dedicated to the qualities of the animal and its purpose (besides serving as food) on this earth.

◆ Research your religion's stance on diet, and find out the official stance, if any, on this particular animal.

◆ Invent a new food that tastes just like the animal you're giving up. (Maybe you could be a little creative here and try *not* to make it taste just like chicken.)

Veggie Soup for the Soul

Think of someone who has inspired you to eat less meat. Was this person shouting "Save the cows!" outside a burger joint? Was it a vegetarian who appeared friendly, attractive, in shape, active, and bright-eyed and made you wonder if you might look that good if you went meatless? I bet I can guess your response. Just for fun, visit Vegetarian Pages at www.veg.org. This site has a huge list of famous vegetarians!

Think about why you want to go on this new diet, and choose your changes carefully because you want to make it last. Maybe you're making this dietary change for your health and in consideration of the people who care about you, so you can continue to run, play, walk, talk, and thrive with them until your time comes.

But if that's not enough motivation for you, you'll find out in later chapters how your choice to give up meat affects all sorts of other things in the world. And that's something to feel good about, too!

Meatless Tuesdays

Still some skeptics out there? All right, let's try an easier approach. Instead of choosing one animal to eliminate at a time, why not work on choosing a day of the week on which you eat no animal flesh at all? Let's say that every Tuesday you have a straight vegetarian meal for breakfast, lunch, dinner, and even snacks.

Make it fun. Tuesday is your day to experiment with this new way of eating. Look forward to it. Start planning on Monday night. Imagine all the animal fat oozing from your veins in excitement. You'll be giving your digestive system, heart, veins, kidneys, and liver all a big break for a whole day! Do this every week, and when it feels right, make Wednesday vegetarian, too.

Do What Works for You

Going vegetarian is a personal choice, and your route to eating meatless is personal, too, so do whatever feels right to make the transition easier for you. If eliminating a certain animal product is difficult at first, and if Meatless Tuesday doesn't work for you, try a variation of the approaches. If you're a slow starter, you could choose an animal you eat daily—pork, for example—and eliminate all pork products from your diet only one day a week. As you can, work your way up from there: once per week for a week or two, then twice a week, and so on, until you can check pork off your "Don't Eat Anymore" list.

> **Sprouts of Info**
>
> When transitioning from a daily meat-based to a plant-based diet, you might need to eat more than usual to be satisfied enough not to miss meat. Add some fat to your meals, like avocado or olive oil. Fats turn on you satiety buttons in your body, making you feel full faster.

Whichever way you choose, set up a plan to make a shift to the next level of your diet. In other words, if you choose to go vegetarian once a week, do that for two weeks and then move up to twice a week for two weeks, and so on. Set a target date when you are going to be a pure vegetarian (or the vegetarian type of your choice). Mark that date on your calendar—the day you can proclaim yourself vegetarian!

Twelve Weeks to Meat Free

Behavioral psychologists tell us that it takes a consistent amount of time—about 12 weeks—of doing something repeatedly before it becomes habitual. Humans are creatures of habit, so why not make some new meatless ones?

The following two tables walk you through a 12-week transitional period and help you switch to a meatless diet. Decide which of the following statements matches your intentions, and then, if you're ready, skip to the appropriate table to get started:

◆ *I would like to transition to a vegetarian diet one day per week.* Skip to the "Twelve Steps for Going Meatless" table for your game plan.

◆ *I want to start by eliminating one main animal product at a time.* Skip to "The Meat-Free Transition Diet, Per Animal" table.

Twelve Steps for Going Meatless

			Food Suggestions for …		Optional
Week(s)	Day	Breakfast	Lunch	Dinner	Snack
1, 2	Mondays	fruit and soy yogurt smoothie	hummus and veggie pita wrap and chips	lentil loaf, mashed potatoes, and green vegetable	fruit
3, 4	Add Tuesdays	tofu scrambler and hash browns	veggie chili and cornbread	Indian Dinner*	Celery sticks with nut butter
5, 6	Add Wednesdays	breakfast burrito (leftover tofu scrambler wrapped in wheat tortilla)	baked potato covered with salsa and vanilla soy yogurt	Mediterranean Meal*	carrot sticks with spinach and artichoke dip
7, 8	Add Thursdays	bowl of oatmeal with raisins and rice milk	large Greek-style salad	Spaghetti Squash and Falafel Balls*	wild rice sticks
9, 10	Add Fridays	carrot juice and a handful of raw cashews	veggie soup, fresh spring salad, and wild rice sticks	Vegetarian Lasagna*	popcorn sprinkled with yeast flakes and tamari
11, 12	Add Saturdays	tofu French toast with Boca sausage patties	Baked sweet potato and corn chowder	Veggie Pizza*	dried fruit and nuts
Full-time vegetarian	Add Sundays	potato veggie scrambler covered with melted soy cheese	black bean burger with guacamole dressing and french fries	Mexican Dinner*	smoothie

Find recipes for these foods in later chapters!

The Meat-Free Transition Diet, Per Animal

Week(s)	Animal or Product to Eliminate	Replacements
1, 2	red meat	vegetarian burgers, fried tempeh falafel balls, tofu balls, textured vegetable proteins, lentil loaf, tempeh sloppy joes (Tofu can be made in many ways to resemble and taste like beef.)
3, 4	pork	tofu pups; veggie sausage patties; fake bacon cubes; marinated, breaded, and fried tofu; fake pepperoni products; fake bacon bits
5, 6	poultry (turkey, chicken, duck, etc.)	stir-fries with tofu strips, nonchicken nuggets, tofu cordon blue (The good news about tofu is that it can be made to taste like anything, and the chicken taste isn't hard to copy. Use vegetable bullion cubes to replace chicken stock.)
7, 8	fish and seafood	veggie sushi (Tofu can be made to taste and look just like fish and seafood. Try seaweed for the iodine you may crave.)
9, 10	eggs	tofu scrambler, egg replacer, soy- or grape seed–based eggless mayonnaise
11, 12	dairy	soy milk, rice milk, nut milks, soy cheese, rennetless cheese, ghee, tofu everything from ice cream to yogurt, sour cream, soy-based margarine, nutritional yeast flakes
		in place of butter on popcorn and other foods, plus all the vegetables, fruits, grains, nuts, seeds, nut butters, breads, pasta, cereal, crackers, chips, fruit juices, vegetable juices, herbal teas, vegetarian soups, chili, sandwiches, stir-fries, and other wholesome foods you want!

Of course, the meals and types of food I share here are just suggestions. They're mostly hearty meals with plenty of meat replacements so you won't feel meat-deprived. Someday you'll probably look back at this chart and think, *Ugh, how could anybody eat all that food in one day?* But as a meat-eater, your body is used to working hard to digest heavy protein and fats all the time, and it will take your body a while to adjust.

Sprouts of Info _____

Tofu can take some getting used to. Plain tofu isn't anything special, but it can be made into incredible dishes. Think of tofu as clay and you as the sculptor. Try soaking it in tamari, dipping it in breadcrumbs, and frying it, or mix it with oregano and crumble it on pizza. Yum!

If you find the suggested meals don't fill you up, don't hesitate to go back for seconds. Most vegetarian meals contain much less unhealthful fat than you would get in meaty meals, so chow down! If you want to follow my meal suggestions exactly, go for it! Either way, take it at your own pace and enjoy your transition.

The Replacement Diet

The replacement diet can be used *holistically* to make your entire diet better and more healthful. You can start by using replacement foods for meat and animal products and then move on to replacing unhealthful foods such as sodas and other sugary foods, salt, and processed foods with more healthful options.

Lettuce Explain _____

Holistic, from the Greek word *holos*, which means "whole," is used as a philosophy and way of approaching and correcting health dysfunction that takes into consideration all influences on the person, including diet, nutrition, exercise, mental outlook, and spirituality.

Meat replacement foods can look, taste, and smell so much like the real thing that some long-time vegetarians won't even eat them! Such foods make delicious replacements for the real thing and can be a welcome substitute, especially if you're just starting on a vegetarian diet.

Steer Clear _____

During the time you're transitioning to a meatless diet is not the time you should start worrying about losing weight. It's best if you get used to the way you feel without eating meat first. The weight loss, if you need it, will come soon enough, although you might notice that you lose excess water weight right away. This can initially be due to a decrease in sodium, which is found in excess in animal products.

Fake and Bake

Now that you've chosen your path—once a week, cold turkey, or one animal at a time—let's talk about what types of foods you might choose during your transition and how to sneak some meat replacements into the food of your unsuspecting roommate or other household members.

You'll sometimes find that you wind up liking the meat replacement food better than the meat. In other cases, you won't be able to tell the difference between them. If you're planning to trick your family into going vegetarian on the days that you want to eat veggie, it's best not to serve up a lentil loaf and try passing it off as a meatloaf. They will surely be on to you right away.

Here are some more subtle suggestions for slipping in a fake-and-bake once in a while:

◆ Use textured vegetable protein (TVP) in chili in place of ground beef. (See Chapter 3 for more on TVP.)

◆ Try Boca or Morningstar Farms brand sausage patties in place of pork sausage patties.

◆ Pour rice, soy, almond, or oat milk on your morning cereal.

◆ Try tamari-marinated tofu cubes, breaded with seasoned breadcrumbs, fried, and added to stir-fries in place of chicken.

> **Sprouts of Info**
>
> Trying to avoid flour products such as bread and refined crackers? Try Ryvita or Wasa crackers, found at most health food stores. They contain whole grains such as sesame seeds, rye, and wheat germ, and only a bit of salt. They're hearty-tasting, low in fat, and high in fiber, and make a great substitute for bread.

> **Sprouts of Info**
>
> Sometimes when you want something to taste like meat and it doesn't, you end up feeling cheated. To avoid this, make it a point to vary your new vegetarian menus with items that don't even resemble meat. This can get you used to the idea of not having to base your entire diet around meat products.

Sometimes "tricking" your family with meat replacements doesn't go over well. In such cases, try presenting your new food choice as a fun thing that everyone can be involved in. Start by giving your family this book and getting them to choose some meatless recipes to try. Or try a meal that's completely different from what your family normally eats, like an Indian feast (see Chapter 21) or a Mediterranean spread (see Chapter 23). And don't prepare the replacement foods like you would prepare their meat counterparts. You might be surprised at how quickly everyone adopts the new foods as favorites!

This Is Getting Cheesy

It's easy for many people to eliminate meat from the diet, at least occasionally, but often they give up the beef and increase the cheese. This is no better than the meat because cheese is itself a concentrated animal product with its own list of pitfalls.

Now, don't worry, I'm not going to take away your cheese just yet; but I do want you to know that jumping off the meat wagon doesn't mean you have to jump into the cheese vat! In this section, I fill your mind with many different options for meat replacements. You can then fill your cabinets with these items, and you won't need to fall into the trap of replacing one evil for the other. You might be surprised to find that you have more variety in your diet than you ever had as a meat-eater.

Educating Your Taste Buds

I recommend a slow, deliberate transition to your new diet, not only because this will help it last longer, but also because you need time to retrain your taste buds. The good news is that most of our tastes are acquired and, therefore, can be changed.

Maybe you remember from science class that the tongue has different areas for tasting salty, sweet, and bitter flavors. Your taste buds are designed to protect you and send signals to the brain about what you're eating. These signals tell the rest of the body, like the digestion system and the immune system, what to prepare for. Most poisons, for instance, are extremely bitter and, when tasted, cause you to spit out the substance immediately. The system breaks down, though, because we can train our taste buds to accept new and different things by simply eating or tasting something over and over. Eventually, your taste buds recognize the new substance as "tasty."

Some people have genes that make their taste buds more sensitive to bitter tastes. Many health-promoting substances have a somewhat bitter flavor—such as flavonoids in grapefruit, gluosinolates in kale and cabbage, and isoflavones in soy products like tofu and tempeh—and these sensitive tasters generally avoid all these goodies, therefore putting them at greater risk for ill health. If you or a family member suffer from picky taste buds, you can disguise many of the problematic foods with other foods that complement the food and cancel or override the bitter.

Sprouts of Info

Babies receive acquired tastes through their moms while they're in the womb and through breast-feeding, so pregnant moms should eat a variety of healthful foods during and after pregnancy to help set the stage for the child to crave health-promoting foods later in life.

For instance, dark leafy greens include kale, spinach, and arugula, among others, and also include lots of potassium, folate, and fiber. (See Chapter 14 for more on fresh greens and some great recipes.) Always serve fresh lemon wedges with these cooked foods or add lemon juice to the recipe. The sourness of the lemon helps with any bitterness. Most of my greens recipes also include cheeses, which take away the bitter as well.

Lettuce Explain

Cruciferous vegetables are those vegetables that belong to the *Brassicaceae* or *Cruciferae* family and include broccoli, cabbage, kale, Brussels sprouts, bok choy, horseradish, arugala, and watercress, to name a few.

Another good tip for helping your taste buds respond to the stronger-tasting *cruciferous veggies* like broccoli, cabbage, and Brussels sprouts, is first to not *overcook* these veggies. Overcooking them brings out a more pungent flavor, making them even more dislikable to some sensitive tasters. Always steam these veggies until they're bright green, and no more. The texture should be crisp-tender. Adding strong flavors such as toasted pine nuts, fake bacon, and strong cheeses makes them so yummy, picky tongues will ask for more! (See Chapter 16 for recipes and more on the health benefits of these veggies.)

If you start off slowly, even masking the food with condiments when you have to, at some point your tastes will change and you will learn to like the food. In fact, research shows that it takes kids sometimes up to 15 tastes to appreciate a new flavor. Adults who were raised as vegetarians say, when asked why they don't eat meat, that they've never had the desire to eat flesh. It's that simple. You, too, will lose your desire for meat and animal products over time, as long as you go meatless long enough to let the remnants of all those meat residues leave your body.

From Bitter to Better

Now that you know how you can change your tastes, why not begin by choosing a substitute for an animal product? For example, buy a carton of soy, oat, or rice milk instead of cow's milk the next time you go to the market. Use this in place of cow's milk in cooking and on cereal first. You'll get used to the new nutty flavor, and you'll eventually develop a taste for it. In addition, you'll find that not only do you like soy milk, but you'll lose your taste for cow's milk.

Keep doing this, and your body begins to change and adjust. Really, your body likes these new healthful things. As you continue with your clean diet, your body evolves. Soon you lose your desire for heavier foods and eventually find that you cannot tolerate meat or even the smell of cooking meat. Isn't that amazing?

In general, your body adjusts as best it can to the type of diet you feed it, so why not feed it the best diet you can? The goal here is not only to leave out the meat, but to help you learn to feed yourself good, wholesome foods in place of meat to promote nourishment, strength, and health. To help you get there, the next chapter provides a shopping list and walks you down the health food store aisles. So grab your grocery list, and let's talk shop!

Veggie Soup for the Soul _____

Even if you aren't consciously trying to be a full-time vegetarian, your body tends to get used to your new diet rather quickly, which can cause you to become ill after eating a heavy meat-based meal. I have yet to meet a vegetarian who has gone without meat for six months, ate red meat for some reason, and didn't have his or her body react negatively for several hours and sometimes days afterward. The good news is that the illness from the "meat bomb," as I call it, is usually dramatic enough to keep you from ever going back to meat again (although I do not recommended trying it).

The Least You Need to Know

◆ Celebrating each stage of your transitional diet makes a psychological impact that keeps you committed to your new changes.

◆ Creating a plan to transition to a plant-based diet slowly helps make the change permanent.

◆ Many tasty meat, egg, and dairy substitutes can make your initial transition to meatless easier.

◆ Some meat substitutes are so meatlike that your nonvegetarian housemates might not know the difference!

◆ Tastes are acquired and can change over time. You can retrain your taste buds and your body to enjoy vegetarian foods—and eventually lose your desire for meat.

Let's Talk Shop

In This Chapter

◆ Plan your shopping list

◆ Meet the variety of meat substitutes

◆ Learn why and how to choose produce wisely

◆ Equip your vegetarian kitchen

So now your mind is full of new ideas, but your cupboards are bare! You need to go shopping. As a vegetarian in transition, the shopping experience may be a whole new event for you. That's what this chapter is for. In these pages, I help you plan a shopping list for the staple vegetarian foods you can stock up on and some things you might want to equip your new veggie kitchen with so you can cook some of the delicious recipes in Chapters 7 through 26!

Here I also discuss some foods you might want to try but maybe aren't familiar with, such as tofu, Quorn, and tempeh. I also give you the lay of the land in the health food store so you won't be looking in the canned food aisles for that package of tofu!

Before You Go to Market

Because of the growing demand for more healthful alternatives and vegetarian items, large companies such as Kraft, Colgate, and Dean Foods have purchased and are purchasing smaller health food manufacturers. As a result, you're now able to find natural products and meat and dairy alternatives widely available.

Veggie Soup for the Soul

If you skipped it, please go back and read the section titled "About the Recipes" in the introduction, where you'll find some notes to consider before shopping for any of the recipes (and also when cooking the recipes).

Even if you aren't lucky enough to be in an area where health food stores exist, you should be able to find a growing number of alternatives at your regular grocer. Most large grocery chains also carry a selection of organic produce, too, so going organic is becoming an easier option.

Before you go to the health food store or your supermarket, you need to think about how far you want to take your new diet. Are you going for it all at once or just weekly for now? Are you going to be a pesco vegetarian, a lacto vegetarian, an ovo vegetarian, or a strict vegetarian? These things, of course, will help shape your shopping list.

Yes, I said shopping list. It's always good to make a list. A list can help you spend less and make smarter choices, and can ensure that you get everything you need—or at least that you don't go home *without* the two things you need the most. A list is especially helpful now that you're going vegetarian because you're likely adding some unfamiliar foods to your cart. For now, let's take a look at what you're going to need.

What to Find and Where in the Health Food Store

On your first trip to the store as a vegetarian, you might want to stock up on some basic staple foods, or those foods you'll use often. If you keep staple goods in your pantry or freezer, all you'll need to purchase every week are a few fresh vegetables, and you'll have everything you need to make countless veggie meals. Stocking either your freezer or your pantry helps you turn your kitchen into a place where meatless gourmet meals are never-ending (or, at least, you can fill up those barren cupboards).

Some good choices for vegetarian staple foods that store well include ...

Bulk foods (if your store doesn't have a bulk section, you can also find most of these foods prepackaged): raw nuts (cashews, almonds, or pistachios), grains (rice, couscous, quinoa, barley, bulgur, oats, whole-wheat berries), granola, nutritional yeast flakes, textured vegetable protein (TVP), sesame and sunflower seeds, dried beans and bean flake powders, hummus mix, tabbouleh mix, organic spices, and sesame sticks, carob chips or flour (in place of chocolate), and dried fruit.

Prepackaged and dried goods: Point your cart to the prepackaged and dry goods sections to find nonbulk items such as prepackaged grains, cereal, couscous, vegetable bouillon, spices, hummus, falafel, tofu scrambler mix, tabbouleh, dehydrated refried beans, dehydrated soups, dehydrated mashed potatoes, and egg replacer.

Sprouts of Info

Grains and mixes store for long periods in glass jars. Store tofu, tempeh, soy hot dogs, and most meat substitutes in the freezer until preparation time.

Get familiar with your health food store before you find yourself looking for tofu in all the wrong places!

Frozen foods or items you can freeze for later: tofu, tempeh, Quorn, bean burritos, lentil loaf, french fries, frozen vegetables, filo dough, egg roll wrappers, shredded soy or regular organic cheese, Gardenburgers, vegetarian sausage patties, vegetarian bacon, and tofu hot dogs.

Canned goods: vegetarian refried beans, water chestnuts, diced chilies and jalepeños, veggie soup (Health Valley makes excellent organic vegetarian soups), veggie broth, tomato sauces or paste, veggie chili, artichoke hearts, and bamboo shoots.

In the refrigerated produce sections, you'll find tofu, tempeh, organic yogurts and cheeses, and seitan.

Other: pita pockets, whole-wheat tortillas, blue corn tortillas (all can be frozen), Ryvita crackers, nut butters (these keep a long time in the refrigerator), soy milk, oat milk, almond milk, rice milk (purchase small individual boxes of milks; they keep a long time unopened), stevia, frozen juices, olive oil, soy sauce (referred to as the low sodium, tamari in my recipes), and toasted sesame seed oil. Cooking oils: coconut, peanut, grape seed, canola, and olive oil (see Chapter 22). And be sure to pick up a can of spray olive oil; it comes in handy for many cooking uses.

> **Sprouts of Info**
>
> Bring along your own paper or cloth shopping bags when shopping at a health food store. It's better for the environment to reuse bags, and most stores give credit for it. Always store a few bags in your vehicle to be sure you have them.

Produce that keeps a while: hard squashes such as spaghetti squash and acorn squash, onions, garlic, potatoes, and apples.

You should also consider which meals you want to prepare for the week and determine any other ingredients you might need.

Shop Hopping

Now you know what you need, but where do you go shopping? Here are some places that carry the vegetarian items on your list:

Health food stores. Find one in your telephone book.

Cooperatives. Usually referred to as co-ops, these stores were started to meet the demand for hard-to-find health foods. Most offer just about everything you need as a vegetarian. Most co-ops are open to the public for shopping, but if you become a member, you'll probably receive a discount.

Chain stores. Many large grocery store chains now have entire sections dedicated to health foods and health-related books and products. These stores are like a mini health food store within a large store.

Grocery stores. Local grocery stores are now carrying more health food items, so if you're in an area where you cannot find what you need, ask your local grocer to help you.

Import or ethnic shops. Look in your Yellow Pages for Indian, Asian, Mediterranean, or other specialty food stores where you can find many vegetarian foods.

Introducing Meat Substitutes

What's it going to be for dinner? Gardenburgers? Black bean burgers? Tempeh sloppy joes? Nature burgers? Tofu burgers? These tasty processed meat substitutes are a tempting alternative to your typical hamburger—and are loads better for you. Meat substitutes are big business, so you'll find plenty of different types available. Some are strictly vegetarian; others contain eggs or cheese. And of course, you can always make your own from a recipe in this book!

Steer Clear

Just because it says "meatless" on the package doesn't mean it's vegan, so be sure to read the label. Whole foods are always the best choice, but it can be difficult to avoid *all* processed foods, even in the most healthful of diets. Reading labels is a good idea when taking more responsibility for your diet, and is especially useful when changing the way you eat. Reading labels helps raise your awareness of exactly what you're eating and can help you avoid unnecessary chemical additives such as MSG, food dyes, and coloring, which are unnatural substances to the body.

Let's look at what some of these meat substitutes really are.

Tofu for You

Did you ever wonder what the curd was that Little Miss Muffet, who sat on her tuffet in the nursery rhyme, was eating? It was probably a *tofu* dish! Tofu is a curd made from soybeans. Tofu is white, resembles cheese, and usually comes in blocks in packaged tubs of water and sometimes vacuum packed. A typical package of tofu weighs about 1 pound. Tofu is a favorite of many vegetarians because it makes a great meat substitute and soaks in the flavor of anything you cook it with. Its natural taste is fairly plain, and that's exactly what makes it so versatile.

Tofu comes in different textures, from soft to extra firm. Tofu labeled "soft" is usually used to make things like tofu cheesecake, dips, and spreads; tofu labeled "firm" or "hard" or even "extra firm" can be cut in pieces and used in stir-fries or other dishes in place of meat. If you're watching carbs, tofu is also an excellent food choice, as it's low in calories and high in protein. Read the labels for calories or protein; they vary with the different textures. If you're new to tofu, you'll have to experiment to find the textures that appeal to you most. I always use firm tofu in my main dish recipes, but feel free to substitute to your liking.

Find tofu in the refrigerated produce section usually, often where the organic produce is displayed, or in the dairy section next to the cheeses. Silken tofu, which does not require refrigeration before it's opened, might be found on the shelves along with Asian foods. Silken tofu has a texture similar to the white of a hard-boiled egg.

> **Sprouts of Info**
>
> Be sure to squeeze out the excess water from tofu before you cook it, especially if it has been frozen and thawed. Tofu is porous and soaks in the juices and spices you cook it in. Squeezing the excess water from it makes it a bit more receptive to flavorings.

After you unpack tofu at home, store unused portions covered with fresh water in a container and in the refrigerator, changing the water daily. Tofu keeps for several days this way. Freezing tofu makes it more porous and gives it a gritty texture that makes it even more meatlike.

Tofu is high in protein, low in calories, low in carbs (the firmer tofu is generally the lower in carbs), cholesterol free, and full of calcium and iron. Some tofu is certified kosher.

Tempting Tempeh

Tempeh is a mix of whole fermented soybeans, sometimes mixed with grains such as millet or rice, and made into cutlet-shaped patties. Its use dates back more than 2,000 years in its native Indonesia. Tempeh has a pale brown color and a bumpy-looking texture that I can only describe as resembling alligator skin.

Tofu (right) and tempeh (left) are both versatile, soybean-based meat substitutes.

Tempeh has a somewhat nutty flavor, is hearty, and is used to replace meat and to make vegetarian dishes more filling. It contains no cholesterol and almost no fat and is high in protein and fiber.

Find tempeh in the frozen foods or dairy section, usually in shrink-wrapped plastic packages or in reusable plastic zippered bags.

Textured Vegetable Protein (TVP)

Textured vegetable protein, or *TVP*, is a meat substitute made from soya flour. It has a tough, chewy texture much like beef steak. It is grayish-brown and is sold either in bulk or prepackaged in small chunks, or shredded and flavored to taste like meat. Use TVP to add a meatlike texture to vegetarian foods such as bean burritos and chili, or to boost a meal's nutritional content.

Steer Clear

Some TVP is high in fat content, so read the label. TVP made from defatted soy flour is low in fat.

What the Devil Is Seitan?

Seitan (pronounced *SAY-tahn*), or wheat meat, is a brown, slick-textured, high-protein, low-fat form of wheat gluten found in health food stores, generally near the tofu. It's made from whole-wheat flour and is used in sandwiches and stir-fries and as a meat substitute; in this book, I use it in my Nonchicken Nuggets recipe (see Chapter 13). It's low in fat and high in protein.

Seitan seems to be as versatile as soy, as manufacturers make premade seitan in different flavors such as chicken and steak.

Quorn ... Off the Cob

Quorn can be a nice alternative to soy products for the lacto ovo vegetarian, but strict vegetarians, take note: it does contain egg whites and whey. Quorn is a brand name of a meat substitute and is a mycoprotein product, which is made from the fungi *Fusarium Venenatum. Wait*, you might be thinking, *she wants me to eat something made from a fungus?* Don't worry. Mycoprotein is a fungus that contains high-quality protein, containing 9 essential amino acids and fiber. It's also low in fat and calories, and contains no cholesterol.

Quorn is typically substituted for chicken and is usually stocked in the freezer section.

This is what to look for when looking for Quorn—this is the Naked Cutlets style.

A plate of Quorn's Naked Cutlet, a salad, and a steamed veggie makes a great high-protein, low-carb, lacto ovo vegetarian lunch.

A Closer Look at Produce

As a vegetarian, you'll want to become more familiar with your produce and choose it carefully. After all, vegetables and fruit are the focus of your new diet, so you want to get everything you can from these foods.

Unfortunately, these days, not all vegetables are created equal. Remember, food production is a business, and making food more profitable doesn't necessarily mean that it's better for your health. If you are what you eat, you should know what you are eating.

A Question of Genetics

You've no doubt heard about genetic engineering, and you'll probably run across references to GMOs, or genetically modified organisms, when shopping or in the news. What does genetically engineering or altering foods mean? It means that scientists have changed what occurs naturally in a plant by manipulating or cross-breeding its DNA. For instance, most commercially grown tomatoes are now genetically altered to remain firmer so fewer are lost by crushing during shipping. Sometimes plants are spliced with genes from completely different organisms, including bacteria, fish, and insects—combinations that could not happen naturally.

Many crops are altered to resist strong herbicides and pests. About half of the United States' soybean crops are genetically engineered, as well as about one third of the corn. The U.S. Food and Drug Administration (FDA) assures us that these foods are safe for consumption, but still there's much debate.

> **Steer Clear**
>
> Some years ago, genetic DNA from a Brazil nut was crossed with soybeans. With nut allergies so common, some feared that unsuspecting consumers could have allergic reactions when eating these genetically manipulated soy products. This brings up more issues about labeling our "natural foods."

If you want to avoid such foods, pay attention to labels, especially on foods that contain soy. If the company does not use genetically altered food in its products, it says so on the label.

Some food companies have shown their concern over genetically altered foods and have promised to stop using them in their products. Baby food makers Heinz and Gerber have said they will discontinue using genetically modified soybeans, and Japan, one of the world's largest tofu makers, is phasing out purchasing genetically altered soybeans. Some beer makers have cut out the use of genetically altered corn in brewing their beer.

Going Organic

One of the main reasons to go organic is because there's simply no taste comparison in organic versus commercially grown produce. Organic foods taste fresh and just *good*.

In the organic section, you might notice that foods such as tomatoes, apples, cucumbers, and strawberries, among others, are smaller than their commercially grown counterparts. They may not be spiffed up with waxes, polish, or dyes, and a few may be a little misshapen just as Mother Nature grew them. Don't let this distract you from buying them. As long as they're fresh and not wilted or overripe, I can almost guarantee they'll taste better. I believe organic fresh produce tastes better because, without the scientific "tinkering" involved with making fruits and vegetables perfectly round, harder, or more resistant to rotting, organically grown veggies reach the size they're meant to reach—with their fullest flavor intact.

> **Sprouts of Info**
>
> To compare the tastes of organic and commercially grown produce, try a ripe freshly picked strawberry from nature, a ripe, regular-size organic strawberry, and a ripe, commercially grown gigantic strawberry from a grocery store. I bet your taste buds will be convinced.

Another reason to go organic is to lower your daily toxic chemical exposure. Toxins are everywhere. They can be found in the air you breathe, on and in foods, and in your drinking and bathing water. There's no way to completely eliminate exposure to chemicals throughout your life, so your best bet is to choose foods free from pesticides. So besides better-tasting produce, organic is better for the environment. It keeps toxic pesticides from getting into our water, air, and soil. And of course, choosing organic foods helps limit your personal exposure to such pesticides.

Now, although it does help, going organic won't completely eliminate 100 percent of the toxins in your life. Testing individual food items for "safe" levels of pesticides doesn't take into account how many pesticides you've eaten in a day or over a lifetime. Pesticides and other chemicals add up over time and can leave residues in your body tissues. The information on pesticides and organically grown produce is so vast, I could go on several more pages. The bottom line: limiting the amount of toxins you knowingly expose yourself to daily is a good, commonsense safeguard. Organic foods can help with that.

Work on your health preventively and actively. It's much easier to maintain your health than it is to try to reclaim it later. Choosing organically grown foods when possible is an easy preventative step you can take.

Vaccinated Vegetables?

How would you like to be vaccinated against the Norwalk virus when you eat a banana? Some researchers in the United States have been experimenting with adding bacterium to fresh produce that reacts with the plant's own structure to create different types of vaccines in the fruit itself. The purpose is to create edible vaccinations that consumers can ingest in their uncooked foods. If this is done, you'll need to give serious consideration to whether you want to consume such foods. Educate yourself on the effect of vaccines, the research on the aftereffects of vaccines, and the related risks versus benefits of inoculations in general if you're not aware of this information. This should prove to be a very interesting and controversial subject.

> **Sprouts of Info**
>
> For an interesting look at exactly how many chemicals you're getting in your food and what effects these pesticides and chemicals can have, visit www.foodnews.org. The interactive questionnaire lets you check off what you've eaten in a day, and the results show a breakdown of the chemicals you've consumed.

For now let's stick to foods. Just keep in mind that foods from nature are the perfect foods. Read the signs and labels, even on fresh produce.

Ripe for the Pickin'?

Try to get your fruits vine-ripened, when possible. Most commercially grown produce is picked green, and much of it is then gassed and dyed to the color that appeals to the consumer—oranges are made oranger, for example. When you eat unripened fruit, such as a green orange, its acids are not yet fit for consumption and can stir up your own body acids, creating discomfort. You also miss out on nutritious phytochemicals that are created only by nature through vine-ripening.

> **Sprouts of Info**
>
> Bananas don't ripen on the tree; they're harvested green and ripen after picking. Refrigeration slows this process, whereas warm temps speed it up. If you want to slow down the ripening, put your bananas in the fridge after they reach the ripeness you like. Even though the skin turns brown, the fruit inside should remain steady for a few more days.

Take some of your food lessons from nature. Notice that animals don't eat fruits or vegetables from your garden until the food is ripe. (The critters think you're growing it for them, you know!) Their instincts tell them when foods are ready for consumption.

Humans not only have altered their taste buds over time, but, through the use of chemically laden foods, have deadened their natural instincts related to food and eating. As you turn more and more toward whole foods, your taste buds and eating instincts will come back to life, and you'll learn to enjoy obeying them. You'll even come to understand how well these natural instincts serve you!

Budget Tips

Eating meatless won't necessarily cost you more money, but when you find all the great veggie-friendly foods available to you, you might run up your bill at the health food store! Here are some budget tips for the frugal vegetarian:

Buy in bulk. It saves packaging and labeling costs.

Eat more whole foods and fewer processed foods. Whole foods naturally cost less than prepared processed packaged foods, which require more handling.

Don't buy nonfood items at health food stores. Items such as aluminum foil and sandwich bags are generally more expensive in health food stores than at regular grocery stores. This can run up your food bill in a hurry.

Purchase a juicer and make your own juices, nut butters, and soups. Have a free day off? Spend the day with your juicer, making these items all at once and then freezing them for use later. This saves not only money, but time!

Avoid prepared foods except for certain occasions. Deli items and prepared foods can be delicious and convenient, but they cost more.

Before you spend money for a prepared food, consider whether you could make it yourself almost as easily. If so, you can save a bundle. Consider buying tabbouleh in bulk, for example, versus premade or boxed. All you need to do to bring dehydrated tabbouleh to life is add water. Besides, dried tabbouleh keeps much longer than prepared tabbouleh from the deli.

This Gadget's for You

If you're going to become a vegetarian gourmet, a few appliances are essential to your kitchen. A well-equipped kitchen for the vegetarian might include the following:

- Wok to whip up stir-fries (See more on woks in Chapter 22.)
- Cutting board designated for produce only

- Sprouter to make your own alfalfa or other bean sprouts

- Bamboo steamer to steam vegetables lightly

- Strainer to drain pastas and rinse fruits

- Grater for grating lemon to make lemon zest and for grating ginger root, carrots, and hard cheeses

- Spray olive oil (This helps you use less oil in cooking and is excellent for greasing cookie sheets or pans.)

- Mortar and pestle to grind whole herbs such as cloves into powders

- Juicer to make your own vegetable and fruit juices

- Blender for making smoothies and sauces

- Food processor to make applesauce, veggie dips, and spreads, and to quickly and easily slice, shred, or dice veggies

- Vegetable brush for cleaning vegetables and fruits

- Vegetable wash to remove outer wax, pesticides, and dirt (Find this spray in the produce section.)

- Rice cooker to perfectly cook rice and other grains

- A thermos or slow cooker to slow cook grains to keep them alive

- A slow cooker to make soups, stews, chowder, and chili (See more on slow cookers in Chapter 12.)

- Clear jars to store all your bulk items, nuts, mixes, etc.

- Salad bowl

- Waterless cookware for cooking without the use of water (It can be expensive, but it keeps the nutrients in the foods intact.)

- Skewers for making vegetable kabobs for barbecues

- Reverse osmosis water filtering system

> **Steer Clear**
>
> If you share a kitchen with a meat-eater, be sure to keep separate cutting boards. One should be used only for produce and the other only for animal products. This helps avoid contaminating the vegetables with bacteria spread by raw meat and eggs, and is especially important when eating produce raw or steamed.

Sprouts of Info _____

Feel like shopping? A Vita-Mix (www.vitamix.com) is an all-in-one blender that does the job of 10 kitchen appliances. It makes whole juices without eliminating the pulp and has at least 40 other functions. Nature's Sunshine Products (www. naturessunshine.com) offers a nice selection of waterless cookware and a highly rated reverse osmosis water unit, Nature's Spring.

Now you have the information and ideas you need to have your kitchen equipped, your fridge stocked, and some new meat substitutes to try. If you're hungry and ready to cook, this can be a good time to skip to the recipe chapters beginning in Chapter 7! Or if you want to stay with me, I'll make it worth your while with the upcoming chapters on the vegetarian lifestyle, including the next chapter on meat-free traveling and dining out. *Ciao!*

The Least You Need to Know

◆ Meat replacements, like tofu and tempeh, help round out your vegetarian diet.

◆ Purchase the majority of your produce in as close to a natural state as possible, including vine ripened, pesticide free, nongenetically altered, and nonvaccinated.

◆ Eating vegetarian can be very economical.

◆ Vegetarian cooks can benefit by having some special kitchen equipment to prepare fresh, wholesome vegetarian snacks and meals more easily and economically.

Chapter 4

Have Veggies, Will Travel

In This Chapter

◆ The office vegetarian

◆ Discover sources of hidden animal ingredients at restaurants

◆ Plan ahead to get what you need when traveling

◆ Find out how to say "vegetarian" in different languages

Don't despise empiric truth. Lots of things work in practice for which the laboratory has never found proof.

—Martin H. Fischer (1879–1962), German-born U.S. physician and author, in *Fischerisms*

Although I've given you shopping tips and lists in the preceding chapter, and in later chapters I give you all kinds of yummy vegetarian recipes, you can't stay in your kitchen forever (as much as some of us would like to!). This chapter helps you come out of your kitchen and step into the world as a vegetarian.

Although it might seem unnecessary to read about how to live as a vegetarian when working, traveling, and dining out, when you take your new diet out there and realize how deeply others are entrenched in their meat-eating ways, you might be glad for the interesting and even face-saving tips offered here!

And as a bonus, every time you speak up for your needs, you expand another's perceptions and can help make more healthful options available for everyone. Look at you, you pioneer!

The Vegetarian at Work

What do you do when you're trapped in a business luncheon meeting and the caterer brings in all meat items? Hopefully, you can use some of the following tips before starving to death—or at least be able to change things for the future.

When you get caught in a catered meeting and you didn't have the heads-up to make a "vegetarian options, please" request, if there's nothing for you to eat, you'll certainly draw attention to yourself if you simply sit quietly and abstain from eating *anything*. When asked why you're not eating, explain that there's nothing being served that you can eat and make a suggestion for future meetings. Most people care about making others comfortable and are happy to make a change for the next meeting.

Sprouts of Info

When requesting vegetarian items at a buffet luncheon, make suggestions. Most lunches are served with some type of salad or other items that don't depend on meat. A few examples include pasta salads, hold the ham; green tossed salads, no egg, dressings on the side; and beans or bean salad, no bacon.

If you catch the caterers as they're setting up, rush the buffet and scope out everything available. If there's nothing for you to eat, you still have time to run to a local deli or the office cafeteria to get something else or order something in. And if veggie-friendly items are available, by getting your food first, you ensure you'll have food after the meat-eaters get through, and you reduce the risk of the vegetarian items mixing with or getting contaminated by the meat items—a common occurrence in self-serve buffets.

If the buffet has at least a few items you can eat, such as salad and rolls, make a meal of it. Stuff the roll with every vegetable available, and you have a veggie sandwich. Use salad dressing as a condiment and pile up the carrot sticks, salad, and potato chips on the side. Make it colorful and enticing, and I'll bet a few meat-eaters in the group will copy your idea and make their own salad sandwiches!

When you know ahead of time about a catered lunch meeting, talk to the person who does the ordering for the lunches to make your vegetarian request. But be as specific as possible, as this makes it easier on everyone involved. If you just say, "No meat, please" but you don't eat egg, either, the caterer could show up with a cheese omelet for you!

Request that catered meals be served buffet style versus premade. If sandwiches are premade, make a request for yours to include vegetables only, hold the mayo (if you're not an ovo vegetarian). It might be a good idea to bring some of your own condiments to make your sandwich more interesting—keep packets of mustard handy for these occasions.

If the meal is a catered buffet, request that the meat items be arranged separate from the cheese and vegetable items, to avoid cross-contamination. (If you've ever eaten a piece of lettuce that had been sitting under a piece of bologna, as a vegetarian, you'll know what I mean about contamination.)

You can get through a business lunch without starving, but you might have to use your creativity. Think of it as an opportunity to showcase your wonderful problem-solving skills! And remember to stay professional. Don't sulk if you hate the food, and don't even think about telling your boss what's really in her bologna sandwich!

Dining Out, Vegetarian Style

Dining out and grabbing food on the run shouldn't be a stressful experience, but just keep in mind that as a vegetarian in the minority, the norm isn't leaving meat out of the dish. Therefore, a little planning, forethought about where you go, and clear requests can go a long way toward getting your needs met. Let's think about the different types of restaurants so you can find your best bets!

Steer Clear

Sit-down, family-style chain restaurants usually have at least one vegetarian item on the menu these days, but check the menu before sitting down! If nothing on the menu will work for you, don't assume the cook can make something special for you. Most items are premade, and removing the meat from the sauce, and so on, isn't possible.

Belly Up to the Trough

Vegetarians can fill up on foods from most restaurants offering buffet-style dining. (Try to keep it to your two handfuls maximum here, eh?) Don't let the word *steakhouse* fool you. As long as it's a buffet-style place, you can usually find a surprising selection of salad fixings, veggie salads, vegetables, soups, fruits, breads, pastas, and rice. Many of these places offer baked potatoes and sometimes taco salad fixings, too.

Fine Dining

Finer restaurants are usually much more willing and able to accommodate your requests than the family-style chains. The classier restaurants usually make meals per request, not en masse, so they have more flexibility in their output. Even so, it's not wise to show up expecting the chef to fulfill your requests.

It's best to call ahead and find out whether the chef can make you something vegetarian or vegan. Be specific about which ingredients you do not eat. I've been to places where the chef thought vegetarians eat fish, for example. You are the expert on your diet, so help others accommodate you by being clear about your needs.

> **Sprouts of Info** _____
>
> It's best to call a restaurant beforehand to find out if vegetarian items are on the menu or if the chef is willing to accommodate you. Sometimes the folks who answer the phone aren't able to give you a good answer because they aren't familiar with vegetarianism. Check their menu online or ask them to fax you a copy so you can decipher it for yourself.

Creative Dining à la Chain

You're meeting your friends at a meat-oriented chain-type place they picked to celebrate a birthday, watch the big game, grab a few drinks, etc. You want to go, even knowing the type of food served there. Should you eat before? Bring snacks in your purse/pocket? Eat later (even though you're hungry *now*)? Try to find something on the menu? All are viable options (except maybe bringing in the snacks—some restaurants don't allow that), but if you plan on muddling through it, here are some tips on finding something to eat.

> **Veggie Soup for the Soul** _
>
> Sometimes the waitstaff can be very helpful if you let them know you are vegetarian. I am often surprised at how many waiters/waitresses tell me they are vegetarian, too, and they generally make great suggestions.

Scan the entire menu for à la carte items, garnishes, or side dishes—beans, avocado, various vegetables, and rice or potatoes—that are okay for you to eat. Check the appetizers section, too, and don't forget the pasta section for meatless sauces. Come up with your own combination of these items.

Read the description of the sandwiches and meat items, and check out the rest of the ingredients. Many dishes can be made without the meat. Consider the grilled chicken sandwich with grilled peppers, onions, tomato, and avocado, served with a veggie pasta side salad—hold the chicken—for a satisfying meatless meal.

Can Fast Food = Healthful Food?

As demand grows for more healthful organic and vegetarian fare, more and more fast-food places are responding with vegetarian menu options. When you're not in the mood for fast food, even healthful fast food, grab lunch or dinner at your local grocery store's soup or salad bar. And by now you should be familiar with your local health food store; if you're lucky enough to have one with a deli, you know where to go for lunch.

Another good fast lunch can be found at your local bagel shop. Many of the bagel chains now serve lunch, making sandwiches with bagels. You'll find plenty of vegetarian choices, and they usually have good soups available, too.

Fast-Food Alternatives

If you've got a hankering for some junk food or are secretly adding to your collection of fast-food-restaurant kids' toys, here are some tips on what to order at some of the major fast-food joints.

Burger King now has a meatless burger, and at McDonald's you can ask for a Big Mac with *no meat*, which is sort of a veggie sandwich—all the fixings without the meat: special sauce; processed American cheese product; shredded, nutritionally void iceberg lettuce; pickles; and a bun with as much sugar as a cinnamon roll—who could resist? In Europe, you might find different things on the McDonald's menus—I've had a veggie burger at McDonald's in Germany that included an actual meatless patty. It was quite delicious!

Wendy's hamburgers can also be ordered without meat, but Wendy's restaurants also have some things for vegetarians the other burger joints don't—namely, baked potatoes and a salad bar. And Jack in the Box offers many food items that can be made to accommodate you, such as teriyaki bowls, salads, pita sandwiches, and other items.

Arby's offers baked potatoes and garden salads. Taco Bell offers veggie wraps. Pizza Hut has mini cheese pizzas—call ahead, and they'll be ready to pick up in less than 10 minutes. Most Pizza Huts also have salad bars.

Any fast-food restaurants offering subs can accommodate you with a vegetarian sub and usually a salad as well. See how easy this is getting?

Veggie Soup for the Soul _____

Fast foods should be eaten only occasionally, if at all, because the calories add up! But if you must, go to the fast-food places that can accommodate you best. Chains in Europe and in major metropolitan cities tend to offer more vegetarian menu choices, such as falafel sandwiches and tofu and veggie pitas. And chains everywhere are starting to offer salads.

Good in a Pinch

It can be hard to find vegetarian fare in rural areas. I remember being in the boonies in northern Montana and having to survive on iceberg lettuce salads and grilled cheese sandwiches for a few days! When you find yourself in a place that offers nothing that isn't deep fried in lard or boiled in chicken stock, it can wear on your vegetarian soul, so always plan ahead if possible. If you can't, here are some worst-case-scenario survival foods:

◆ Peanut butter and jelly sandwich

◆ Grilled cheese sandwich (if you're a lacto vegetarian)

◆ Pasta with plain tomato sauce or olive oil and parsley

◆ Bread and whatever raw veggies are available—make your own sandwich

◆ Oatmeal or other breakfast foods that might still be available later in the day

◆ Baked potato topped with raw vegetables, salsa, beans, or guacamole

Sprouts of Info _____

Ethnic restaurants can be a wonderful source of vegetarian foods. Some even cater to a vegetarian clientele. It's worth seeking out a good Indian restaurant, for example, because even if it's not completely vegetarian, many have some vegetarian options on the buffet so you can experiment and not worry about finding meat in a sauce. Call ahead to find out.

Finding Meat in All the Wrong Places

Even when items are labeled vegetarian on the menu, you still need to find out what a particular establishment thinks "vegetarian" means. No meat, probably, but how about dairy? Eggs? Fish? You will often find that meatless items contain cheese or egg. Although some vegetable soups do not contain pieces of meat, such as tomato bisque or vegetable soup, the base is often chicken stock or beef bullion.

Sorry, but it's just the way restaurants work, so you'll have to plan ahead and watch your step until you find some favorite restaurants with reliable veggie foods on the menu. To help you narrow it down, here's a list of some items where you would never expect to find meat.

Steer Clear

In Thai and other Asian restaurants, watch out for the fish sauce, which is commonly poured over steamed vegetables or rice but is not necessarily listed on the menu.

Hidden Animal Ingredients in Restaurant Foods

Food	Often Contains
Vegetable soup	chicken, pork, or beef stock
Baked beans	ham
Bean soup	bacon
Biscuits	lard
Broccoli soup	pork, cheese
Caesar salad	anchovies alone or in the dressing
Chili	ground beef (unless it says "vegetarian chili")
Cooked greens	salt pork (more prevalent in the southern United States)
Flour tortillas	lard
French onion soup	beef stock
Fried rice	eggs
Greek salad	anchovies, feta cheese
Green beans	bacon
Green chili (used as a sauce in many Mexican dishes)	pork
Marinara sauce	beef
Pasta salad	ham
Pie crust	lard
Potato salad	eggs, sometimes bacon

continues

Hidden Animal Ingredients in Restaurant Foods   (continued)

Food	Often Contains
Potato soup	bacon
Refried beans	lard
Sautéed vegetables	simmered in chicken stock (not always, but ask)
Spinach salad	bacon, eggs
Steamed rice	chicken stock
Stir-fry	oyster sauce
Tossed or dinner salads	eggs, bacon bits

For a free 16-page fact sheet listing more than 200 animal ingredients used in food preparation or other items, along with their vegetarian alternatives, contact People for the Ethical Treatment of Animals (PETA) at 757-622-PETA (757-622-7382) or www. peta-online.org.

Vegetarian Travel Advice

Probably the most important component in getting your vegetarian needs met while traveling is proper planning. When you travel, you don't always have access to a kitchen, and certainly not your *own* kitchen. You will be at the mercy of unknown restaurants, train dining cars (or, more often, train cart food, if you're lucky), room service, vending machines, and airline food. When you're on a road trip, whether in your car or via bus, you'll be at the mercy of bus station cafés, designated pit stops at less-than-desirable greasy spoons, and truck stops. This just means you'll have to do a little planning.

Consider what type of transportation you'll be taking: plane, train, car, bus, cruise ship, or a combination. Will you have the use of a vehicle when you get where you're going? How long will you be gone? Will you be staying at a condo or another place with a kitchen available? Will your destination be rural (far from restaurants), in a city (walking access to what you might need), or in a foreign country (won't know what to expect)? The rest of the chapter addresses why you should be asking yourself these questions. But first, a few more important guidelines.

How You Say ... *Vegetarian?*

One essential element in making sure you get what you need is proper communication with those in charge of ordering and preparing your meals for you. Remember that it's important to be concise, up front, and clear with your restaurant server when requesting or inquiring about a vegetarian meal.

If you're in a place where you don't speak the language, being clear will be a little more difficult, obviously. The good news is that I've vacationed and lived in different countries and managed to get vegetarian meals just about everywhere. I learned from the locals how to say "no meat" or "vegetarian" in different languages, and I've included a little list.

Translating "Vegetarian" to Other Languages

Language	"Vegetarian"	"No Meat"
Arabic	*bela lahem*	*bela lahem*
French	*végétarien*	*pas de viande*
German	*vegetarier*	*kein Fleisch*
Hindi	*shakahari'*	*shakahari'*
Italian	*vegetariano*	*nessuna carne*
Polish	*wegetarianin* or *jarosz*	*dieta beztluszczowa*
Russian	*vegetarianskii*	*Ya ne yem myaso!* (I don't eat meat!)
Spanish	*vegetariano*	*nenhuma carne*
Swedish	*vegetarisk*	*aucune viande*

You can see that the word *vegetarian* is quite similar in most languages, so that's a help, but try to memorize the words in the appropriate language to be sure to get your meal with no meat. If you're afraid of forgetting, write it down.

Frequent Flying

Flight services sure have changed over the years, especially since the last edition of this book in 2000. Most airlines don't serve meals, especially if the flight is less than three hours. But at least many airlines are now offering food to purchase in flight, and the options generally can accommodate most vegetarians. And on longer flights, most airlines that serve meals can accommodate vegetarian palates; just request a vegetarian meal when purchasing your tickets. On airlines that are still offering in-flight meals, your request will go into the system, and you'll be served your special meal on your flight.

Even if you've forgotten to request a vegetarian meal when you purchased your tickets, you can call *up to 24 hours* before your flight, which is always a good idea anyway because I've found that special meals are frequently forgotten unless you call again a day or two before your trip.

Here's a list of some of the major airlines and their vegetarian choices (they have other meal options, but I've listed only the vegetarian ones):

Steer Clear

Flight attendants use seat numbers to deliver special meals, so if you happen to switch seats with someone in another aisle, be sure to notify the flight attendant that you have a special meal coming and that you have changed seats.

Sprouts of Info

As a business traveler, be sure to tell your travel agent to make a permanent note in your profile that you are a vegetarian. If you forget to request your special meal, at least there will be a chance your travel agent already took care of it.

Canadian: Asian vegetarian, lacto ovo vegetarian, pesco vegetarian (seafood), fruit plate, vegan, and Hindu vegetarian.

Continental: strict vegetarian, lacto ovo vegetarian, Asian vegetarian, Hindu. (Theirs is most likely vegetarian, but be sure when you call.)

Delta: fruit plate, vegetarian, lacto ovo vegetarian, Asian (Hindu), and pure vegetarian. (You need to give them only 12 hours' advance notice.)

Northwest: specialty meals come in four choices: low calorie, low fat, low cholesterol, or low sodium (the same attributes of most vegetarian meals). These meals are not necessarily vegetarian, so inquire when you order.

Southwest: no in-flight meals offered, but nuts are served on all flights.

Swissair: claims to be the first airline to serve naturally grown foods. It offers strict Asian vegetarian (Indian style), Hindu vegetarian, kosher fish or a vegetarian variant, Western vegetarian (no meat or dairy), and Western lacto ovo vegetarian.

TWA: strict vegan.

United: lacto ovo vegetarian (actually, strict vegan meals; however, those in first or business class can have some dairy appetizers or desserts, if they choose) and Asian vegetarian (includes egg-free pastas, tofu, nonmeat/dairy gravy).

USAir: fruit plate, lacto ovo vegetarian, nondairy vegetarian, Asian vegetarian. (Some of these meals require only a 6-hour heads-up!)

Road Trip!

In some ways, it's a lot easier to get decent vegetarian food on road trips because you have a car, which means you have more freedom to drive to a health food store and get what you need. However, interstate travel can still leave you hungry for good food, as most of the food you'll find close to the interstate consists of fast foods, truck stops, and greasy spoons, which are not always vegetarian friendly. It's always a good idea to take foods to eat at the rest stops.

Traveling by bus is even worse because the busses seem to stop only in the greasiest of spoons and coffeehouses. Be sure to take an assortment of backup snacks with you on bus trips. Don't forget the moist towelettes, either!

Here are some things to make an emergency food kit when you're traveling by car. Fill up your kit with your favorite sandwich items, such as precut fresh veggies, pita pockets, sprouts, mustard, and vegetarian turkey slices. Be sure to prewash, cut, and slice all sandwich fixings and put them in individual baggies, to keep them from spoiling and to make sandwich assembly easy. Add fresh fruit slices, dried raw nuts and seeds, sesame sticks, and salsa and chips, too, as they're all great for supplementing. Soy yogurts are a great snack or breakfast food—just don't forget the plastic utensils. Add some chilled bottles of water or chocolate soy milk, and you're ready to roll! Here are some other items and tips for your kit:

- *Large cooler* to store all your refrigerated food items. Bring your cooler into your hotel room when you arrive; don't let it sit in a hot car.

- *Straws* to put in bottled juices and other beverages when you can't properly clean the container.

- *Plastic utensils* for preparing sandwiches and for eating.

Steer Clear

If you're hungry, don't wait for the train ride to find vegetarian cuisine (or much of any good food). The trains I've been on throughout Europe and Asia all seemed to have either no food or food I wouldn't want to eat, meat-eater or not!

- *Aluminum foil* to wrap sandwiches and leftovers.

- *Zippered baggies* to hold the rest of your tomato or avocado after you slice it.

- *Bottle opener* to open bottles of natural soda.

- *Paper plates* to put your veggie sandwiches on or to use as a cutting board. Can also serve as a clean barrier between your food and a dusty picnic table.

- *Gallon jug of pure water*—you don't want to run out of pure water, and it can come in handy for rinsing the fresh fruits you purchase along the way.

With all these items, you can make yourself sandwiches and even whip out a salad for a great roadside picnic. Plan to hit a supermarket along the way once in a while to stock up on more fresh produce.

The Least You Need to Know

- Most airlines offer a vegetarian meal, but be sure to order ahead of time and call again 24 hours before your flight to confirm it.

- Learning how to say "no meat" in the local language can come in handy.

- Always call ahead to check on restaurant and food options, whether you're flying, cruising, or staying at a hotel.

- Hidden animal ingredients are often found in vegetable-based foods, including soups, sauces, rice, and beans; eggs, cheese, or fish are often added to salads. Always ask before you order.

Chapter 5

Veggin' Out for Health and Beauty

In This Chapter

◆ Checking out the digestive system

◆ Meat and the circulatory system

◆ Tips for weight loss and management

◆ Be a vegetarian, have better skin

We all want to be healthier, have more energy, feel good, and look our best, right? This chapter helps you understand why you feel healthier, have more energy, and look your best when you eliminate meat from your diet. Here you get the lowdown on how your body digests food, learn about the effects of meat-eating on your heart health, and get tips for weight loss. Let's start with digestion.

The Truth Is Hard to Swallow

Were humans truly designed to eat meat? This is a question that's been debated for decades. Let me tell you a little bit about how the human digestive system works and compare some of that to a carnivore's system. You can decide for yourself what to believe.

Chew On This

Digestion begins in the mouth with chewing. Your body is designed to work best if you chew your food thoroughly—29 times, we're told—using your molars to grind down the food, allowing time for your saliva to mix completely with it. Your saliva contains enzymes that begin the digestive process for starches.

Compared to a strictly meat-eating lion's teeth, human teeth are noticeably different. First, humans don't have sharp fangs for ripping open tough animal hide and sharp claws that tear through prey, nor do humans have a jaw that's limited to an up-and-down movement like the carnivore's. The human jaw allows teeth to move in a lateral motion as well as up and down. This motion enables the grinding of foods before swallowing and encourages the proper enzymes to be released from salivary glands to begin digestion of starches. Lions are not designed to chew their food 29 times before swallowing like we are told to do. They also don't have all the flat molars we do for grinding and chewing grains, nuts, seeds, and vegetation.

> **Sprouts of Info**
>
> The teeth are tiny samplings of the condition of the rest of the bones in your body. If you're suddenly having dental problems but haven't changed your dental hygiene, it could be a clue that your body is overacidic due to poor diet. Cavities could indicate poor calcium absorption and mineral imbalance. Work with your dentist and nutritionist to help get the supplemental nutrition you need to counteract the problem. If you can get your teeth in shape by improving your nutrition, you can bet you're doing the rest of your bones good as well.

Digestive Systems Compared

Generally speaking, most lions and other strict carnivores gulp down the flesh of their prey. Not that you haven't seen a family member do this at Thanksgiving, but this fact brings us to the next striking difference between a typical carnivorous animal and a typical human animal—the rest of the digestive process.

When you swallow, food enters your stomach, where bacterial enzymes and hydro-chloric acid (HCl) are released to help break down and sterilize your food particles.

A more significant amount of HCl is needed to break down meat compared to vegetables.

After the food is sufficiently broken down in the stomach, it's called *chyme*. The chyme passes into the small intestine, where it's slowly pushed through the 20-foot-long tubelike intestinal tract by wavelike movements called *peristalsis*. Fingerlike projections inside the small intestine are called *villi*. It's through these villi that you absorb most of your nutrients. The mostly digested food then passes into the large intestine, also known as the colon or lower bowel, where more minerals, vitamins, and excess water are absorbed. The final material is then passed to the rectum, where it's eliminated from the body. The entire digestive process in a healthy, functioning human body takes approximately 12 to 18 hours. This is called *transit time*.

> **Steer Clear** _____
> Eating meat creates uric acid in the body, and uric acid overload can lead to many health conditions. A carnivore's body produces uricase, which breaks down uric acid. Humans do not produce or have uricase.

Now for the digestive system of a strict carnivore. First, the lion's stomach makes about 10 to 15 times the HCl a human's stomach produces. Remember, the HCl is for breaking down all the meat the lion eats.

In addition, the lion has a small intestine, the length of which equals only about three times his trunk length and is less than half the size of a human's intestinal tract. So when the lion eats its prey, the meat passes through its short digestive system and the waste products from the meal are eliminated rather quickly. There's no time for the meat to sit and fester, as it does in the human system.

When meat enters the human digestive system, it is subject to a warm, moist environment for a long period of time (12 to 18 hours, remember). In this type of environment, meat begins to rot and decay, creating *free radicals*. This is another reason why overall, vegetarians have a lower risk of colon cancer; they get more fiber and don't have meat hanging around in the colon and causing free radical cell damage.

> **Lettuce Explain** _____
> **Free radicals** are unstable and destructive oxygen atoms created by the body's natural processes. Excess free radicals increase the risk for cancer, premature aging, and other degenerative conditions.

In addition, when your body breaks down the complete proteins from meat, it naturally creates an abundance of nitrogen by-products, such as ammonia and urea. This can lead to a buildup of uric acid, symptoms of which include sore, achy, stiff joints. When uric acid crystallizes, it forms glasslike splinters that can then cause sharp pains, arthritic problems, gout, and neuritis.

The longer waste materials stay in the colon, the more likely you are to become constipated. The colon absorbs water from the matter in the bowel, and if the fecal matter sits too long, it becomes dried and hard, making it very difficult to pass. Constipation leads to autointoxication and can be linked to more health ailments than I have room to list here, including the harboring of parasites. Meat goes through your system slower than other foods, which slows your colon transit time and adds to the possibility of chronic constipation. Most pure vegetarians do not have troubles with digestion or constipation; however, lacto ovo vegetarians might because cheese, other dairy products, and eggs tend to be constipating.

So as I see it, the human digestive system is not fully designed for eating meat on a regular basis. Eating meat is like putting green logs in your fireplace—they might still burn, but not as well as cured logs. Fortunately for vegetarians, our digestive systems seem to be more designed for a broad range of whole grains, nuts, seeds, and fresh fruits and vegetables.

Meatless for a Healthier Heart

People die from circulatory system diseases daily. You hear about strokes, heart attacks, high cholesterol levels, angina, arteriosclerosis, high blood pressure, and bypass surgery all the time. Although these diseases and treatments are abundant in our world, especially among North Americans, they are almost nonexistent among vegetarians. And coronary heart diseases and some forms of cancer are at the top of the list when it comes to the leading causes of death. Meat-eaters, take note: both of these diseases can be either prevented or made worse by diet!

Veggie Soup for the Soul _____

Reports show that only 1 percent of what the average American eats comes from whole-grain foods, even though there's overwhelming evidence showing that adding more whole grains to the diet lowers the incidence of heart disease and cancer. Surveys show that most Americans say they want more whole-grain foods in their diet but are confused about what whole grains are. See Chapter 18 to learn more and get recipes featuring whole grains.

Circulating Rumors About Cholesterol

Let's start with how eating meat and animal products adds to or creates circulatory system problems. Most of these problems start with eating too much saturated fat, which is found abundantly in all animal flesh and animal products. Too much dietary fat can lead to high cholesterol levels, which begins most types of diet-related heart problems.

Of course, it's not just too much saturated fat that causes high cholesterol—stress is a big factor in both high cholesterol and blood pressure, as is too many refined carbohydrates. So consider all lifestyle factors when working to prevent or control these imbalances.

It All Adds Up

Most meat-eaters eat meat or some animal product at every meal. Some people believe that eliminating red meat from their diets lowers their cholesterol or blood pressure. Although this can be somewhat effective, a lot depends on what type of foods they replace the red meat with.

Remember that animal products such as eggs and cheese are included in a lacto ovo vegetarian diet. Foods like milk chocolate, French toast, and other seemingly non-animal products still contain hidden animal fat, and that fat builds up in the body and can lead to disease.

Blood Pressure and Your Kidneys

Because your kidneys play a role in regulating your blood pressure, meat and animal products affect them, too. When your body breaks down animal protein, it creates uric acid and ammonia by-products, which the kidneys have to filter, making the kidneys work much harder than if they had to break down only plant protein.

Processed meats contain high levels of nitrates, preservatives, and other toxins, and the kidneys have to filter some of these toxins from the body as well. And all animal flesh, processed or not, contains high amounts of sodium; when you eat the flesh, you get the sodium. When you take in an excess of sodium, the sodium attracts water.

Veggie Soup for the Soul

Lipemia is a condition in which dietary fat accumulates in the blood. This condition lasts for about four hours after you consume fat as the liver attempts to break it down and eliminate it from the body.

When you have too much sodium in your diet, you might notice bloating, swollen fingers, and bags under the eyes, and you may feel and look puffy. Although your body is holding excess water, your kidneys are unable to release it because the sodium in your body and blood is holding on to the water. The excess sodium and water in your blood increase the volume of liquid inside your arteries, and the result is high blood pressure.

Please *Don't* Pass the Salt

Your sodium should come from plant life such as celery and strawberries. The sodium in animal flesh and animal products, table salt, and processed foods is inorganic and is too concentrated for your body to process easily. An abundance of inorganic sodium in your diet depletes the amount of potassium in your body. Remember that your heart is a potassium-loving organ. When an excess of sodium is in your body, it can rob your heart and other muscles of the extra potassium needed to balance the excess sodium.

Potassium helps keep the body flexible, and when you have a potassium deficiency, you also get hardening of tissues, such as hardening of the arteries, muscle cramps, and hardened skin and other organs. Symptoms of a deficiency include muscle weakness, paralysis, and confusion. Fresh vegetables and fruits are naturally rich in potassium.

Balancing Deposits

How does all this relate to the kidneys? While all this fighting among minerals is going on, the kidneys continue to try to maintain your mineral balance. For your body to maintain its proper functioning, it constantly attempts to manage the correct balance of minerals and other nutrients in the right proportions. Chemical signals trigger the body's demands for sodium and water.

These signals cause the walls of your kidneys to become more or less permeable to these substances, which are reabsorbed accordingly from the urine, which again leads to overworked kidneys. On top of it all, you still have high blood pressure because you have too much sodium, and more than likely your arteries are clogged and hardened with plaque.

> **Sprouts of Info**
>
> A 1999 University of Minnesota study suggests that if Americans ate one whole-grain product every day, death rates from cancer and heart disease would drop 8 percent. That's 120,000 lives saved every year.

Now that you've taken a look inside your body and have seen what all that meat and animal food can do to it, you can rest much easier eating your tofu, vegetables, fruits, nuts, seeds, beans, and grains, knowing that not only will your circulatory system thank you, but so will your liver, your kidneys, *and* your insurance company.

Weighing In on Being Vegetarian

Not all vegetarians are lean, and not all meat-eaters are overweight. Everyone has his or her own makeup and body shape, metabolism, and eating habits. But vegetarians who follow a healthful balanced vegetarian diet, eat whole foods, and limit the amount of refined carbs they eat are likely to be slender, as are most occasional meat-eaters who balance their diet and eat mostly vegetarian foods.

Hold the Water

As I've mentioned, meat and animal products contain a high amount of sodium. Excess sodium consumption makes you retain water. Water retention tends to make you look and feel puffy and bloated. This makes you feel or look fat by causing puffy eyes, a full face, a bloated abdomen, swollen ankles, and swollen fingers.

The more whole, fresh foods you eat, the faster your body settles at your ideal weight. Taking in a proper amount of water every day throughout the day helps you retain less water.

Steer Clear

Sixty to eighty percent of your foods should include foods with a high water content, like fruits and vegetables. Also try to eat only one concentrated food at any meal. A concentrated food is one with little or no water content, including bread, most starches, cheese, and meat products. If you eat this way, you will lose weight naturally.

Feast or Famine?

Another thing you need to understand when attempting weight loss is that your body is primitive, in that it genetically still "remembers" times of famine. This is exactly why you cannot starve yourself by severely restricting your calories and achieve permanent weight.

In the past, primitive peoples didn't get to run to a grocery store when they were hungry. They had to forage and round up what they could find, and sometimes had to go long periods without food. Primitive people's bodies learned how to store food energy for long periods.

Your body has kept this amazing ability to store reserves of food. Unfortunately, it isn't very discriminating. It can also hold on to toxins, fat, waste products of all kinds, mucus, chemicals, excess water, and so on. This fact is key in understanding why dieting and severely limiting calories for periods of time does not work for long-term weight loss. When the body detects that famine is setting in, it slows down your *metabolism*. When your metabolism slows, you naturally burn fewer calories, your energy levels decrease, and your body holds on to your foods for longer periods. You can think of it as your body rationing out the fat because it believes famine has set in, and it wants to make every calorie last as long as possible. Your body actually believes you're starving, and it's trying to help you survive.

Lettuce Explain _____

Metabolism refers to the ongoing interrelated chemical activities in your body that process and provide the energy and nutrients to sustain life. Your metabolism is controlled by glandular activities in your thyroid, adrenals, and pituitary glands, and can be slowed or increased depending on how your glands perceive the needs of your body. A slow metabolism can be linked to weight gain.

Stuck on the Plateau

So although you might initially lose weight by severely restricting your calories, your body slows down and plateaus rather quickly. When you restrict your caloric intake, you do something unnatural because you make an effort to hold back from eating. You eventually go back to eating the amount you are comfortable with. No one can live with restrictions forever—it's just too tense a way to live.

But while you were restricting your calories, your body got ready for a famine. Now when you go back to eating normally, your body quickly grabs all the calories and hoards them for later! Suddenly you're back to the weight you were—or more.

Sprouts of Info _____

Your body is not your enemy. It wants what is best for you and does what it can to keep you alive. Your body works hard to keep you going despite the abuse and neglect it withstands. A little body awareness can help you become healthier—and thinner—just by paying attention to what your body is trying to tell you.

Reverse Training

You have effectively trained your body to *lower* the amount of calories you are able to survive on effectively. Therefore, if you go back to the amount of food you used to eat, you will likely gain weight consistently.

So how do you change this vicious cycle? Fortunately, you can retrain your metabolism by allowing yourself to eat as many wholesome, fresh vegetarian foods as you want on a consistent basis. By eating primarily vegetarian fare, you naturally keep your quantity of food up but your calories—along with fat and other elements you don't need—at a moderate level.

Be sure your food pyramid looks mostly like this one if you're trying to lose weight. All you need to do is leave out animal products and replace pastas and refined bread products with whole grains. If you get hungry, fill up on high-protein foods like tofu, beans, fatty fruits such as avocados, fruit that goes through your system more slowly (like bananas), or a handful or two of cashews. Check out the following table for some healthful replacements.

The weight-loss food pyramid.

Oils
Sweets
Nuts & Seeds

Fresh Fruit

Cooked Vegetables

Meat Substitutes, Tofu, Tempeh, Beans, Legumes

Fresh, Raw Vegetables, Salads

Slow Cooked Whole Grains (No refined flour products or pasta)

10+ glasses of pure water daily, fresh air, exercise, positive affirmations, family & friends, religious/spiritual values

The "Good Stuff" Replacements

Replace This ...	With This ...
Soda	water
Candy	fruit
Dairy products	vegetables
Meat	tofu
Cow's milk	rice, soy, or nut milk
Chicken eggs	egg replacer
Refined flour products	whole grains
Flour-based crackers and bread	rye crackers
Table salt	bulk kelp and/or capsicum
Sugar	stevia, honey, molasses
Starving yourself	eating lots of foods high in water content
Refined carbohydrates (pasta, flour products)	whole foods
Inactivity	exercise
Negative self-talk and excuses	positive affirmations

Instead of trying to give up the things you know are bad for you, keep adding good things until one day you find you no longer have room or desire for the bad. At some point, something has to go. I'm betting your old eating habits, and your excess weight along with them, will soon be extinct.

Building Good Habits

See how it works? As you continue to fill your life with all the good things, you have no room for the bad! You would have to create tension just to shove down that piece of cake, really!

Here are some things to keep in mind when you want to lose weight:

◆ Don't fight to be thin. Let yourself become thin by making better food choices.

◆ Understand that you are what you eat, and eat that way. (i.e., lean, low-fat, clean, organic, toxin-free, high-water-content foods).

◆ Eat all the veggie foods you want, and avoid the processed foods. Eating whole foods means you can eat all day long. Have a banana, a handful of raw cashews, or a glass of cold carrot juice for a snack instead of a Pop-Tart, and you won't have to worry about calories.

◆ If you're not feeling satisfied, go for some protein and/or vegetable fat—nut butters or soy yogurts generally do the trick. Snacking on refined-carb snacks like low-fat cookies can cause binging.

◆ Make 60 to 80 percent of your foods high-water-content foods, like fresh fruits and vegetables.

◆ Eat only one concentrated food at any meal. Concentrated foods include most starches (bread, pasta, potatoes) and foods that do not contain much water.

◆ Avoid refined carbohydrates such as breads and crackers.

◆ Eat only two handfuls of food at a sitting, and stop eating at least four hours before bedtime.

◆ Hang out with active people who inspire you to be fit.

◆ Exercise at least five days a week. Weight-train three days a week and do cardio the other two or three days. Take a cardio class of some type— make it fun!

◆ Drink plenty of clean water. Divide your bodyweight in half to figure out how many ounces you should get daily, and add more when you're losing weight or cleansing.

◆ Envision yourself at your best.

> **Sprouts of Info**
>
> Simply by substituting all the high-calorie drinks with pure water will cut your average caloric intake by about 225 calories per day. Replacing just one soda a day with water can help you lose more than 10 pounds in a year!

Don't force or rush yourself to lose weight! Let yourself be thin by adding more and more quality foods and good things to your life. Let yourself evolve over time naturally. Remember, don't starve yourself. You'll just mess up your metabolism.

Finally, good self-talk is just as important as healthful habits. Wake up each morning and ask yourself, "What positive things am I going to do today to achieve my goals?"

Vibrant Vegetarian Skin

Whether or not beauty is only skin deep, your skin is still your largest organ and needs proper care. Although you probably take your skin for granted, it is a living, breathing part of you that serves to protect your insides from invaders and deserves to be taken seriously. Besides, the health of your skin reflects how it looks, which affects your appearance.

Beautiful Bioflavonoids

Plant foods like fruits and vegetables contain phytochemicals called *bioflavonoids* that give the plant's skin strength and integrity. In your body, bioflavonoids have many purposes, including nourishing and strengthening the cellular walls of the tiny blood capillaries found throughout your body. Broken blood capillaries, also called spider veins, are tiny red or purplish splotches on your skin. They can be anywhere, but many people find them on their legs, nose, and cheeks. Delicate skin and areas where skin is exposed to the elements are more vulnerable to broken capillaries.

By eating lots of fresh fruits and vegetables with the skins, you will certainly get plenty of bioflavonoids, which can help you avoid weakened blood vessels. Weakened blood vessels can cause you to bruise easily and can produce unsightly broken blood vessels that make your skin appear blotchy.

Greasy Kid Stuff

Your skin contains oil glands. These glands help lubricate your skin to keep it young, glowing, and supple-looking. But if you have too much fat and oil in your system due to meat and dairy consumption, these extra fats can cause a greasy complexion that can easily break out with pimples.

The extra fat from a meat-based diet can clog your system with sludgy, oily substances and might contribute to overactive oil glands, which cause acne. By eating a vegetarian diet, you will have lots of variety and less than half the amount of greasy oils you get from eating meat and cheese. Overall, the vegetarian diet helps keep your skin from being too oily, so there's another reason a plant-based diet can help you have better-looking skin!

> **Steer Clear**
>
> Coffee beans sometimes contain a great deal of oil, especially the flavored coffees, which can be made by spraying flavorful oil over the beans. If you have an acne problem and are drinking a lot of coffee, try limiting your intake for a few days and note the difference.

The Least You Need to Know

◆ Non-meat-eaters naturally eliminate excess sodium in the diet, which has been linked to high blood pressure.

◆ Animal flesh and animal products are high in saturated fat, which can lead to high cholesterol. Vegetarians often don't have high cholesterol.

◆ Never starve yourself. It only slows the metabolism and makes you gain more weight later.

◆ Vegetarians must avoid loading up on refined carbohydrates such as flour-based products and pastas, which can easily turn to fat in a sedentary person. Instead, fill up on vegetables and high-protein meat substitutes to lose or maintain ideal weight.

◆ Vegetarian diets contain lots of bioflavonoids, which strengthen blood capillaries and can help keep skin looking beautiful.

Chapter 6

A Passion for Compassion

In This Chapter

- The environmental effects of eating meat
- Learn about the irradiation of foods
- Discover the unbelievable cruelties of factory farming
- Find out how to live and shop cruelty free

Now that you've learned many of the health and nutritional aspects associated with your diet, I'd like to share how your food choices influence other areas of life. I'm sure you'll be pleased to discover how much excess water consumption, land waste, pollution, and world hunger you *won't* contribute to simply by eliminating meat from your life! Your choices truly do make a difference.

Draining Us Dry

As a vegetarian, you're certainly doing a lot of good for the earth's water resources because you're not contributing to the demand for meat, which takes a tremendous toll on the water supply. How? Farmers need plenty of water to raise agricultural crops for human consumption, but they actually use *more* water to raise crops that are grown and harvested for animal feed!

Sprouts of Info _____

Agricultural wastes are more often being detected in local water supplies. This means more chemicals must be used to clean the water, which uses up even more resources just to manage drinking water supplies, fueling the vicious cycle of chasing symptoms with more poisons.

This is due to the rise of feedlots for cattle, pigs, and other farm animals. About 50 percent of the water consumed in the United States is being used to grow crops used for grain-fed animals, whereas only about 35 percent of water used for irrigation is for food crops meant for humans. It's estimated that 2,500 gallons of water produce a 1-pound beef steak. That's about 15 times the amount of water needed to produce the same amount of protein from plant sources.

It doesn't take such enormous amounts of water to produce fruits and vegetables. For example, it takes only about 23 gallons of water to produce 1 pound of tomatoes, 25 gallons of water to produce a pound of carrots, and 33 gallons to produce 1 pound of wheat! So when you eat a plant-based diet, you use water much more efficiently and conserve a precious resource.

It's a Dirty Business

The vegetarian diet conserves water directly, and it also lessens water pollution due to agricultural waste products. Animals living in the wild who are free to roam excrete their wastes over a large area. These waste products return to the soil and are properly recycled by the earth's natural processes. In modern industrial farming, animals are corralled in feedlots or live in more crowded conditions that produce an overwhelming amount of manure concentrated in one area. Nature can't absorb these abundant wastes back into the land safely. That leaves the excess to wash off or soak in and pollute rivers and streams.

Steer Clear _____

Wastes from both pig and poultry factories serve as a catalyst for _Pfiesteria_ outbreaks, a toxic form of algae. This toxin has killed billions of fish and causes memory loss in humans who come in contact with it. Pig waste creates ammonia, which evaporates into the air and contributes to acid rain, again polluting the water and soil.

If nothing else, the vegetarian lessens the demand for these damaging and polluting factory farms.

Logical Land Use

Raising grain for livestock to produce meat on cropland is an inefficient use of the land. Why not just eat the soy burger (made from soybeans raised for livestock feed) with an ear of corn (a grain raised for livestock feed) on a whole-wheat bun (another grain used for feeding cattle) to get your supply of protein? Wouldn't this be more efficient than waiting for that steer to be fattened up on practically the same foods and then eating 1 pound of the animal's body?

Something's in the Air ...

Naturally occurring chemicals can be just as bad as the manufactured kind. Farm animals produce quite a few of them; in fact, they account for about 10 times more waste than the human population.

Cattle naturally produce methane gas. Methane gas makes up 9 percent of the gasses creating the greenhouse effect, which is directly linked to global warming. Livestock, and especially cattle, also produce waste that is high in nitrous oxide, another greenhouse gas. Animal waste is the second largest source of emissions of this gas; cattle waste makes up 95 percent of it.

Deforestation of the rain forests for the purpose of raising cattle contributes to the greenhouse effect and global warming, and some scientists believe that this throws the earth's natural climate control out of whack.

Runoff from manure and dairy-house milk wash contains high amounts of nitrogen, phosphorous, pathogens, and detergents. These can flow directly into waterways, creating ideal conditions for the rapid growth of algae. Algae eat up significant amounts of oxygen and, in turn, can suffocate and damage fish habitats.

Transportation of cattle and swine to slaughterhouses via semi trucks contributes to diesel fuel emissions.

The list could go on and on, but I think you get the point.

X-Rated Meat?

The U.S. Food and Drug Administration (FDA) has approved the irradiation of red meat, and other foods, such as poultry. And fresh produce and spices are already being bombarded with this radiation.

Lettuce Explain _____

Irradiation is a process that showers foods with powerful radiation after the foods are placed inside a secure chamber. The purpose is to burst apart the DNA molecules of any food-borne bacteria that could cause food poisoning.

Irradiation kills organisms such as salmonella, listera, and E. coli that cause food poisoning without harming the food, says the FDA. The foods are placed in a secure irradiation chamber and blasted with a powerful electron beam that scans the food and breaks the DNA bonds of bacteria that could be lurking on it.

Food irradiation is not new—in fact, the patent that paved the way with an x-ray process to treat meat was granted in 1921. This form of discharging kiloGrays (lethal to humans) onto foods is expected to be used more frequently in the future, especially as food-borne illness scares increase.

The following table shows the known effects that irradiation has on food and gives some thoughts to ponder.

Irradiation Facts

Fact	Commentary
Irradiation produces about the amount of nutrient loss in foods as other processing methods such as canning.	Whole, live, enzyme-rich foods direct same from nature nourish your body. If irradiating fresh produce makes the food equivalent to a canned or otherwise processed food, why bother with the fresh produce?
Irradiated strawberries and other fresh fruits last significantly longer than produce that has not been irradiated without rotting or molding, and potatoes are stunted and can, therefore, be stored longer.	If we get life from the foods we eat, why would we want to purchase fresh produce that has effectively been embalmed?
Irradiation causes the skins of some fruits to soften.	Could this be anything like what radioactive fallout does to human skin?
Irradiation causes undesirable flavor changes in cheese, milk, and other dairy products.	Pew!
Irradiated meat tends to have a darker color and smells "off."	Your nose knows!

No matter which side of the fence you are on about irradiation, there are a few things you need to know. If it makes you feel safer to eat irradiated foods or if you would like to avoid these foods entirely, you should look for the following symbol in the figure when grocery shopping.

Since 1986, all irradiated products sold in stores must carry this international symbol, the radura.

This symbol is required to be posted near or on irradiated foods. Although you can seek or steer clear of foods with this symbol at your grocery store, restaurants and hospitals are not required to disclose this information when the foods are served.

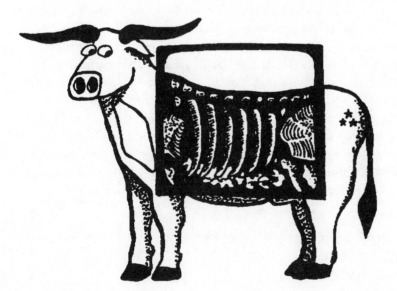

The FDA now allows irradiation of beef to kill bacteria.

(Drawing by artist Glenn Beckmann, Kenai, Alaska)

Support Your Local Organic Farmer

Some farmers and field workers do have a special affinity for nature. They see how nature works and understand the gifts the earth provides. Talk to some of them, and you will see. The farmer who is in touch with nature is usually a good man or woman with good intentions. Support these people with your pocketbook by purchasing their foods.

Wouldn't you rather support the good old-fashioned farmer who works with the earth to bring you wholesome, nourishing, unadulterated, nonhybrid, pesticide-free, non-waxed, vine-ripened food? Ahh, utopia!

The Horror of Factory Farms

To any person with a compassionate bone in his or her body, the realities of slaughterhouses and factory farming are easily enough to drive a person to give up meat for good.

To spare you all the unbelievably horrific but unfortunately realistic details, simply put, the factory farming system of modern agribusiness is designed to produce the maximum amount of meat, milk, and eggs as quickly and cheaply as possible, and in the least amount of space. Cows, calves, pigs, chickens, sheep, goats, turkeys, ducks, geese, rabbits, and other animals raised in factory farms are kept in the smallest areas possible, often restricting their movement so they are not even able to turn around. These farm animals are deprived of exercise, sunshine, and any sort of natural environment so that all of their bodies' energy goes toward producing flesh, eggs, or milk for human consumption. They are fed growth hormones to fatten them faster and are genetically altered to grow larger or to produce more milk or eggs than nature intended. They are loaded with antibiotics and other drugs to keep them from being taken over by bacteria and viruses. They live a life of suffering from the beginning to the end.

Here are some more personal things you can do as an activist to protect farm animals from abuse:

- Become a strict vegetarian or vegan.
- Boycott restaurants that serve veal and let them know why.

◆ Fill out comment cards in restaurants requesting more vegetarian items on the menu.

◆ Ask your state legislators to sponsor bills that would prohibit the use of veal crates.

◆ If you do choose to eat meat or other animal products occasionally, buy organic, free-range products when possible.

Sprouts of Info

Vegetarians should be happy to know that the Farm Animal Reform Movement (FARM, www.farmusa.org), the Farm Sanctuary, and similar organizations are fighting to improve factory farm situations.

Cruelty-Free Living

One of the greatest powers we have is our buying power. Money runs the economy, and your money contributes to the demand for certain products. It drives what kinds of items are manufactured and made available. This same rule of supply and demand holds true for other consumer goods, from the obviously cruel products like fur to the not-so-obviously cruel products like many hairsprays, cosmetics, and household items.

Most people already know not to drink shampoo, eat a tube of toothpaste, or flush their eyes with toilet bowl cleaner! However, many companies continue to force-feed these substances to rabbits, rats, mice, dogs, cats, guinea pigs, and other animals because it has been industry standard to do so. However, cruelty-free companies have found alternatives to conducting these animal tests. Consumers can help make these practices more the norm by supporting these companies and letting the other companies know they will only purchase cruelty-free products.

Needless Cruelty

The FDA does not require animal testing for beauty products. It requires only that each ingredient in a cosmetic product be adequately substantiated for safety. These safety tests can be done without the use of animals. Millions of animals suffer terribly and are killed in the name of testing products despite the lack of requirements to use animals. In addition, the makers of household items, such as cleaning formulas and the like, are also not required by their governing body, the Consumer Product Safety Commission (CPSC), to test their products on animals, but many manufacturers do it anyway.

Manufacturers determine testing methods. Many companies like the idea that their products were tested on animals because they feel it is a good defense in the face of possible consumer lawsuits. Others believe that testing on animals helps them compete in the marketplace because consumers demand products with exciting new ingredients, and animal tests are often considered the easiest and cheapest way to prove that new ingredients are safe. The reality is that animal tests are not necessarily the best, cheapest, or most accurate.

Animal Test Alternatives

Hundreds of cruelty-free product manufacturers of household and beauty products refuse to engage in animal testing. Manufacturers that do not use animals can substitute cell and tissue cultures, corneas donated from eye banks. Many vegetarians help reduce animal suffering by becoming organ donors. Ask for the designation when you get or renew your driver's license. Companies also use sophisticated mathematical models and computer programs to determine the safety of products. (After all, we are living in the age of computers—why should our testing methods stay in the Dark Ages?)

These manufacturers tend to choose ingredients for their products that already have proven track records. These companies maintain and use databases that show ingredient and formula information they've gathered from other companies that have already performed safety tests in vitro, in human clinical studies, or both. Many of these companies do not use toxic or dangerous ingredients in their products and instead take advantage of the many safe ingredient alternatives available—even fruits, vegetables, and grains!

To be sure you don't contribute to the needless suffering of animals used in product testing, patronize companies that do not test on animals. PETA can give you a complete list of such companies. Contact them at:

> **PETA (People for the Ethical Treatment of Animals)**
> 501 Front St., Norfolk, VA 23510
> 757-622-PETA (757-622-7382)
> Fax: 757-622-0457
> info@peta-online.org
> www.peta.org

Hidden Animal Ingredients

Here's a sampling of some hidden animal ingredients and their vegetarian alternatives. For more on ingredients in food and cosmetics, consult *A Consumer's Dictionary of Cosmetic Ingredients* by Ruth Winter (Three Rivers Press, 1999) and *A Consumer's Dictionary of Food Additives* by Ruth Winter (Three Rivers Press, 1999).

Ingredient	What It Is	What It's Used In	Veg Alternative
Adrenaline	from adrenal glands of animals	medicine	synthetics
Allantoin	uric acid from cows	creams and lotions	comfrey root extract, synthetics
Carmine, cochineal, carminic acid	red pigment from crushed female cochineal insect	used to color items red; commonly found in lollipops, red apple sauce, shampoos, cosmetics	beet juice
Egg protein	poultry eggs	shampoos, skin-care items	plant proteins
Keratin	protein from ground animal horns	shampoos, permanent wave solutions,	soy protein, almond oil, rosemary

Look for the Logo

Although switching to all non-animal-tested (cruelty-free) products can be a tedious process at first, the work is over after you find your favorite brands. It is unlikely that any company with a no-testing-on-animals policy would suddenly decide to switch to animal testing.

Look for this cruelty-free logo on cosmetic and household products. This international logo can be used only on packaging and advertising by manufacturers that sign the Corporate Standard of Compassion for Animals, a strong pledge stating that the manufacturer does not conduct or commission animal tests for their products, nor does it use ingredients or formulations that are tested on animals. In addition, once the logo is licensed, the manufacturer agrees to an independently commissioned audit to verify its compliance with the standard.

The international cruelty-free logo used by manufacturers of cosmetic and household products that do not test on animals.

(Logo used here with permission from the Coalition for Consumer Information on Cosmetics)

The CCIC (Coalition for Consumer Information on Cosmetics) logo is the international symbol used by manufacturers of cosmetic and household products that comply with the Corporate Standard of Compassion for Animals. The logo program is supported by a unique coalition of more than 50 animal advocacy organizations worldwide and was launched in 1998.

> ### Veggie Soup for the Soul
>
> The Coalition for Consumer Information on Cosmetics (CCIC) works to ensure that companies using its logo do not conduct or commission animal testing. Most products manufactured with compassion may be safer for the earth and safer for you, anyway, because these products tend to be more natural, more environmentally friendly, and less toxic overall.

If you find that you use some products that aren't cruelty free that you just cannot live without, write the company to tell it you will boycott unless it comes up with alternatives to animal testing. This consumer feedback works! Many companies that once tested on animals have switched to other methods. At the least, you will get a response telling you where the company stands on the issue, and you can decide from there whether you can continue to support it with your patronage.

When you get the swing of it, you'll see that cruelty free is an easy way to live, eat, and shop.

The Least You Need to Know

◆ A vegetarian diet uses about 15 times less water than a meat-based diet, which helps conserve one of earth's natural resources.

◆ Arguments exist for and against the irradiation of meat and produce. Investigate the issue for yourself, and look for the radura symbol when you purchase food.

◆ Animal factory farming manipulates and interferes with natural processes to produce more animal products at the expense of the animals' welfare.

◆ Using cruelty-free products ensures that you do not contribute to unnecessary testing of cosmetics and household products.

Part 2

What's for Breakfast?

Good morning! Welcome to Part 2, where the recipes begin. We start with breakfast, naturally, a very important part of everyone's day for the best health and well-being. I also discuss the pros and cons of eating eggs because, no doubt, some of you are ovo vegetarians. And of course, because bacon isn't on the vegetarian breakfast menu, I offer nearly 15 balanced—and bacon-free!—breakfasts you can try instead. So take a fast break for breakfast, and get your day started right!

Chapter 7

I Brake for Breakfast!

In This Chapter

- ◆ Eating breakfast is *so* important—don't skip it!
- ◆ Understand how breakfast affects hormones
- ◆ The importance of steady blood sugar
- ◆ Satisfying breakfast recipes

Ready for breakfast? Some people tell me that if they eat breakfast, they're constantly hungry the rest of the day. To avoid feeling the all-day need to gorge, eat a protein-rich meal in the morning. Most of the breakfast recipes you'll find in this and the next two chapters are rich in protein, like the Artichoke and Goat Cheese Tofu Scramble (Chapter 8) and the Whey Good Smoothie (Chapter 9). Before you skip breakfast again, give some of these a try.

But before we get to the recipes, allow me to explain a little more about why it's important for you to eat something in the morning and how eating breakfast, especially the right kinds of foods, contributes to hormonal and blood sugar balance—which can make a huge difference in the way you feel for the rest of the day.

Breakfast and Metabolism

Your metabolism is generally higher during the day and slower in the evening. That means you can get away with eating more in the A.M. and less in the P.M. without turning those meals into extra pounds. Plus, by eating earlier, you have all day to burn off those meals.

It's important to your metabolism and general hormonal balance to eat at least some type of healthful snack in the morning. Breakfast not only stimulates your digestive system to begin working and signals your bowels to eliminate yesterday's intake, but it also helps keep your *cortisol* levels balanced.

Lettuce Explain

Cortisol is a steroid hormone secreted by the adrenal glands and regulated by the brain in response to stress. Cortisol is needed to maintain normal physiological processes during times of stress; without cortisol, the body would be unable to respond effectively to stress. An effective cortisol metabolism is important to maintain balance in the body.

Cortisol is a double-edged sword of a hormone—too little or too much can create immune system problems, blood sugar problems, weight gain, and a host of other issues. However, the right amount of cortisol helps normalize blood sugar, regulate the immune system, control inflammation in the tissues, protect cells from excess insulin, and balance blood pressure.

Cortisol levels tend to be higher in the morning, which helps you wake up, and then drop off rapidly after about 10 A.M. Eating something by or before 10 A.M., when your cortisol levels naturally drop, is a good way to help steady cortisol in your system for the rest of the day and help keep your glucose balanced and your metabolism buzzing, which, in turn, helps keep you feeling more relaxed and your appetite more reasonable.

Sprouts of Info

If you aren't hungry in the morning, it could mean you have a sluggish liver that's not metabolizing glucose efficiently. Try knocking off the sugar and dairy for a few days and eat lots of beets and salads. You can also take some liver-detoxing herbs or supplements such as N-acetyl cysteine and/or milk thistle to help the detoxifying process and protect your liver.

Breakfast and Blood Sugar

As with cortisol, you need to keep your blood sugar (glycogen) within proper levels. When you eat, your blood sugar rises and your pancreas secretes a proper amount of insulin to keep your blood sugar levels from getting too high. Continual high blood sugar causes diabetes and a host of other health problems. Too-low blood sugar is termed *hypoglycemia*, and severe cases cause fainting. And because glucose is the main food for the brain, severe or prolonged low-blood-sugar causes brain damage.

Keeping blood sugar steady is important to proper metabolism, weight management, clear thinking, overall health, and a balanced appetite. Exercise, food, and drink all affect blood sugar.

Here's how breakfast fits in: during sleep, the body is in a fasting state. With no food going in, the body works on healing, repair, cleansing, and rebuilding. By the time you wake up, your glucose level is naturally low, which, in most cases, stimulates hunger, therefore signaling breakfast time. When you eat something healthful (like any of the following breakfast recipes!), your blood sugar steadies and you are on track for at least the next three to five hours. After that time, your blood sugar again begins to fall and triggers you to eat. Eating a little bit of good food—not sugary snacks!—every three or four hours is a great way to keep your metabolism buzzing and your blood sugar steady.

Lettuce Explain

Hypoglycemia is an abnormally low level of sugar (glucose) in the blood. Symptoms may include headache, shakiness, sweating, fatigue, intense hunger, and spacyness. Prolonged and/or severe drops in blood sugar cause brain damage.

Sprouts of Info

Sleep is very important to health and metabolism. Many studies show a high correlation between people who are sleep deprived (getting fewer than eight hours of sleep each night) and obesity.

However, if the first thing you do in the morning is take in caffeinated coffee, the caffeine stimulates your adrenals, which temporarily lowers your appetite, removing that natural hunger you woke up with. If you skip breakfast, especially under the influence of caffeine, your blood sugar soon plummets, leaving you with an intense hunger, especially for the wrong type of foods, such as sugar or refined carbs. Worst of all, this intense hunger generally leads to overeating. You may also feel somewhat fatigued the rest of the day due to the internal damage that takes place when blood sugar falls so rapidly.

Even without the influence of caffeine, blood sugar levels as well as cortisol levels continue to drop naturally without breakfast. Eating foods that are high in fiber, protein, and/or fat is ideal for helping you keep your blood sugar levels balanced throughout the day.

Eating foods rich in fiber helps your body absorb sugar more slowly, which is another way to keep your blood sugar from spiking. Fats such as butter have a similar effect. Fat also signals satiation in the brain so you feel full. That's why a bowl of oatmeal with a little bit of butter or cream is a great start to any day. Although oatmeal is high in carbs, it's also high in fiber, which counteracts some of the carbs, and the fat from butter or cream adds to the satiation factor, giving you longer-lasting energy from your meal.

Steer Clear

"What goes up must come down" and "the taller they are, the harder they fall." Likewise, eating such things as high-sugar cereal, a glass of fruit juice, and/or a doughnut for breakfast causes your blood sugar to go up fast and high, which always follows with a plummet. That plummet promotes cellular damage and contributes to poor health.

Work It Out

We should all exercise at least five times a week for a healthy, fit body. But keep in mind that exercise also affects you hormonally. In particular, cardiovascular exercise raises cortisol levels and burns sugar from your muscles—which also uses up some insulin to keep the sugar getting into the cells, which also helps keep blood sugar more balanced.

It can be more comfortable to exercise with an empty stomach, but be sure to have some type of proper nutrition at least a few hours before exercising. It takes your stomach about 2 to 4 hours to empty after a regular meal. Having some protein, such as a protein shake, in your system prior to exercise keeps your blood sugar from getting too low during exercise, which helps prevent the damage hypoglycemia can cause.

Muesli: The Perfect Breakfast Food

Muesli could very well be the perfect breakfast food; it contains just about all the great things your body needs for health in one small but powerful meal.

Muesli was introduced by Swiss physician Dr. Maximilian Bircher-Benner in the early 1900s. Dr. Bircher-Benner promoted vegetarianism and ran a sanatorium in Zurich that focused heavily on a raw fruit, nut, and vegetable diet as part of the healing therapy for patients. Around the same time, Dr. John Harvey Kellogg, also a vegetarian, was doing similar work in the United States. And if that name sounds familiar to you, Dr. Kellogg is most famous for his introduction of Kellogg's Corn Flakes cereal.

The following recipe for Coconut and Blueberry Muesli is great for breakfast because you get a little bit of everything—whole, raw grains for fiber; minerals and B vitamins to feed your brain; raw nuts and seeds for essential fatty acids and protein; low-fat yogurt for additional protein; and fresh fruit such as blueberries, which give you phytochemicals and enzymes.

Sprouts of Info

Blueberries contain nutrients that protect your eyesight—especially protection from night blindness. They also have some of the same substances cranberries contain that help protect your bladder from infection. Blueberries are higher in potassium than bananas are, so they're great for the body if you work out. Potassium feeds the muscles and can help eliminate muscle fatigue and/or cramping with strenuous exercise.

When making muesli, you can have what I call the "cereal and milk syndrome"—add too much muesli and you need more yogurt; add too much yogurt and you need more muesli. Soon you can have a whole mixing bowl full! This is a filling food, so the key is balance. I like to use a small juice glass to mix my muesli, to help control portions. Try ½ cup dry muesli and ½ cup yogurt to start. Add a little more yogurt for a creamier texture and a little more muesli for a crunchier texture.

The longer the muesli sits in the yogurt, the softer it gets as the grains and nuts soak in the yogurt and enzymes from the fresh berries. You can vary this recipe with any of your favorite fruits. I also like adding some banana slices to this recipe. For "wetter" consistency, add watermelon chunks. For a crunchier consistency, add chopped apple or pear.

Veggie Soup for the Soul

You can eat the dried mix as a cereal with any plant- or nut-based milks if you'd rather not have it with yogurt.

Next come the recipes! This chapter includes some recipes for big meals for breakfast. Of course, not everyone has the time (or desire) to have such a big breakfast every day. So some of these recipes may be more of a treat for weekends or brunches, whereas a protein smoothie (see Chapter 9) or the muesli recipe would be easier, quicker, and more practical on a daily basis. Whatever you choose, go enjoy your breakfast and have a great rest of the day!

The Least You Need to Know

◆ Metabolism is higher in the day and slower in the evening, so eat your larger meals early and then take in less as the day goes on, to avoid your meals turning into excess pounds.

◆ Foods containing fiber, protein, and fat aid blood sugar balance.

◆ Caffeine, sugar, and refined carbohydrates are the worst choices for breakfast, as they make the blood sugar plummet; that can wreak metabolic havoc.

◆ Blueberries are rich in potassium, which feeds the heart and muscles. Some of their other phytochemicals can protect eyesight and promote bladder health.

Coconut and Blueberry Muesli

The slightly crunchy and creamy texture of this chilled muesli complements its semisweet and nutty flavor. Fresh blueberries give each bite an extra moist pop of texture.

4½ cups rolled oats

1 cup unsweetened, shredded coconut

1 cup raisins

½ cup toasted wheat germ

½ cup oat bran

¼ cup raw chopped cashews

¼ cup raw sunflower seeds

½ cup low-fat vanilla yogurt or soy yogurt

Fresh blueberries

Serves: 8
Prep time: 5 minutes
Serving size: 1 cup muesli

1. In a large mixing bowl, combine oats, coconut, raisins, wheat germ, oat bran, cashews, and sunflower seeds. Mix well. Store unused portion in an airtight container in a cool, dry place.

2. Add about ½ cup muesli to a serving cup or bowl. Add yogurt to muesli and mix well. Fold in fresh blueberries.

3. Let sit for 5 to 20 minutes to get the consistency you like. Serve chilled.

Sprouts of Info

Find premade muesli in the bulk section of your health food store or prepackaged. When you get it home, store muesli in an airtight container. This recipe keeps for about two months at room temperature.

Mountain Man Breakfast

This hearty breakfast ensemble consists of Tofu Scramble, Meatless Breakfast Patties, Hash Browns, and an English muffin. Topping it off with a handful of fresh alfalfa sprouts and a couple slices of fresh orange as a raw garnish provides enzymes and phytochemicals.

Serves: 1 or 2	
Prep time: 5 minutes	
Cook time: 15 minutes	
Serving size: 1 large plate or 2 small-medium plates	

2 cups frozen hash browns or about 2 medium-large potatoes, cut into ½-in. cubes or shredded

6 TB. olive oil

2 meatless breakfast patties, frozen

1 slice whole-grain bread

⅔ lb. firm tofu, drained and crumbled

Freshly ground black pepper

1 TB. dried basil

⅓ cup artichoke hearts, chopped

½ cup crumbled goat cheese

Butter or soy margarine (optional)

1. Cook hash browns as directed on package. Or if making your own, heat 2 tablespoons olive oil in frying pan over medium-high heat. Add potatoes in single layer and cover. Turn over potatoes when brown, and cook on other side.

2. In a smaller skillet, add 2 tablespoons olive oil and fry meatless patties until heated through. If using frozen patties, this usually takes 4 to 6 minutes per side.

3. Toast bread.

4. In large nonstick skillet, heat remaining 2 tablespoons olive oil over medium-high heat. When hot, add tofu and sauté until light brown. Add black pepper, basil, and artichoke hearts, and sauté until heated through. Fold in cheese crumbles until melted.

5. Serve hot with hash browns; meatless breakfast patties; and a crispy toasted, buttered (if using) toast. Add fresh orange slices, alfalfa sprouts, and a sprig of parsley as garnish if desired.

Veggie Soup for the Soul

Think of the tofu in this recipe as a scrambled egg replacement, and prepare it like you would scrambled eggs. Depending on how you like your eggs—firmer or runnier—cook the tofu similarly by either adding more water-content items like artichokes to make the tofu runnier or draining the artichoke hearts from the oil (same goes if you purchased them packed in water) and use less cheese for firmer. You can also give the tofu a few good squeezes over the sink before crumbling it to remove excess water. Or cook the tofu a little longer to make it firmer.

This meal is completely vegetarian, but it's hearty enough to satisfy a hungry mountain man!

"Bubble and Squeak" Breakfast Burrito

A mix of spicy artichoke and goat cheese tofu scramble, meatless breakfast patty chunks, crunchy hash browns, and salsa warmed and wrapped in a large, organic whole-wheat tortilla make this a filling breakfast option.

Serves: 1 or 2
Prep time: 2 minutes
Cook time: 4 minutes
Serving size: 1 burrito

Leftover tofu scramble, meatless breakfast patties, hash browns, and tofu scramble (from Mountain Man Breakfast)

1 whole-wheat, organic tortilla

Salsa (optional)

1. Spray a skillet with olive oil and set over medium-high heat.

2. Chop meatless breakfast patties and warm in the skillet. Mix in leftover hash browns and tofu scramble.

3. When warmed, remove contents from the skillet and place in tortilla. Add salsa (if using), roll up, and enjoy your breakfast burrito!

Variation: If you're not in the mood for frying, you can microwave the burrito contents instead.

Veggie Soup for the Soul

I learned of Bubbles and Squeak from London menus. Traditionally, Bubbles and Squeak was last night's dinner leftovers all mixed together and fried. Each menu varied the ingredients, but typically peas, mashed potatoes, cabbage, and some ham or boiled beef were included. The name "bubbles" comes from how the vegetables sounded when boiled, and the "squeak" apparently comes from the squeaking sounds when you fry everything together.

Hash Brown and Veggie Skillet

The starchy, soft texture of potatoes in this meal complements the slightly crunchy, zesty, water-content fresh veggies and the refreshing cilantro. The optional cheese folded in at the end binds it together.

1 TB. olive oil

3 large russet potatoes, shredded

1 medium onion, chopped

1 medium green bell pepper, ribs and seeds removed, and chopped

1 medium red bell pepper, ribs and seeds removed, and chopped

1 medium zucchini, sliced

2 TB. chopped fresh cilantro

Freshly ground black pepper

1 cup shredded mozzarella cheese

Salsa and sour cream (optional)

Serves: 2
Prep time: 5 to 10 minutes
Cook time: 20 to 30 minutes
Serving size: about 2 cups

1. Heat olive oil in large frying pan over medium-high heat. When hot, add potatoes and cover. Turn potatoes when browned on one side, about 15 minutes.

2. Add onion, green bell pepper, and red bell pepper. Cover and cook for about 5 minutes or until hash browns are about half-done.

3. Add zucchini, cilantro, and ground black pepper. Mix and sauté all vegetables until zucchini slices are desired softness.

4. Turn off heat, and fold mozzarella into veggies. Serve immediately with salsa and/or topped with sour cream (optional).

Sprouts of Info

Use your favorite types of potatoes in this and all recipes that call for potatoes. There are too many varieties to cover, but potatoes range in textures from more creamy, sweet to more dry, from purple to white, red and typical brown skin russets. Russets are the most common. Have fun trying them out!

Chapter 8

Scrambling for an Egg Alternative

In This Chapter

◆ To eat eggs or to not eat eggs?

◆ Finding a good egg substitute

◆ Making eggs a healthful choice

◆ Yummy eggless recipes

If your taste for eggs is something you don't want to give up or if you're on the (chicken wire) fence about whether to eat eggs, this chapter gives you the reasons many vegetarians skip eggs—but also gives the positives about eggs and informs you ovo vegetarians how to make good egg choices. In this chapter, you'll find recipes for some of my favorite egg substitute meals to expand your breakfast choices. Enjoy!

Too Chicken to Eat Eggs?

You might be too chicken to eat eggs when you realize that the shells of eggs are a breeding ground for *salmonella* bacteria, which causes many violent episodes of food poisoning every year. The eggshells get contaminated with this bacterium in many ways, including contact with chicken feces. Although most people discard the eggshells, contamination can occur if any part of the egg comes in contact with the shell when the egg is broken open. Even if you're careful when handling raw eggs and their shells, you still might not be protected from salmonella poisoning. Researchers have discovered a new evolved strain of the salmonella bacteria that's found in the egg yolk itself.

Veggie Soup for the Soul

Salmonella is a bacteria commonly found in and on eggs and in and on poultry products, such as chicken. Three types exist. The two common strains of salmonella cause the food poisoning called *salmonella gastroenteritis*, which creates acute symptoms such as diarrhea, cramps, fever, and vomiting, and can be fatal for immuno-suppressed individuals. A third type of salmonella is responsible for typhoid fever.

Steer Clear

Raw eggs and their shells carry salmonella, which causes acute illness. Did you ever accidentally drop an eggshell into the cake batter after you cracked it? Even if the yolk wasn't carrying the bacteria, you probably contaminated the batter with the eggshell. Don't let your kids lick the bowl or spoon when making foods that include raw eggs.

The problem with salmonella is compounded when the carcasses of dead chickens carrying the bacteria are ground and added to chicken feed, allowing the bacteria to continually circulate inside and outside the chickens and their eggs.

Salmonella is effectively killed by thoroughly cooking eggs or chicken. Unfortunately, the poisoning does not always come from the eggs themselves. The most prominent problems occur when food handlers touch a contaminated eggshell and pass it on to other food.

Contamination is also transferred via cutting boards where eggshells or chicken flesh have been. And, of course, you can get salmonella poisoning by eating egg-containing products that are not cooked thoroughly enough to kill the bacteria. Mayonnaise and potato salad are frequent trouble spots.

Getting a Rise Without Eggs

Okay, so how do you cook without eggs? Here are some simple substitutes to use in place of eggs for cooking:

◆ Ener-G Egg Replacer is a powdered mix made primarily from potato starch and tapioca flour, and can be found where health foods are sold. One box is the equivalent to about 120 eggs and, therefore, lasts a long time. Furthermore, you don't need to worry about it spoiling like eggs would!

◆ Use half a smashed ripened banana in cooking to give stickiness to your baked goods.

◆ Mix 1 teaspoon soy flour with 1 tablespoon water to substitute for 1 egg in baking.

◆ If you like eggs for breakfast, try some tofu scramblers or frittata recipes in this chapter. Squash firm tofu with a fork or through your fingers to make a texture similar to scrambled eggs.

Steer Clear

Animal lovers who choose to go veg many times give up eggs and chicken because of the conditions that factory-farmed chickens go through such as de-beaking, extremely cramped pens, uncomfortable temperatures, unsanitary living conditions, hormonal manipulation, and the incredible stress to the animals that all these factors cause.

The Sunny Side of Eggs

Eggs are a whole food. They are high in protein and low in carbs, and the yolk is rich in the nutrient lecithin, which is actually a fat emulsifier many people take in supplement form to help lower high cholesterol. Eggs are a wonderful food, especially for those vegetarians who feel they need more protein to feel satisfied.

You can make eggs a healthful part of your diet by preparing them properly, and you can avoid contributing to inhumane practices by supporting organic, free-range farmers and ranchers.

Steer Clear _____

Ninety percent of all commercially sold eggs come from chickens raised on factory farms where conditions are horrible, to say the least. Ovo vegetarians who are concerned about farm animal welfare generally consume eggs only from free-range chickens and/or organic or smaller farms. Labeling on egg cartons indicates this information.

The best way to eat whole eggs is poached or soft-cooked, as poached or soft-cooked eggs tend to maintain most of the nutritional value without overcooking the benefits out of them. If you scramble them, fry them in a healthful oil like coconut oil or olive oil spray and throw in some fibrous veggies. If you're watching your fat intake, try egg whites only. They're a great protein source without the fat.

Avoid the excess hormones and antibiotics and suffering that come from the mass-produced henhouses by purchasing your eggs from the organic farms raising free-range, organically fed, and healthy chickens. The farmers who provide a low-stress environment for their hens have happier chickens, which generally means healthier chickens that produce more eggs. For you, that means a healthier food without the guilt!

That said, the following recipes are all eggless, but ovo vegetarians can use these same recipes with eggs—free-range and organic, of course!

The Least You Need to Know

- Eggs can be breeding grounds for bacteria such as salmonella that can cause serious illness.

- For baking, many egg substitutes exist such as Egg Replacer made from tapioca flour; soy flour; or a ripe, mashed banana. Tofu can be used in place of scrambled eggs.

- Eggs are an excellent source of protein and, when eaten in moderation and prepared properly, can be a healthful part of an ovo vegetarian diet.

- Ovo vegetarians who are concerned about the humane treatment of animals should try to obtain eggs from free-range and organic farms where the animals are not subjected to inhumane conditions.

Artichoke and Goat Cheese Tofu Scramble

Sautéed crumbled tofu folded with melted goat cheese, artichoke hearts, and fresh basil give this tofu scramble a Mediterranean flavor and flair.

2 TB. olive oil	**2 tsp. dried basil**
⅔ lb. firm tofu, drained and crumbled	**⅓ cup chopped artichoke hearts**
Freshly ground black pepper	**½ cup crumbled goat cheese**

Serves: 2
Prep time: 5 minutes
Cook time: 10 minutes

1. In a medium skillet, heat olive oil over medium-high heat. When oil is hot, add tofu, pepper, basil, and artichoke hearts, and sauté until heated through.

2. Add goat cheese and cook until melted. Serve hot.

Artichoke and Goat Cheese Tofu Scramble—shown here served with Boca link sausages and a whole-grain English muffin.

Eggless Quiche

This tender-crisp mix of broccoli, zucchini, carrots, and artichoke hearts with Monterey Jack and Parmesan cheeses is seasoned with garlic and turmeric and baked to perfection in a whole-wheat and asiago cheese crust.

Serves: 4
Prep time: 15 minutes
Cook time: 40 minutes
Serving size: 2 slices (¼ pie)

1½ cups whole-wheat flour

⅓ cup asiago cheese

½ cup butter, melted

3 TB. water

3 tsp. olive oil

½ tsp. garlic powder

½ cup sliced carrots

1 cup broccoli florets

½ cup sliced zucchini

1½ cups sour cream

2 TB. arrowroot

¼ tsp. freshly ground black pepper

Pinch turmeric

½ cup grated Parmesan cheese

1 cup shredded Monterey Jack cheese

¾ cup water-packed artichoke hearts

Steer Clear

If you don't eat eggs, don't be fooled on menus if you see "vegetarian" or "vegetable quiche." This generally just means that the quiche contains vegetables instead of meat, not that the quiche is eggless.

1. Preheat the oven to 400°F.

2. In a large bowl, blend together flour, asiago cheese, and butter. Add water a little at a time to form dough. Pat crust dough into the bottom and along the sides of a 9-inch Pyrex pie or quiche pan. Prick well with a fork. Bake for 8 minutes.

3. In a skillet, heat olive oil over medium-high heat. Add garlic and carrots, cover, and cook for 10 minutes, stirring occasionally. Add broccoli and zucchini, and cook 5 more minutes.

4. In a separate large bowl, combine sour cream, arrowroot powder, pepper, and turmeric. Add Parmesan cheese and ½ cup Monterey Jack cheese. Fold in cooked vegetables and artichoke hearts. Pour mixture into the quiche pan, and top with remaining ½ cup Monterey Jack cheese.

5. Bake for 40 minutes or until the edges of quiche are browned and center is slightly golden. Allow quiche to set several minutes before cutting and serving.

Eggless French Toast and Syrup

These thick slices of whole-grain bread dipped in a nutty, sweet soy milk spiked with cinnamon and vanilla and topped with homemade thick, organic strawberry syrup will quickly become a breakfast table favorite.

3 cups soy milk

¼ cup unbleached all-purpose flour

2 TB. *nutritional yeast flakes*

1 tsp. stevia

¼ tsp. vanilla extract

2¼ tsp. ground cinnamon

8 thick slices whole-grain bread

2 TB. vegetable oil

⅔ cup plus 2 TB. grape juice

1 cup chopped strawberries

1 TB. arrowroot

Serves: 4	
Prep time: 5 minutes	
Cook time: 15 minutes	
Serving size: 2 slices	

1. In a mixing bowl, whisk soy milk, flour, nutritional yeast, stevia, vanilla extract, and 2 teaspoons cinnamon. Pour mixture into a wide, shallow bowl or pie pan. Soak bread slices in mixture until soft. (You might have to do this in batches.)

2. Heat vegetable oil in a skillet over medium heat. Fry each bread slice until both sides are golden brown and crispy, about 5 to 7 minutes per slice. Keep warm.

3. In a small saucepan over medium heat, combine ⅔ cup juice with strawberries and remaining ¼ teaspoon cinnamon, and bring to a boil. Reduce heat to simmer, and simmer for 5 minutes.

4. Stir remaining 2 tablespoons juice into arrowroot powder until dissolved. Add this mixture to the saucepan and simmer, stirring, until syrup thickens. If syrup becomes too thick, thin with a little more juice. Serve over hot French toast. Top with stevia powder if desired.

Lettuce Explain

Nutritional yeast flakes (or powder) is deactivated yeast used as a supplement, cooking ingredient, and condiment. Its nutty, cheesy flavor makes it useful in a variety of recipes (it's great on popcorn!), and it creates a creamy texture when mixed with liquids. It's rich in protein and vitamins and is particularly high in B-complex vitamins.

Spanish-Style Tofu Frittata

Seasoned tofu layered with artichoke hearts, sautéed zucchini, asiago cheese, and Roma tomatoes; topped with melted Monterey Jack cheese; and sprinkled with Italian parsley makes this high-protein, low-carb eggless frittata truly a taste for all seasonings!

Serves: 4
Prep time: 10 minutes
Cook time: 20 minutes
Serving size: 1½ cups

1 lb. firm tofu, squeezed

⅔ cup nutritional yeast flakes

2 TB. garlic powder

3 TB. dried oregano

1 whole scallion, minced (about 2 TB.)

4 TB. shredded asiago cheese

1 (6-oz.) can artichoke hearts, drained and sliced

1 cup zucchini, sliced

1 clove garlic, minced

2 TB. butter

3 Roma tomatoes, sliced

1 cup shredded Monterey Jack cheese

Fresh Italian parsley for topping

Salsa

Sour cream

Guacamole

Steer Clear

Frittatas are generally made from eggs, so, as with vegetarian quiche, if you don't eat eggs, beware of frittatas on menus; the main ingredient, unless specified otherwise, will be eggs.

1. In a large bowl, mash tofu with nutritional yeast flakes, garlic powder, and oregano until thoroughly blended. Stir in scallions, 3 tablespoons asiago cheese, and artichoke hearts.

2. In a skillet over medium-low heat, sauté garlic and zucchini in butter until softened. Add tofu mixture, stir, and press tofu mixture evenly over the bottom of the skillet. Cover and cook for 10 minutes or until hot throughout.

3. Place Roma tomato slices on top of the frittata in the skillet. Sprinkle remaining 1 tablespoon asiago cheese on tomatoes, and layer Monterey Jack cheese over frittata. Cover and cook until tomatoes are done and cheese is melted. Top with fresh chopped Italian parsley. Serve with your favorite salsa, sour cream, and guacamole.

Chapter 9

Making a *Smoothie* Transition

In This Chapter

- ◆ Smoothies for any occasion
- ◆ The nutritional benefits of nuts and seeds
- ◆ The wonderful benefits of fruit
- ◆ Whey—hey, it's good for you!
- ◆ Some yummy smoothie recipes

If you've followed along with me and the breakfast chapters so far (Chapters 7 and 8), you know the benefits of eating a healthful breakfast. Your blood sugar levels, your metabolism, and your overall health all benefit from a good, nutritional start to the day.

But if you don't have much of an appetite in the A.M., or if you simply don't have a lot of time, smoothies and protein drinks can make wonderful liquid breakfasts—and fast ones, too. Plus, they can have all the benefits and more of solid food. And smoothies are an easy way to help meet your daily fruit requirements.

Read on to learn about some of the ingredients you can use and how to make some quick and nutrient-rich liquid breakfasts.

Smooth Starts

Smoothies, shakelike drinks, have become very popular in recent years—and not just among vegetarians. Smoothies can serve as a full meal, a dessert, a pre- or post-workout nutritional boost, or just a refreshing snack. The smoothie's cold, fresh creaminess makes it appealing, and smoothie recipes are as varied as the people who make them! You can have totally vegan smoothies, lacto smoothies, even lacto ovo smoothies—all depending on what you like.

You don't need much to make a smoothie: just a blender, some ice or another liquid base like yogurt or juice, and a main ingredient—usually fresh or frozen fruits. If you keep a few basic ingredients on hand, your smoothie recipes can be endless—and you can whip one up in no time.

> **Veggie Soup for the Soul**
>
> Juice bars, health food stores, and many health clubs boast smoothie bars, where you can order a fresh smoothie on the spot. Many health food stores sell different smoothie varieties premade, too. Look for them in a refrigerated area, usually near the produce or dairy sections.

Be creative! Raw fruits, nuts, seeds, yogurt, and even some raw grains all can be included to make delicious and refreshing smoothies.

Any of the following ingredients can serve as your base ingredient(s) for a smoothie:

- ◆ Yogurt (soy yogurt for strict vegetarians or organic yogurt for lacto vegetarians)

- ◆ Soy milk

- ◆ Rice milk

- ◆ Almond milk

- ◆ Fruit juice of any kind

- ◆ Tofu (preferably silken or soft)

- ◆ Cold filtered water and ice

And that's just to get started. Read on for more delicious smoothie ingredient ideas.

Eat Your Fruit

Fresh fruit—it's bright, colorful, sweet, and nourishing, and you know you should eat lots more of it. Most fruit contains high amounts of water, minerals, vitamins, and enzymes. Plus, it's easily digested, and the usable vitamins and minerals contained in fruit are absorbed quickly into the body. Fruit also contains fructose, a natural form of sugar. We use fruit to decorate drinks and other foods, we use fruit to make juices to drink and to sweeten candy, we use fruit skins as natural dyes and their rinds for flavor and nutrients, and we use grapes to make wine. Well, that should make it easy enough for you to incorporate more fruit into your diet, shouldn't it?

Steer Clear

Enjoy fruits, but don't count on them to sustain you unless you have a very clean diet and a system that can survive on frequent fruit snacking.

If you're going to eat only fruit in the morning, be sure to have something else available to snack on within the next few hours because you'll probably be hungry again. A handful of cashews, pumpkin seeds, or raw almonds makes a great protein snack an hour or two after you eat a piece of fruit. Or make it easy and throw them all in a blender and make a smoothie!

You can use any fresh or frozen fruit to make your smoothie. I've listed a few here that you might enjoy, along with some nutritional tidbits:

- Strawberries (good source of sodium, used to nourish the joints and the stomach lining, rich in vitamin C)

- Pineapple (high in enzymes, which aid digestion)

- Bananas (good source of potassium; help replenish muscles after a workout; slower to digest, which makes it a good fruit for those with a tendency toward blood sugar imbalance)

- Mangoes (excellent source of enzymes)

- Papaya (used by some people to expel parasites, also serves as a wonderful digestive aid)

- Blueberries (strengthen blood capillaries, have been used therapeutically for eyesight improvement)

- Pears (help purge the gallbladder of excess bile)

- Coconut (rich source of fatty acids)

> **Sprouts of Info**
>
> When your bananas get too ripe to eat fresh, peel them, put them in a freezer bag, and store them in the freezer. When you're ready to make a smoothie, chop and add the frozen banana pieces. The blended frozen banana not only adds flavor, but also makes the smoothie creamy and cold.

A Little of This, a Little of That …

In addition to fruits, consider keeping the following on hand to make all sorts of yummy recipes. A pinch of these ingredients can add heartiness or a complementary flavor to your base ingredients:

- *Carob* powder (Carob is a natural ingredient used as a chocolate substitute. It looks like chocolate and has a similar taste, but it doesn't contain any caffeine. It's somewhat bitter, so add a little sweetener if you want.)

- Your favorite raw nuts, such as cashews, almonds, or walnuts

- Pure vanilla extract

- Nut butters

- Cinnamon

> **Lettuce Explain**
>
> **Carob**, also called locust bean, is a tree prized for its bittersweet, leathery seed pods that are harvested to make carob powder. The tree is native to the Mediterranean area and other warm climates. Carob is frequently used as a chocolate substitute.

If fruit alone isn't enough to sweeten your smoothie, consider the following:

◆ Honey

◆ Stevia

◆ Blackstrap molasses

◆ Maple syrup

◆ Grape juice

You can throw almost any ingredient into a smoothie after you have your basic "stock" ingredients in there.

Nutrient Boosts

Smoothies are an excellent way to drink your supplements. Here are some nutritional items you can add to your smoothies for their therapeutic benefits:

Flaxseeds can be used as a bulk laxative. They are a good source of essential fatty acids that nourish the brain and circulatory system. Some folks use flax to help lower high cholesterol levels.

Psyllium hulls are an excellent source of fiber. Fiber is necessary in the diet to keep the colon clean and lowers the chances of colon cancer and other diseases.

Aloe vera juice is a mucilaginous-type laxative used for those who cannot tolerate rough fiber such as psyllium. Aloe is rich in vitamins and other nutrients, and is used for soothing irritated tissues, cleansing the bowels, eliminating wrinkles, and boosting the immune system.

Chlorophyll liquid is the blood of plants and can be used to thin the blood slightly, deodorize the body, protect from pollutants, and provide iron to help with anemia; it's also a body cleanser and builder.

Sprouts of Info

For people who have trouble swallowing pills, a smoothie makes a delicious liquid carrier for supplements like fiber pills, vitamin C, or essential fatty acid capsules. (Be sure to taste test before you pour, as some herbs are bitter, and too much can ruin the flavor of your smoothie.)

Some super athletes who need extra protein before and after workouts use *protein pow-der.* Adding protein powder to a smoothie is a delicious way to get your daily dose.

Dehydrated goat whey is not for strict vegetarians, but it is one of the richest sources of natural sodium, choline (a substance that may improve brain function), and other nutrients. Goat whey has been used to promote joint health and can serve as a mineral supplement.

Good Morning, Protein

In the last chapter, I mentioned the importance of protein in the morning. Protein is slower to digest, lasts longer, and is therefore more sustaining. Protein is made up of amino acids that rebuild our muscle cells and tissues, and is the building block for all body repair and restoration. Protein needs less water to digest than carbs and so can help you keep off excess water weight. Protein doesn't spike blood sugar levels and helps keep everything in balance.

Now, how do vegetarians get their proteins without eating meat? Many ways! About all natural foods such as nuts and seeds contain protein. Protein in the morning is especially important. It gives you substance and therefore sets the stage for your bio-chemistry to remain more steady throughout the rest of the day, and it's one of the best remedies for maintaining blood sugar levels.

Go Nuts for Protein

Nuts are a plant's shell-covered fruit, and a *seed* is the actual embryo of the plant, but it doesn't usually have a hard shell. The two are closely related and have similar nutritional values; however, there are differences.

Lettuce Explain

Nuts are the fruit of a plant and usually have a hard shell. **Seeds** contain the embryo of a new plant. You can think of them as the eggs of the plant kingdom.

Most nuts are rich in protein and minerals. They provide the body with an alternate source of protein and are best eaten raw or in a nut butter form. A sliced apple dipped in cashew butter makes an excellent satisfying snack. I like to eat a handful of whole raw cashews and a banana after a workout—I get my protein, potassium, and calcium, all of which nourish my structural system. And after you spend an hour working out, it's not a bad idea to give your body the nourishment it needs to rebuild strong muscle tissue.

Seeds contain the embryo of the plant and so contain everything they need to nourish a growing baby plant. Seeds are concentrated nutrition and can have a therapeutic value as well. And because seeds are part of a plant's glandular system, they can also be good for our glandular systems.

Pumpkin seeds, high in zinc, have been used as an herbal supplement for men with prostrate troubles. Flaxseeds, rich in essential fatty acids (covered more in Chapter 1) are used by many, not only to help clean the bowels, but for all sorts of glandular imbalances, from PMS to endometriosis. Another popular support for the glandular system is evening primrose oil, which is derived from the seeds of the evening primrose flower (*Oenothera binennis*). Evening primrose oil is used to help women ease PMS, aid menopausal symptoms, and even help the pancreas balance blood sugar.

Both nuts and seeds provide these general nutritional benefits:

- ◆ They feed us essential fatty acids needed for the circulatory system and brain nourishment.

- ◆ They are rich in protein.

- ◆ They are concentrated nutrition and can make us feel satisfied.

- ◆ They have anticancer properties.

Because nuts and seeds contain natural oils, they should be stored in a cool place to preserve their freshness and to protect the oils from turning rancid. Rancid oils are full of free radicals known to cause cancer.

Testa **Time**

A seed is a self-contained unit within a protective coat called a *testa*. The testa prevents the seed from germinating (growing) at inappropriate times. In other words, if you ripped open a bag of birdseed and it scattered across your kitchen floor, the seeds wouldn't automatically start sprouting. Seeds are programmed to know when the conditions are just right to begin growth. When they find a place that has soil, water, enough air, and warmth from sunlight, the message goes out and off they go.

Lettuce Explain

A **testa** is the protective coating on the outside of a seed that keeps it from germinating until conditions are right. The testa also serves as an enzyme inhibitor and can inhibit our ability to digest them. Therefore, it's best to eat your seeds ground or chew them thoroughly.

That's great if you're a seed. For us, though, it means we need to get around a seed's protective coating, to the good stuff inside. The best way to eat them is ground a little, maybe as a nut/seed butter. If nothing else, be sure you chew seeds thoroughly to help digest them.

Sesame seed butter is an excellent example of a nourishing way to consume sesame seeds. When the tiny seeds are ground a bit, it breaks the testa and exposes the nutrients you body is looking for. Because most seeds are small, many people have a tendency not to chew them very well. But a seed that's not digested goes right through you and offers no nutritional benefit.

Why Whey?

Whey is a protein derived from milk and has many benefits. One recent study in the *American Journal of Clinical Nutrition* reported that whey might curb the effects of carbohydrates on blood sugar and help stop blood sugar from spiking when taken with the carbs—beneficial for folks with diabetes or anyone wanting to help keep their blood sugar more balanced.

Whey also assists the liver in producing glutathione, a vital antioxidant important in detoxifying and protecting the liver. Whey is rich in minerals and also has been linked to helping suppress appetite, boost immunity, lower cholesterol levels, and promote lean muscle mass.

Sprouts of Info

Smoothies are best made in a blender or Vitamixer but can be made in a versatile juicer or even a handheld mixer if you have one.

You can get organically derived whey protein powder in most health food stores to add to your smoothies. Adding some fruit and/or spices or extracts can add flavor. But you can also try flavored whey powders, such as chocolate, vanilla, or strawberry—as always, of course, try to limit the additives and artificial ingredients in all your choices. Look for protein powders sweetened with natural sweeteners like stevia, not with sugars or neurotoxic ingredients like aspartame.

The Least You Need to Know

- Smoothies can serve as an excellent breakfast, a snack, or a way to get your supplemental nutrition, and can be made from a variety of ingredients.

- Raw nuts, seeds, and nut butters are an excellent way to add protein and essential fatty acids to your smoothies.

- Whey is a dried dairy product rich in protein and has numerous benefits to the body, including detoxifying the liver, balancing blood sugar, and promoting lean muscle.

- Having some protein, such as a protein smoothie in the morning, is important in helping to balance blood sugar levels for the rest of the day.

Whey Good Smoothie

Banana, chocolate whey powder, and coconut milk make this smoothie taste like a candy bar, although it's rich in protein and good for your whole body.

Serves: 1
Prep time: 3 minutes
Serving size: 8 to 10 ounces

4 ice cubes

3 rounded TB. chocolate whey protein powder

½ cup water

⅓ frozen banana

2 TB. coconut milk

Nutmeg

1. Place ice in a blender, and chop for a few seconds until crushed.

2. Add whey protein powder, water, banana, coconut milk, and nutmeg, and blend on high until smooth.

Sprouts of Info

Whey is derived from dairy and contains glutathione, which is a substance known to help detoxify the liver. Many people notice a distinct "lift" after having a quality whey protein drink.

Yogurt and Nut Butter Smoothie

This smoothie is creamy, sweet, and nutty. Mixing cashew butter, sweet dates, and rich yogurt gives you a sweet protein shake.

2 ice cubes	**2 TB. cashew butter**
2 dates, pitted	**½ cup plain yogurt**

Serves: 1
Prep time: 3 minutes
Serving size: 8 ounces

1. Place ice in a blender, and chop for a few seconds until crushed.

2. Add dates, cashew butter, and yogurt, and blend on high until smooth.

Sprouts of Info

Sometimes using whole yogurt instead of low-fat or nonfat yogurt is beneficial because, although whole yogurt is full fat—and therefore richer than the others—it also gives you more satiation, which can last longer. For breakfast and smoothies, sometimes it's a good choice.

Oatmeal and Date Smoothie

The oatmeal gives you something to chew on while enjoying this rich, cinnamon-spiked yogurt and date smoothie.

Serves: 1
Prep time: 3 minutes
Serving size: 8 ounces

3 ice cubes

2 dates, pitted

½ cup oats

½ cup plain yogurt

Cinnamon

1. Place ice in a blender, and chop for a few seconds until crushed.

2. Add dates, oats, yogurt, and cinnamon, and blend on high until the consistency you desire.

Sprouts of Info

Chewing ignites different parts of the brain, which can help make you feel fuller and more satisfied, especially when you're having a liquid meal. Take the time to chew each bite of your smoothie. To help, make your smoothies crunchier by not blending the ice too fine. This also makes it thicker so you can eat some of it with a spoon.

Banana, Cherry, Nut, and Yogurt Smoothie

This is the banana split of smoothies. Rich, vanilla yogurt blended with raw almonds, frozen banana, and dark cherries make this a perfect blend for a rich, sweet and nutty shake.

4 ice cubes

½ cup vanilla yogurt

Handful raw almonds

½ frozen banana

Handful frozen dark cherries

Serves: 1
Prep time: 3 minutes
Serving size: 8 ounces

1. Place ice in a blender, and chop for a few seconds until crushed.

2. Add yogurt, almonds, banana, and cherries, and blend on high until consistency you desire.

Sprouts of Info _____

Dairy-free vegetarians can substitute soy yogurt for cow's milk yogurt.

Part 3

What's for Lunch?

Ah, lunch—my favorite meal of the day. In Part 3, we dig into all the typical lunch foods—sandwiches, salads, soups and chowders, and even some kid favorites. And speaking of kids, in the following pages, I give you some vegetarian nutrition tips for nearly every stage of life: moms-to-be, infants, toddlers, and teens. Here you learn about the health benefits of eating raw foods like salads, get tips for making slow-cooker stews and soups so they're waiting for you when you get home for lunch or dinner, and discover some very different types of sandwich ideas—with or without using bread! Let's do lunch!

Chapter 10

On a Roll: Sandwiches

In This Chapter

- ◆ Condiment substitution ideas
- ◆ Garbanzo beans—funny name, good for you
- ◆ Sandwich-making tips
- ◆ Delicious veggie sandwich recipes

The sandwich is perhaps the most versatile meal in the world. You can change the total nature of a sandwich just by changing the type of bread it's on or the condiment used. Sandwich options are endless, even for vegetarians.

This chapter covers a few different vegetarian-suitable condiments for your sandwiches, different types of breads and their benefits, and even bread-less sandwiches for those wanting to cut back on carbs. And, of course, I've added some of my favorite sandwich recipes at the end of the chapter.

Veggie Condiment Choices

You've probably seen the commercial claiming "A sandwich just isn't a sandwich without *[insert condiment name here]*." That particular condiment notwithstanding, there is some truth to that statement. Fortunately, with the exception of Worcestershire sauce (which contains anchovy—fish), Caesar dressing (anchovies again), and mayonnaise (eggs), most condiments like mustard, vinegar, olive oil, relish, and ketchup are vegetarian friendly.

Veggie Soup for the Soul

The name *sandwich* is said to have originated in the mid- to late 1700s by the Fourth Earl of Sandwich. When he didn't want to take the time to sit down at the dinner table for a real meal, he would ask the cook to just put some meat between two pieces of bread for him. As the story goes, others caught on and would say, "I'll have what Sandwich is having." The rest is history.

A grilled soy cheese sandwich paired with warm tomato soup makes a simple and satisfying lunch.

Hold the Mayo?

But what if you want to make a vegetarian potato salad or other recipes in which mayonnaise is a key ingredient? Mayonnaise is made from eggs, and many vegetarians don't eat eggs *and* want a more healthful alternative than artificial replacements. Never fear. A few healthful options can easily take the place of mayonnaise.

Try mayos made from soy such as Nayonaise, found next to the mustards and ketchups in the health food store. This eggless mayo is made mainly from soy milk and soybean oil, is totally vegan friendly, and contains no cholesterol. Nayonaise also comes in Dijon style.

If you're simply tired of doing everything soy, try my latest personal favorite, Veganaise, found in the refrigerated section of the health food stores. This mayo substitute is made from grapeseed oil and distributed by a southern California vegetarian restaurant and health food store called Follow Your Heart. Veganaise is great for low-carb diets, and grapeseed oil can have a beneficial effect on your high-density lipids (HDL) and low-density lipids (LDL) cholesterol. Keeping the HDL high and the LDL lower is important to cardiovascular health.

Sesame Tahini

Sesame tahini is made from ground sesame seeds. It has a nutty flavor and is an excellent addition to any sandwich that needs a little something extra. It can also be used as a dressing, as a dip for fresh fruit or veggies, or as a topping over falafel (see the following section). And in addition to the other benefits of seeds (see Chapter 9), sesame seeds in particular contain high amounts of calcium, so they can be good for your bone and muscle strength.

Keep tahini in the refrigerator, and take it out a while before you want to use it so it can soften, making it easier to spoon, drizzle, or spread on sandwiches.

> **Sprouts of Info**
>
> All seeds, nuts, and butters made from seeds have high oil content, so store them in a cool place to protect the oils from going rancid.

The Many Tastes (and Benefits) of Garbanzo Beans

Garbanzo beans, or chickpeas, are legumes high in protein and fiber, and rich in iron and thiamin (vitamin B_1). Garbanzo beans can be made into hummus or falafel and make a great gluten-free flour for baked goods.

Vitamin B_1 is known as the "morale vitamin" because it has such a huge effect on nourishing the nervous system and mental health. Studies have shown that thiamin can help improve learning capacity. Although severe thiamin deficiency is rare, some signs of mild deficiency include loss of mental alertness, confusion, fatigue, and irritability. So if you have a thiamin deficiency, you actually can *feel awful*—so think *falafel* to get back some of that thiamine and not only enjoy your meal, but feel better mentally!

Never Makes You Falafel

Falafel (pronounced *fa-LOFF-ul*) is a mix of spices and ground, dehydrated garbanzo beans. You prepare falafel by mixing it with water and deep-frying it. It can be used to make falafel balls to replace meatballs or as patties in place of hamburger patties, and it's a delicious choice for use in salads and sandwiches.

Falafel is hard to describe, and although it can't really be compared with any meat flavor, it is uniquely delicious. It has a distinctive flavor that is somewhat nutty and a bit sweet, like corn.

You can sometimes find falafel mix in the bulk section of health food stores, but it also comes prepackaged, usually in a box. I have found boxes of falafel mix, tofu burger mix, Nature's Burger mix, and Perfect Burger mix near the spices section in grocery stores, but in health food stores they're usually on the shelves along with other dry goods. I've also found bagged, premade falafel balls in the refrigerated sections by the tofu and tempeh.

Hummus Among Us

Hummus is a food made by mixing mashed garbanzo beans with a little oil, lemon, and garlic. Hummus can be a veggie dip or a sandwich spread. Hummus is also great spread in a pita pocket with veggies or as a base spread for a veggie wrap. (See my recipe at the end of this chapter for Raw Hummus Romaine wraps for a breadless hummus sandwich.)

Find raw garbanzo beans in the bulk section of your health food store. They also come canned. Prepared hummus is found refrigerated, normally by the refrigerated salsas, tortillas, and tofu. Dried hummus mixes are found in either the bulk sections or the boxed sections with the falafel and Nature's Burger mixes.

> **Sprouts of Info** _____
>
> While you're looking for hummus and falafel, you might want to look for dehydrated tabbouleh to keep in your pantry for when you want to whip up a Mediterranean plate and don't want to start everything from scratch. Tabbouleh is a mixture of grain and parsley, and can be used as a side dish or even added to a hummus pita sandwich.

How Much Bread Do You Knead?

One thing vegetarians rarely have a problem with is getting enough carbs. Many times the problem is too many refined carbs. Excess carbohydrates that the body can't use turn to excess pounds. So just because you've cut out meat doesn't mean you can't gain weight if you're eating too many refined carbs, such as bread, crackers, pastas, and other flour-based products.

Bread can be one of the biggest carb culprits. So let's think alternatively—or think outside the bun, as one commercial touts! The occasional sandwich-eater won't need to worry about too much bread, but those who want to drop a few pounds might consider alternatives such as lower-carb tortillas and light bread with lower net carbs. You may also consider putting your sandwich spreads on Ryevita crackers; corn tortillas; or whole-grain, sprouted, live breads that contain a great deal of fiber and lower the carbohydrate content of your sandwiches. These fiber-rich alternatives also enhance the nutritional value of your meal.

Wrap It Up, I'll Take It

Veggie wraps or roll-ups are a great way to limit big bread intake. You can find lower-carb tortillas in many grocery stores these days. Even if the total carb content looks high, always read the fiber content as well. Total carb count per serving minus fiber content per serving equals your total *net carbs*. Because fiber causes you to burn energy while digesting it, it basically gives you points against the total carbs!

Most of these lower-carb tortillas are made of whole wheat, so check the labels on the brown-colored tortillas before reading the white ones. Remember, there's more fiber in less-refined products.

> **Lettuce Explain** _____
>
> **Net carbs** equal the total amount of carbs per serving minus the total amount of fiber per serving.

Pitas and Flatbreads

Pitas are a simple bread made from flour and water, and have no rising agents in them. This generally makes them sugar free, yeast free, and lower in carbs and calories. When you're looking to fill up on the goodies in the sandwich versus the bread, consider stuffing your sandwich spread into a pita pocket. Toasting a pita lightly gives it a crisp texture.

Flatbread is usually a little doughy and thicker than pitas but is great for piling with chopped veggies. If you have a gas stove, try toasting flatbreads quickly over an open flame to puff them up a bit. Next, spread on some whipped cream cheese. Top with some chopped fresh veggies like baby carrots, cucumber, and red bell pepper. Then pile on the sprouts, sprinkle with balsamic vinegar, and top off with some toasted sesame seeds. Fold and enjoy!

Lettuce *Not* Eat Bread

To go totally carbohydrate free and skip the bread, use romaine lettuce leaves or any type of larger leafy lettuce leaves big enough to roll up or hold your sandwich ingredients. My Tofu Salad recipe later in this chapter works great in romaine, and so does hummus. See my Raw Hummus Romaine Roll-Ups recipe later in this chapter.

The Least You Need to Know

- Garbanzo beans are a good source of thiamin (B_1), which nourishes the nervous system and can make you feel good.

- Consider using lettuce leaves, pita pockets, or low-carb tortillas to keep your carbs in check when eating sandwiches.

- Hummus and falafel are both made from garbanzo beans, which are high in protein, fiber, B_1, and iron.

Tofu Salad Sandwich

Tamari-flavored crumbled tofu combines with crunchy fresh veggies and sunflower seeds to create a complementary, creamy, chunky, protein-rich sandwich spread.

1 lb. firm tofu, squeezed and drained

⅛ cup tamari or to taste

⅓ cup nutritional yeast flakes

1 cup shredded or finely chopped carrots

1 cup chopped celery

⅔ cup chopped scallions, including green tops

⅔ cup chopped green bell pepper

⅔ cup chopped red bell pepper

½ cup shelled, raw sunflower seeds

¼ to ½ cup eggless mayonnaise or to taste

Freshly ground black pepper

Pita pockets, tortilla, or sandwich bread, toasted

Alfalfa sprouts

Serves: 8	
Prep time: 10 minutes	
Serving size: 1 sandwich	

1. Put tofu in a large mixing bowl, and mash with a fork. Add tamari to tofu, and mix thoroughly. Sprinkle with nutritional yeast flakes, and mix well.

2. Add carrots, celery, scallions, green bell pepper, red bell pepper, and sunflower seeds, and mix well. Add eggless mayonnaise until mixture reaches the desired consistency. Season with pepper, and mix thoroughly.

3. Spread Tofu Salad into toasted pita pockets, top with alfalfa sprouts, and enjoy!

For a hearty and healthful lunch, try a Tofu Salad Sandwich, shown with baby greens on the side.

Falafel Ball Sandwich

This is a vegetarian version of the meatball sub: flavorful deep-fried chickpea balls layered on a deli hoagie roll, smothered in warm marinara sauce, and topped with melted mozzarella cheese.

Serves: 4
Prep time: 20 minutes
Cook time: 15 minutes
Serving size: 1 sandwich

1¼ cup (about 10 oz.) bulk falafel mix

1¼ cups cold water

Vegetable oil

Canned or homemade spaghetti sauce

Shredded mozzarella or provolone cheese

4 hoagie rolls

1. Empty falafel mix into a large bowl, add water, and mix well. Let stand for 15 minutes.

2. Heat 1 inch vegetable oil in deep, medium-size pan until hot.

3. Roll falafel mixture into meatball-size balls, add to the pan, and fry until brown and crunchy on one side. Turn balls over and brown the other side. Balls should be evenly brown and crisp on the outside. Remove balls from the pan and place on a paper towel–lined plate to absorb excess oil.

4. In a saucepan over medium-high heat, warm spaghetti sauce stirring occasionally.

5. Preheat the broiler.

6. Slice hoagie roll (toasted first, if you like), and add falafel balls. Cover with spaghetti sauce (bread will soak up a bunch of sauce, so be liberal) add cheese, and put under the broiler for a minute or 2 or until cheese melts.

Variation: Make this a totally vegan meal by leaving off the cheese or using a vegan cheese. Or lower your fat and calorie content by using low-fat/part-skim mozzarella.

 Sprouts of Info

Consider making the falafel balls ahead of time and refrigerating or freezing them. Defrost to add to salads or sandwiches—or eat as a snack by themselves!

Raw Hummus Romaine Roll-Ups

Rich, creamy, garlic-flavored garbanzo bean spread on a crisp, chilled romaine lettuce leaf topped with chunks of feta cheese, cucumber, and tomato make this a delicious, breadless raw food sandwich.

1 cup sprouted garbanzo beans (or steamed)	**Salt**
½ cup tahini	**Pinch cayenne**
1 cup olive oil	**Water**
2 TB. fresh parsley	**Large romaine lettuce leaves, washed and patted dry**
2 cloves garlic	**Feta cheese, crumbled**
¼ cup fresh squeezed lemon juice	**1 tomato, chopped**
1 TB. tamari	**1 cucumber, chopped**

> *Serves: 4*
> **Prep time:** 15 minutes
> **Serving size:** 1 roll-up

1. Place garbanzo beans in a blender or a food processor. Add tahini, olive oil, parsley, garlic, lemon juice, tamari, salt, and cayenne, and blend until creamy.

2. Spread several tablespoons hummus into 1 romaine leaf, and top with crumbled feta cheese, chopped tomato, and chopped cucumber. Roll and eat.

Sprouts of Info

To sprout garbanzo beans, soak them in water for 12 hours or overnight and then drain. Let the beans sprout 2 or 3 days, rinsing with warm water daily. Sprouting garbanzos brings them to life, activating the dormant enzymes, which aid digestion and help provide energy. See more on slow cooking grains (which also applies to legumes) in Chapter 18.

Tempeh and Sauerkraut Reuben on Rye

Slightly nutty, salty, tart, and tempting, this sandwich consists of fried tempeh strips topped with warm sauerkraut on hearty rye bread.

Serves: 2
Prep time: 5 minutes
Cook time: 10 minutes
Serving size: 1 sandwich

1 TB. olive oil

1 (8-oz.) pkg. tempeh

¾ cup sauerkraut

4 slices rye bread

2 slices Swiss cheese or soy Swiss cheese

Dijon mustard (optional)

1. Heat olive oil in frying pan over medium-high heat.

2. Slice tempeh in ¼-inch slices, add to the frying pan, and brown on both sides. Turn off heat.

3. Add sauerkraut to the pan and sauté just to warm it a bit.

4. Place tempeh on rye bread, and add warmed sauerkraut on top. Add cheese and Dijon mustard (if using). Melt cheese under broiler for a few minutes. and top with another slice of rye.

Variation: You can also grill this sandwich, or serve open faced and/or with French or Russian dressing for dipping.

Veggie Soup for the Soul

Raw sauerkraut is made from pickled cabbage and is loaded with beneficial *probiotics*—bacteria good for digestion, the intestinal system, and the immune system.

Grilled, Open-Face Tempeh Sandwich

Hot, saucy tomato marinara over nutty, crunchy-fried tempeh slices with grilled onion and melted cheese make this delicious on sourdough bread. Serve open faced and eat with knife and fork.

1 TB. olive oil	2 slices thickly cut sourdough bread
1 (8-oz.) pkg. tempeh	
½ cup sliced onion	2 slices provolone cheese or soy cheese
1 cup spaghetti sauce	

Serves: 2	
Prep time: 5 minutes	
Cook time: 10 minutes	
Serving size: 1 sandwich	

1. Heat olive oil in a frying pan over medium-high heat.

2. Slice tempeh in ¼-inch slices, add to the frying pan, and brown on both sides until crunchy or desired texture. Add onion and sauté until softened.

3. Warm spaghetti sauce in small saucepan over medium heat.

4. Preheat the broiler.

5. Place tempeh and onion on bread, and spoon warmed spaghetti sauce on top. Add provolone, and put under the broiler until cheese melts. Serve open faced.

This Grilled, Open-Face Tempeh Sandwich tastes as good as it looks!

Chapter 11

Satisfying Salads

In This Chapter

- ◆ The benefits of whole, raw foods
- ◆ Go green with healthful raw greens
- ◆ Phyto*what?* Phytochemicals—they're good for you
- ◆ Satisfying salad recipes

Along with sandwiches (see Chapter 10), salads might be the most versatile kind of food. You can make a salad with just about any or all of your favorite veggies. And salads give you the benefits of raw, whole foods; fiber; and many phytochemicals. Plus, they're generally low in calories and rich in antioxidants. So toss together some greens and *lettuce* eat!

A Raw Deal? Think Again!

The concept of eating a *whole food* diet means eating unadulterated foods in their whole, raw state—the way nature produced them. In general, anything you can pick from a tree or a vine or pull from the ground is considered a whole food. Anything that's generally not been altered to change its fundamental properties and has its own enzymes intact is a whole food. Ideally,

Lettuce Explain _____

Whole foods are unprocessed foods created by nature and eaten in their unaltered, unprocessed state. Raw fruits and vegetables and grains slow cooked to bring them to life are whole foods. Salads are a great way to get your whole, raw foods for the day.

we should all be eating only whole foods, but when that's not possible, eating a salad a day is a great way to work some green, whole foods into part of your day.

Whole foods contain all the ingredients in the right proportions the way nature intended. Your body gets more nourishment more easily with foods still in their natural state. You also get the added benefit of consuming everything the entire food has to offer, which makes it—and you—complete.

Enzymes for Life

Enzymes are essential to life. They are present in all organic material and are the catalysts that keep you alive and make things happen. Enzymes are inherent in fruit and vegetables and all living foods and animals. They're manufactured in the body to help with all bodily functions, so it's important to get many of your foods raw, with enzymes intact, to help you break down what you're eating.

Enzymes are crucial to digestion. Your pancreas and liver must produce enzymes to digest processed foods, so eating raw foods like salads takes stress away from these

Steer Clear _____

All food loses some value when it's cooked—enzymes in particular. Enzymes are killed when food is cooked at temperatures over 110°F.

organs. Because your body requires more energy to digest food than almost anything else you do, give your system break once in a while and go for some raw foods like the raw vegetables and fruits in the salads in this chapter, which are rich in their own enzymes. The less your body has to work to digest and make enzymes, the more it can spend on other life processes, leaving you with more energy. This can mean a longer, more vibrant life for you.

Phytochemical Power

Phytochemicals are naturally occurring chemicals found in plants. Scientists continue to isolate and identify new phytochemicals that are touted as healthful. We know that phytochemicals work in combination to provide your body the most benefits. In other words, even though beta carotene is a photochemical that can be isolated from carrots, many other elements in carrots can help make the beta carotene more efficient in your body.

We don't yet know exactly how many more of these phytochemicals will be found, or what good things they can do for our health, but I bet Mother Nature knows! Nature has had some practice in creating a mixture of phytochemicals in naturally grown fruits and vegetables, and she doesn't give up her secret recipe easily. So take it from your "Mother" and eat the veggies and fruits she serves!

Veggie Soup for the Soul

Vegetables are body builders! They pack a powerful punch of vitamins and minerals, and when eaten raw, they contain enzymes. They supply roughage in the diet and give us sustainable strength.

The bottom line is that whole foods promote a balance of phytochemicals, which is thought to be better for you than relying solely on a particular phytochemical (as in a supplement pill) for your plant-based nutrition.

Synthetic Health?

Most processed foods are enriched with synthetically produced chemicals. In other words, food manufacturers take a whole food, or a part of it—wheat, for example— bleach it, cook it at high temperatures (killing the enzymes and destroying nutrients), and grind it down to a fine powder (eliminating the fiber). By the time it's made into flour, especially white flour, the nutritional value is almost gone. The flour is then enriched with synthetic vitamins and minerals.

Scientists haven't isolated every phytochemical in every food, nor is it guaranteed that they ever will, so how can we trust any food manufacturer to know exactly what to put back into the food to keep us healthy? Surely, many substances are inherent in whole foods that researchers have yet to discover. Just to be sure you're getting what your body needs, whenever possible, try to get your nourishment from whole foods like salads.

Steer Clear

Science has shown us that isolating some substances at the expense of others can cause various side effects. This is yet another reason to get your nutrients from fresh, whole, organic foods and herbs versus vitamin pills, which are isolated compounds of a whole plant or food.

Whole in Spirit

Processed foods can weaken the body, and some believe that, over time, they can weaken the mind and emotions as well. Philosophically speaking, let's say you, as a balanced individual and for whatever reasons, choose a person totally lacking in some aspect as your partner (as an analogy for a slightly processed food). Although on the outside this person appears to be complete (like a processed food might), inside they lack self-awareness, emotional stability, and positive thinking, and they might also rigidly refuse to grow or use their talents to make their life better. He or she probably wound up this way because of past "processing" by negative things that didn't nourish them the way they should have been, leaving them far from the well-adjusted person they should be.

Being with a person like this can drain your own emotional, spiritual, and mental reserves, can't it?

It's an uplift to be complete yourself and share your life with another whole, well-balanced person; it's the same uplift for your body to receive whole foods. Incomplete foods force your body to put out without receiving anything back for the extra effort. A whole food nourishes your body, just as a whole person as a partner can nourish your mind, heart, and soul.

Sweet and Low

For an excellent example of a refined, processed item, let's look at refined sugar, one of the most damaging foods to the body. In contrast, its whole form, such as a fresh stalk of sugar cane from a Hawaiian garden, contains many nutrients, enzymes, minerals, phytochemicals, and vitamins, including the B vitamins. Plus it's got fiber, which helps slow absorption of the sugar into the bloodstream, making it easier for your body to metabolize, and helps maintain your blood sugar levels. A fresh stalk of sugar can be a healthful food.

However, when that same sugar cane is refined, subjected to high heat, and processed through charcoal or ground animal bones, all of its nutrients and enzymes are stripped away. Refined sugar is so lacking in nutrients that it actually robs your body of B vitamins, enzymes, and other nutrients just so your body can process it. When the sugar cane was still a whole food, these nutrients were intact, and there was no need to rob your body for them.

One of the most damaging things too much sugar in the diet can do is make your body chemistry more acidic, which forces your body to utilize its own minerals like calcium, magnesium, and potassium to maintain homeostasis and balance out the acid/alkaline pH balance. Your body is made up mostly of minerals, and minerals such as magnesium and potassium make up the muscles, including the heart and bowels, and calcium primarily makes up the bones and lining of the veins, arteries, and nerves. As excess sugar consumption continually robs the body of these important minerals, it can lead to vulnerabilities in any of these areas. In addition, constant overacidity creates an internal environment condusive to cancer.

Furthermore, refined sugar spikes your blood sugar, causing insulin to rise rapidly and eventually crash (see Chapter 7), which is damaging to your cells and can make you gain weight and eventually lead to diabetes. Refined starchy foods like crackers, fruit juices, pasta, and breads can have the same effect as pure sugary snacks, so the best advice is to skip the sugary, refined foods and fill up instead with fresh vegetables, whole grains, raw nuts and seeds, and veggie proteins. And when you want to have something sweet, go ahead and enjoy the sugary snack, but just don't make it a regular habit! (See Chapter 26 for more on sugar and healthy replacements.)

Getting Your Vitamins and Minerals

You've probably seen the new DRIs (Daily Reference Intakes) for certain minerals and vitamins on food packaging labels. (The DRIs replace the old Recommended Daily Allowances and also take into account age groups and specific categories.) The new recommended intakes are set by the Institute of Medicine and the U.S. Food and Drug Administration.

Let's take a look at the recommended intakes:

For every 1,000 milligrams (mg) of calcium daily, you should also be getting the following:

350 mg magnesium

1,000 mg phosphorus

2,500 mg potassium

For every 1 gram of protein, you should be getting 16 times the amount of calcium in milligrams.

These numbers are general averages and are for either male or female adults over age 30. Your needs might vary depending on age, gender, diet, and activity levels.

It's a Balancing Act

To keep your body functioning correctly, you need a balance of minerals, which you can achieve through natural foods. Balance becomes lopsided when we eat overly processed or genetically manipulated foods.

Too much or too little of any element in the body leads to health concerns. Too much of one type of mineral might inhibit how you utilize calcium, for instance, and can even cause calcium loss. A lack of another vitamin or mineral can make calcium ineffective to your body.

The message is clear: you cannot maintain good health by dosing yourself with one mineral or another (unless, of course, you have a deficiency). Health is maintained by a balance of foods, which naturally occurs when you eat plant foods but does not occur with processed foods or animal products. Natural foods keep your body more balanced.

Calcium-Rich Greens and Beans

As a lacto vegetarian, don't rely on cow's milk to be your main source of calcium. Here's a condensed list of vegetarian foods high in calcium:

> **Veggie Soup for the Soul**
>
> Research has found that each quart of cow's milk contains an average of about 600 million somatic cells (pus cells). To help clean up this problem, the dairy industry has begun feeding cows garlic, a natural antibiotic, which reduces the pus count dramatically. Now there's a natural solution!

- Nuts and seeds, especially sesame seeds and walnuts
- All greens
- All unrefined cereal grains
- Sea vegetables such as kelp and dulse
- Carrots
- Beans

If you're a strict vegetarian, you'll get plenty of calcium along with the other minerals you need in a balanced ratio through your plant-based diet. But you might also consider an herbal supplement rich in calcium and other minerals, such as alfalfa, oatstraw, and horsetail, to be sure you get the recommended 1,000 to 1,500 milligrams daily.

It's So Easy Eatin' Greens

All greens contain chlorophyll, which is detoxifying for the body. Chlorophyll is the blood of the plant and is very close to the structure of human blood, so it should be no surprise that chlorophyll can help build your blood count. A healthy red blood cell count is important to protect from anemia, general weakness, and fatigue and is critical before and during pregnancy. Many menstruating women can have subclinically low levels of iron without realizing it, except that they feel fatigued or sore more often. If this is you, consider your iron intake. Dark greens are a safe way to get iron and calcium in your diet. Here's a quick list to help remind you why raw greens are great for you.

Raw greens …

- Help build red blood cells, which boosts energy levels.

- Are natural deodorizers for the body and breath.

- Have a high calcium content.

- Are rich in iron.

- Are high in fiber.

- Help with weight management.

- Help balance blood sugar.

Veggie Soup for the Soul

Fiber not only is critical for proper bowel health, but it also fills you up so you eat less. Fiber also slows the digestion of sugars so your blood sugar stays more balanced, keeping energy levels more steady.

Mix up the greens you eat. Baby greens can have different nutritional properties than adult greens, so be sure to keep variety in your choices to get all the nutrients you can from your salads. These days you can find prewashed, bagged, and organic lettuces of all types in most all grocery stores, making salad prep easier than ever before.

And because you can add just about any raw fruits or veggies, beans, pasta, legumes, nuts, seeds, and even some grains to lettuce to make a salad, raw greens never have to be boring! Turn to the salad and dressing recipes that follow to see what I mean.

The Least You Need to Know

◆ Eating salads helps ensure you get health-boosting enzymes and phytochemicals present in whole foods. Eating whole foods is the most natural way to nourish your body.

◆ Salads are a delicious and creative way to eat raw foods daily.

◆ Raw greens are an excellent source of fiber, which is imperative for bowel health and also helps fill you up.

◆ Greens contain chlorophyll, a natural detoxifier that helps clean and build the blood.

Baby Romaine and Goat Cheese Salad

Mild baby romaine leaves and sweet apple chunks are highlighted by woody pine nuts and pungent, creamy goat cheese and brought together with a splash of tangy balsamic vinegar and peppery olive oil in this delightful salad.

Baby romaine lettuce leaves, washed

½ apple, sliced into bite-size chunks

Pine nuts, toasted

Goat cheese, crumbled

Balsamic vinegar

Olive oil

Serves: 1	
Prep time: 5 minutes	
Serving size: 1 salad	

1. In a salad bowl, combine romaine, apple chunks, pine nuts, and goat cheese to your liking.

2. Add balsamic vinegar and olive oil, and toss until all ingredients are covered. Serve chilled.

You'll love this Baby Romaine and Goat Cheese Salad that includes toasted pine nuts and apples.

Spring Mix with Corn, Tofu, and Sesame Sticks

This spring mix salad with a range of textures—crunchy, salty, nutty sesame sticks, sweet yellow corn, tangy balsamic vinegar, and olive oil topped with tamari marinated tofu cubes—will soon become a favorite summer treat.

Serves: 1
Prep time: 5 minutes
Cook time: 20 minutes
Serving size: 1 salad

1 lb. firm tofu

3 TB. tamari

Spring mix salad, washed

¼ cup frozen golden corn kernels, thawed

¼ cup sesame sticks

1 TB. balsamic vinegar

1 TB. olive oil

1. Preheat the oven to 400°F. Spray a cookie sheet with olive oil spray.

2. Squeeze excess water from tofu and chop into bite-size cubes. Place tofu in a bowl, and pour tamari over cubes. Toss with a spoon to coat, and arrange tofu on the prepared cookie sheet. Bake for approximately 20 minutes or until desired texture. (The longer you cook it, the harder and dryer it becomes.) Let tofu cool.

3. In a salad bowl, combine ½ cup marinated and baked tofu cubes, salad mix, corn, and sesame sticks. Add balsamic vinegar and olive oil, and toss until coated. Serve chilled.

Sprouts of Info

Got leftover tofu cubes? Store the extra cooked cubes in a covered container in refrigerator for future salads or general snacking.

Baby Spinach, Grape, and Walnut Salad

This elegant salad of small, rounded crisp baby spinach leaves with juicy, sweet, red grape slices, and tender walnut pieces tossed in a tangy balsamic vinaigrette can serve as an appetizer or as a light meal.

2 TB. balsamic vinegar

3 TB. virgin olive oil

Freshly ground black pepper

Pinch dried oregano

2 cups baby spinach leaves, washed

⅔ cup red grapes, seedless and sliced in half

¼ cup raw walnut pieces

Serves: 1		
Prep time: 5 minutes		
Serving size: 1 salad		

1. In a medium bowl, combine vinegar, olive oil, pepper, and oregano with a blender, mixer, or fork until thoroughly mixed.

2. Add spinach, sliced grapes, and walnuts to the salad bowl, and toss with vinaigrette. Serve on a chilled plate.

Sprouts of Info

To maintain your frozen vegetables' nutrients, *do not* cook or zap them in the microwave. Instead, to thaw frozen vegetables for a salad, simply put the vegetable(s) in a strainer and run hot water over them for about 30 seconds until they're thawed.

Falafel Salad with Greek Dressing

Spicy, nutty falafel balls make this Greek-style salad filling. Refreshing tomatoes, cucumbers, firm feta cheese crumbles, sweet red onion, and chilled greens tossed with basil and oregano spiked Greek dressing give this salad its Mediterranean flair.

Serves: 1	
Prep time: 8	
Serving size: 1 salad	

2½ tsp. olive oil

Pinch garlic powder

Pinch dried oregano

Pinch dried basil

Pinch freshly ground black pepper

Pinch onion powder

2 TB. red wine vinegar

1½ cups mixed greens

¼ cup red onion, thinly sliced

¼ cup cucumber, chopped

¼ cup Roma tomatoes, sliced

¼ cup feta cheese, crumbled

4 or 5 falafel balls (recipe in Chapter 10)

Flatbread, toasted and cut into triangles (optional)

1. In a blender, combine olive oil, garlic powder, oregano, basil, pepper, and onion powder. Add vinegar and blend until well mixed.

2. Place greens, onion, cucumber, and tomatoes in a large bowl, pour in vinaigrette, and toss to combine.

3. Sprinkle salad with feta cheese, and top with falafel balls. Serve with toasted flatbread triangles (if using).

Lettuce Explain

Pinch is a term used in cooking as an approximate measurement for dried spices and is usually equivalent to about ⅛ teaspoon, or about the amount of a dried spice you can pinch between your thumb and forefinger.

Strawberry and Cucumber Salad

Cool, minty, spicy, tangy, and so refreshing, sweet red strawberries and crunchy, cool cucumbers make an unlikely tasty duo in this chilled side salad.

3 TB. rice vinegar	4½ cups organic strawberries, stemmed and quartered
1½ tsp. chopped fresh dill	
1½ tsp. chopped fresh mint	1 medium organic cucumber, peeled and cut into ½-in. pieces
½ tsp. ground cumin	
½ tsp. paprika	¾ cup chopped Italian parsley leaves
½ tsp. honey	
¼ cup olive oil	4 whole scallions, chopped

Serves: 4 to 6
Prep time: 15 minutes
Serving size: 1 cup

1. In a bowl or a blender, combine rice vinegar, dill, mint, cumin, paprika, and honey. Whisk (or blend) in olive oil until well mixed.

2. In another large bowl, add strawberries, cucumber, parsley, and scallions. Pour in vinaigrette, and toss until coated. Serve immediately.

Sprouts of Info

Cucumbers and strawberries are naturally full of potassium. Potassium helps you regulate your body heat, making this salad great in the hot summertime to keep you cool as a cucumber!

Tahini Lemon and Spice Dressing

Nutty and creamy with a hint of citrus and hot pepper, this thick dressing is good on any salad.

Serves: 6 to 8
Prep time: 5 minutes
Serving size: 1 or 2 table-spoons, depending on salad size

2 cups sesame tahini

1½ cups water

1 cup freshly squeezed lemon juice

1 tsp. ground cumin

1 tsp. dried oregano

Pinch cayenne

Freshly ground black pepper

3 TB. chopped fresh parsley

1. Pour tahini into a large mixing bowl, and whisk in water and lemon juice until smooth and creamy. Add cumin, oregano, cayenne, and pepper, and whisk to combine.

2. Add parsley and mix again. Add additional water, if necessary, to achieve the dressing consistency you desire. Keep refrigerated.

Sprouts of Info

This Tahini Lemon Spice dressing is good for use on any type of salad, but also makes a great condiment for adding on top of pita falafel sandwiches, with cucumbers, tomatoes, and sprouts, or drizzled on any raw veggie sandwiches.

Chapter 12

Delicious Soups, Stews, and Chowders

In This Chapter

◆ The health benefits of soup

◆ Helpful slow cooker tips

◆ Thickening agent hints

◆ Hearty soup, stew, and chowder recipes

What's cozier than enjoying a steamy bowl of soup while relaxing indoors during a big snowstorm? Or settling into camp on a crisp fall afternoon and sipping some soup after a challenging hike up the mountain? And you can't deny the good feeling you get when you're sick and a loved one brings you a hot bowl of nonchicken noodle soup.

Soup can make you feel good and has many health benefits. Just like getting fresh fruit by blending it into a smoothie (see Chapter 9), soup, chowders, and stews are a great way to get your fresh, mineral-potent vegetables.

This chapter includes recipes for soups, stews, and chowders, and also includes some tips on cooking with slow cookers—quite possibly the easiest way to make these recipes. Plus, while you're at work or doing other things, your slow cooker is at home cooking and filling your home with aromatic flavors that make you feel good the moment you walk in the door.

The Skinny on Soup

Lots of dieters know that soup can help you lose or maintain weight. Beginning a meal with a broth-based soup starts to fill you up and helps you eat less of your main course. Eating broth soup fills you up even more than simply drinking water with your meals.

You can make your own vegetable broth easily by simply adding a few spices like bay leaves, thyme, and parsley, and some chopped root vegetables like onions, garlic, turnips, and carrots to water and bringing them to a boil. Then reduce the heat and simmer. After several hours, use a strainer to strain the broth from the vegetables and store the broth in airtight containers in the fridge. Veggie broth has almost no calories but *lots* of nutrients.

> **Lettuce Explain**
>
> **Excitotoxins** are substances added to foods and beverages such as MSG and aspartame that can disrupt and/or destroy brain neurons. For more information, check out *Excitotoxins: The Taste That Kills* by neurosurgeon Russell L. Blaylock, M.D. This is an important read for anyone concerned about mental and nerve health.

Soup can certainly be an economical way to eat and helps reduce waste. You can chop up extra produce that won't last too much longer and make a broth, soup, or stew. Homemade vegetable soup is an excellent source of minerals and vitamins. Season it with natural ingredients such as kelp (for a salty flavor), garlic, cayenne (for some hot spice), and onions. Use purified water, and avoid unnatural seasonings, especially those containing MSG or hydrolyzed vegetable protein, which are *excitotoxins*.

A Quick Course in Slow Cookers

Slow cookers are a great way to make soups and stews. Most recipes simply have you toss in all your ingredients, turn it on, put on the lid, and leave it alone. By dinner time, soup's on!

Here are some tips on using slow cookers to make the best of your slow cooked meals:

◆ Use whole-leaf herbs and spices instead of ground for better flavor, and add them when the cooking is almost done.

◆ Keep the lid on the slow cooker so liquids don't boil away. Lifting the lid to stir causes enough heat to escape to prolong cooking time about 20 minutes. Have patience!

◆ If your stew or chili is too soupy, remove the lid and cook on high for about $1/2$ hour. This thickens your stew or chili and can also help concentrate flavors; it's a process called reduction.

◆ If you're making a recipe that wasn't specifically developed for the slow cooker, reduce the liquid by $1/4$ up to about $1/2$ unless you're cooking rice, which will soak in the water, or if you're making soup.

◆ Foods cook properly at even temperature in a slow cooker filled about $1/2$ to $2/3$ full.

◆ To avoid soggy stew veggies, add your tender vegetables like tomatoes, squash, or mushrooms during the last 30 minutes of cooking.

◆ To deter bacteria that can cause food poisoning, heat the food to 140°F as quickly as possible. Test the temperature after a few hours of cooking on low (which should be at 140°F). If it's lower than this, there's a problem with your slow cooker and you should get a new one.

◆ Don't add frozen foods to a slow cooker. Even if the foods do eventually reach a safe temperature and cook thoroughly, potential bacteria growth in the food can produce toxins that won't be destroyed by heat and can make you sick.

> **Veggie Soup for the Soul**
>
> Spices and herbs contain essential oils that can evaporate or lose their flavor if cooked with the rest of the ingredients for the long cooking period. If adding cayenne or black pepper to your recipe, add it toward the end of the cooking time, as they can become bitter if cooked for long.

> **Sprouts of Info**
>
> Many people have experienced food poisoning and don't even know it because symptoms can be delayed. Mild symptoms can include body aches, slight nausea, headache, and digestive discomfort.

◆ Grains and pasta such as couscous needs lots of liquid to cook properly in the slow cooker and should be added during the last hour of cooking time. Rice soaks up about double its amount in liquid, so be sure you have enough liquid in the recipe for the rice to become tender.

◆ In general, cooking one hour on high equals two hours on low.

◆ You may need to double the cooking time if you live at a high altitude.

◆ Unless a recipe states otherwise, add dairy products during the last 30 minutes of cooking time to avoid spoilage.

And if that weren't enough info, here are some slow cooker cleaning and maintenance tips:

◆ Slow cookers with removable liners are much easier to clean. Either purchase one with the removable liner or purchase plastic bag–type liners.

◆ Never use an abrasive cleaner such as an SOS pad to clean the slow cooker. Instead, when the slow cooker is cooled, let it soak for 15 to 20 minutes in hot, soapy water. Use a sponge or nylon scrubbie to clean. You can also run the crockery insert through the dishwasher.

◆ To remove mineral stains, add 1 cup distilled white vinegar to the slow cooker and fill about ¾ full with hot water. Cover and cook on high for two hours. Then let the slow cooker cool and clean as directed earlier.

◆ To remove water marks from glazed crockery, rub the surface with vegetable oil and let stand for two or three hours. Then fill with hot soapy water, rub the surface, and scrub with a nylon scrubbie pad. Rinse and dry well.

Thickening Agents That Keep You Thin

If you're not using a slow cooker and want to thicken your stew, chowder, or soup, or if you're using a slow cooker but don't want to wait another ½ hour to cook off the excess liquid to get the consistency you want, you can add a *thickening agent*. Thickening agents can also be used in making veggie gravy and other sauces.

Lettuce Explain

A **thickening agent** or **thickener** is a term used in cooking to refer to substances, usually starchy powders, that add body and thickness to foods like soups, stews, chowders, puddings, and gravies.

Most of these starches can be used interchangeably, but here's a quick list of some of your thickener choices, with pros and cons for each.

Thickener	Pros	Cons
Arrowroot powder	holds up to freezing without changing texture of food; neutral flavor; tolerates acidic ingredients; tolerates prolonged cooking	more expensive than cornstarch; turns dairy-based foods slimy
Cornstarch	works best with dairy-based sauces	loses potency when mixed with acidic foods
Kudzu powder	reported medicinal benefits, include calming anxiety and curbing appetite for alcohol	expensive and harder to find
Potato starch	gluten free, kosher	does not tolerate boiling

Thickeners don't add flavor to foods unless they're undercooked, and then you might taste a starchy flavor. Expert cooks tend to choose arrowroot powder when thickening foods with delicate flavors, as it's one of the most neutral-tasting of the starch thickeners.

Veggie Soup for the Soul

No one's sure which came first, the bowl or the soup, but anthropologists' findings of food residue on ancient pots show that man has probably been making some version of soup for thousands of years. The name *soup* supposedly derived from the word *sop*, meaning a piece of solid food such as bread for dipping in a liquid food.

The best way to use starch thickeners is to first whisk or mix the starch with an equal amount of cold water until it becomes pasty. Then whisk it into the liquid you're trying to thicken. Be sure to cook the food for a brief time to remove any starchy flavor. Don't add thickeners at the beginning of cooking because some thickeners break down after a while or at too high a temperature.

The Least You Need to Know

◆ Broth-based soups can help maintain weight if eaten prior to a meal, as they tend to fill you up and make you eat less of the main course.

◆ If cooking a meal in a slow cooker, be sure the food is heated to at least 140°F within $1\frac{1}{2}$ hours to avoid potential bacteria growth and the resulting food poisoning.

◆ When cooking in a slow cooker, add spices toward the end of cooking time, as some spices can turn bitter if cooked all day.

◆ Arrowroot powder is the best thickener to use for delicate flavors, as it's the most neutral-tasting of the thickeners.

Corn Chowder

This filling chowder makes a great comfort food with its thick, creamy, hot, sweet corn chowder with tender crunchy bell pepper chunks and scallions seasoned with a touch of cayenne and fresh dill.

3 (15-oz.) cans vegetable broth

6 medium russet potatoes, cubed

1 medium onion, chopped

1 stalk celery, chopped

⅛ tsp. dried sage

½ tsp. dried thyme

½ tsp. dried oregano

½ tsp. ground capsicum or cayenne

Freshly ground black pepper

1 TB. butter

¼ cup chopped green bell pepper

½ cup minced scallions

3 or 4 cups fresh or frozen corn kernels

¼ cup heavy cream or soy milk (optional)

1 TB. fresh minced dill

Serves: 4
Prep time: 25 minutes
Cook time: 35 minutes
Serving size: 1 bowl

1. In a large saucepan over high heat, bring veggie broth to a boil. Add potatoes, onion, celery, sage, thyme, oregano, capsicum or cayenne pepper, and black pepper. Cover and simmer over medium heat for 15 to 20 minutes or until potatoes are tender.

2. In the meantime, in a small skillet over medium-high heat, melt butter. Add green bell pepper and scallions, and sauté until vegetables turn a bright green, approximately 3 minutes. Set aside.

3. Put potato mixture in a blender and blend in small increments. Add blended chowder back to pot and keep over low heat.

4. Add corn to potato mixture and simmer for 5 minutes, stirring to ensure chowder does not stick.

5. Stir green bell pepper and scallions into simmering chowder. Add cream or soy milk (if using) and dill, and adjust seasonings if needed.

Sprouts of Info

If you are dairy free, you can substitute soy, oat, almond, or rice milk for heavy cream in my recipes. Don't expect it to give the thickness that heavy cream would, though. If need be, you can thicken with any of the thickening agents discussed earlier.

Black Bean Soup

Rich, thick, and hearty, this black bean soup seasoned with garlic, scallions, fresh cilantro, and lime juice and topped with a dollop of sour cream is terrific served with Blue Corn Bread.

Serves: 2
Prep time: 10 minutes
Cook time: 5 minutes
Serving size: 1 bowl

⅓ **cup sliced scallions**

1 tsp. minced garlic

2 tsp. olive oil

1 (15-oz.) can vegetable broth

1 (15-oz.) can black beans, drained

¼ **cup chopped fresh cilantro**

Sour cream

Freshly squeezed lime juice

Blue Corn Bread (recipe follows)

1. In a deep frying pan over high heat, sauté scallions and garlic in olive oil. When scallions and garlic are soft, add vegetable broth, drained black beans, and cilantro, and simmer 5 minutes.

2. Add soup to a blender and purée until smooth.

3. Serve soup with sour cream, a squeeze of lime, and Blue Corn Bread.

Sprouts of Info _____

Thick, hearty soups and chowders can be a meal by themselves, but they're also great accompanied by a slice of freshly baked bread—like the Blue Corn Bread coming right up!

Blue Corn Bread

Buttery, sweet, and moist, this corn bread with chewy, sweet red bell pepper dices and golden corn kernels throughout is best served warm with melted butter.

½ cup butter

1 red bell pepper, diced

1 cup yellow corn kernels, fresh or frozen and thawed

⅔ cup honey

Egg replacer equal to 2 eggs, premixed

1 cup vanilla soy milk

½ tsp. baking soda

1 cup blue cornmeal

1 cup all-purpose flour

½ tsp. salt

Serves: 6 to 8	
Prep time: 15 minutes	
Cook time: 30 to 40 minutes	
Serving size: 1 piece	

1. Preheat the oven to 375°F. Grease an 8-inch square pan.

2. In a large skillet over medium-high heat, melt butter. Add red bell pepper, and sauté until soft. Add corn kernels, and sauté for another minute.

3. Remove the skillet from heat, and stir in honey. Quickly add egg replacer, and beat until well blended.

4. Combine soy milk with baking soda, and stir into skillet mixture. Stir in cornmeal, flour, and salt until well blended and few lumps remain.

5. Pour batter into the prepared pan, and bake for 30 to 40 minutes or until a toothpick inserted in the center comes out clean.

Sprouts of Info

Blue corn is rich in the amino acid l-Lysine, an important supplement.

Cheesy Cauliflower and Potato Soup

Creamy, hot, and cheesy, this cauliflower and potato soup is spiked with fresh dill, basil, and parsley. Green peas and chopped celery add texture interest, and cream cheese adds a hint of sweetness.

Serves: 4
Prep time: 15 minutes
Cook time: 20 minutes
Serving size: 1 bowl

2 TB. butter

1 medium onion, chopped

1 garlic clove, minced

4 medium red potatoes, diced

½ cup diced celery

2 (15-oz.) cans vegetable broth

1 medium head cauliflower, cut in florets

2 TB. fresh slivered basil

1 TB. fresh minced parsley

1 tsp. dried dill

½ cup green peas

Freshly ground black pepper

½ cup soy milk

½ cup cream cheese

1 cup grated cheddar cheese

1. In a deep saucepan over medium-high heat, melt butter. Add onion and garlic, and sauté until onion is softened.

2. Add potatoes and celery, and stir, cooking about 2 minutes. Add broth and bring to a boil.

3. Reduce heat to low. Cover and simmer until potatoes are almost tender, about 10 minutes.

4. Add cauliflower and cook until tender.

5. Add basil, parsley, dill, peas, pepper, soy milk, and cream cheese, and simmer over low heat until heated through.

6. Stir in cheddar cheese just before serving, and garnish with fresh basil leaves.

Variation: For a creamy soup, leave peas aside, add rest of soup mixture to a blender or a food processor, and purée. Fold in peas for added texture and serve.

Veggie Stew

A delicious blend of fresh herbs and spices flavor, this brothy stew is loaded with chunks of onions, leeks, celery, carrots, cabbage, potatoes, and tomatoes. Firm and creamy garbanzo beans add a nice texture, and each bite contains a smooth, buttery aftertaste.

1 TB. butter

1 medium yellow onion, chopped

1 leek, sliced

1 small whole garlic bulb, peeled and minced

3 stalks celery, chopped

3 large carrots, chopped

2 Roma tomatoes, chopped

3 (15-oz.) cans vegetable broth

1 (15-oz.) can garbanzo beans

½ head cabbage, cored and shredded

4 large russet potatoes, chopped into bite-size pieces

2 TB. fresh finely chopped parsley

1 bay leaf

2 tsp. dried dill weed

½ tsp. dried oregano

½ tsp. freshly ground black pepper

Dash cayenne

Grated parmesan or asiago cheese (optional)

Serves: 6 to 8
Prep time: 15 minutes
Cook time: about 4 hours in a slow cooker or 40 minutes on the stove
Serving size: 1 bowl

1. In a slow cooker, combine butter, onion, leek, garlic, celery, carrots, tomatoes, broth, garbanzo beans, cabbage, potatoes, parsley, and bay leaf. Cover, set on low, and let cook for at least 6 hours.

2. About ½ hour before serving, add dill, oregano, black pepper, and cayenne, and mix well. Re-cover to finish cooking.

3. Remove and discard bay leaf. Top with fresh Parmesan or asiago cheese (if using), and serve.

Sprouts of Info

It's easiest to put the ingredients in a slow cooker and leave it to cook all day. You can also speed things up by boiling the veggies in a pot on the stove and simmering for about 40 minutes.

A bowl of hearty Veggie Stew will warm you up and provide lots of essential vitamins and minerals.

What Kids Want

In This Chapter

- ◆ Tips for a vegetarian pregnancy
- ◆ Raising healthy vegetarian children
- ◆ How animal products might influence hormones
- ◆ Kid-friendly recipes

You've traveled the world as a vegetarian and are getting ready to settle down with a vegetarian family of your own, right? Good, because this chapter offers helpful tips on being a vegetarian through a pregnancy. It also helps provide you what you need to know about raising healthy vegetarian infants, toddlers, and teens.

At the end of the chapter, I've listed some kid-friendly recipes—all meat free, of course—sure to soon become kid favorites.

The Pregnant Vegetarian

Congratulations! You're pregnant! Now what do you need to know to get everything you need as a vegetarian? Well, most everything you've learned thus far still applies; however, your needs for certain nutrients will go up

Steer Clear _____

Don't let others scare you about staying healthy as a pregnant vegetarian. What's good for you is good for building a baby—all you'll need is *more* good stuff!

naturally, and I'll give you the rundown. You also may be nauseous, and I'll give you some vegetarian snack ideas to help you through. Other than that, you can continue your vegetarian diet as a pregnant and nursing mom with robust health and be able to get everything you need to build a healthy baby!

As long as you aren't a "junk food" vegetarian, you should have no problems getting nourished for pregnancy. All you really need to do is follow some simple guidelines, such as getting the extra calories you need and making sure you're getting extras of some nutrients listed in the following table. Besides that, work with your trusted doctor and/or midwife to help monitor your prenatal progress and help you with all the other aspects of pregnancy and planning for delivery!

Nutrient	Amount	Why It's Important	Food Sources	Herbal Sources
Iron	30 mg	Keeps mother's blood count up, helps avoid pregnancy-related anemia.	Black cherries, dark greens, blackstrap molasses	Liquid chlorophyll, spirulina, red raspberry leaves
Calcium	1,200 mg	Builds skeletal system for baby, prevents calcium loss from mom (especially now that you're eating more protein).	Tofu, barley, kale, collard greens, carrots and carrot juice, sesame seeds	Alfalfa, parsley
Protein	60 g	Aids baby's development.	Nuts, seeds, vegetables, beans, dairy, whole wheat, tofu	Spirulina, blue green algae

Nutrient	Amount	Why It's Important	Food Sources	Herbal Sources
Folic acid (B_9)	Trace amounts (0.8 mg)	Essential for nervous system, formation of genetic (RNA and DNA) cells, production of hydrochloric acid, essential for B_{12} absorption, essential in red blood cell formation.	Green leafy vegetables, fresh mushrooms, wheat germ, soybeans	Kelp, parsley, spirulina
Vitamin D (calciferol)	40 IU (same as non-pregnant women)	Helps the body utilize calcium.	With adequate sunshine exposure and a healthful diet, you shouldn't need to supplement, but ask your healthcare provider to be sure	Spinach, dairy, egg yolks, alfalfa, fortified cereals
B_{12}	Trace amounts (2.2 mcg)	Essential in fat and protein metabolism, blood cell formation, bone marrow, gastrointestinal tract, and nervous system.	Fortified cereals, most meat substitutes, most milk substitutes, Red Star T-6635+ nutritional yeast flakes, dairy	Alfalfa, bee pollen, spirulina
Daily caloric intake	300 extra calories daily (after first trimester)	Baby needs extra nourishment to grow!	Starchy snacks, thick soups and chowders (see Chapter 12) with grains and beans, thick smoothies added nuts, cereals, bean burritos	Spirulina, blue-green algae

continues

continued

Nutrient	Amount	Why It's Important	Food Sources	Herbal Sources
Water	Extra! (more than half your body weight in ounces)	Water helps keep your body flushed and can help alleviate constipation and toxemia that sometimes accompany pregnancy.	Drink purified, filtered water	
Fiber	Extra!	A change in hormone levels when pregnant makes most women constipated, which also can cause hemorrhoids; take in lots of extra fiber (and water) to avoid these problems and stay regular; staying regular also helps keep you from toxemia.	Raw vegetables and fruits	Psyllium hulls, flaxseeds/flax-seed oil

* Although these are considered safe during pregnancy, please work with an herbalist and/or your doctor to ensure that taking an herbal supplement or any type of supplement is okay for you during gestation and breast-feeding.

Nausea and morning sickness are common among pregnant women. Here are a variety of foods to try to help with your stomach upset. Choose the one that appeals to your stomach the most at the time!

◆ Smoothie

◆ Bagel with nut butter

◆ Warm bowl of oatmeal; grits; or slow cooked wheat kernels, millet, or barley

◆ Cold cereal with soy or rice milk

◆ Ryvita crackers

◆ Bean burrito

Sprouts of Info _____

Ginger tea is an excellent tonic for pregnant women and can also help control nausea and morning sickness.

The Vegetarian Child

Breast milk is the best nutrition you can give your baby. It not only helps his or her digestive and intestinal systems develop properly, but it's invaluable for the immune system. Some studies even show that students who were breast-fed do better on tests than those who were not breast-fed. Other studies show that breast-fed babies are less likely to have problems with allergies later in life and that they are more likely to maintain an ideal weight. And of course, the experience can build a strong bond between mother and child that can last a lifetime. Breast milk contains the foods that have already been digested by the mother, whose gastric juices have done the job for both mom and baby. Mother's breast milk is also a sterile food.

Veggie Soup for the Soul

Mother's milk is the perfect food—for the species it was designed for. For instance, the high amount of protein and fat found in cow's milk is great for a rapidly growing 64-pound newborn calf designed to grow to a full 1,500 pounds in adulthood within 24 months. Human milk is the only milk designed to be the perfect food for a 5- to 10-pound human baby who takes 18 to 21 years to grow into a 100- to 250-pound adult. Nature has figured this out for us: cow's milk is for baby cows.

However, the choice is not for everyone, some babies are adopted, some moms have medical problems that prevent them from nursing, and some moms just plain choose not to for personal reasons. So what can you do instead?

Certified raw goat's milk has the closest makeup to human milk, and your baby can survive on the fresh goat's milk from a healthy goat. The milk needs to be diluted with some pure water. (Although this is not a choice for vegans, if you can find a farmer with a goat that's treated well and is willing to provide you goat milk for your baby, you can avoid the ethical reasons linked to using factory-farmed animal products.)

Steer Clear

Do *not* feed your baby regular rice or soy milk. These are not suitable for an infant. You need formulas specifically made for infants. Your doctor or midwife should be familiar with the use of goat's milk and other milk alternatives; seek his or her advice on which would be the most suitable choice.

Try a soy-based infant formula such as Soyalac, Prosobee, or Isomil. These contain no animal products and are suitable for vegans.

Many infant formulas are based on cow's milk but are altered as in hydrolyzed-protein formulas, which are basically predigested to make the cow's milk protein more digestible for baby and may lessen allergic reactions to cow's milk protein.

Your baby's nutrition is the foundation upon which his or her entire body will grow. Help them build a strong foundation. As with your own diet, go organic when feeding your baby whenever possible to lower their exposure to chemicals, fertilizers, and growth hormones. Earth's Best, made by Horizon, who brings you other organic dairy foods, makes an organic infant formula. More organic infant formulas can be found at BabyOrganic.com, NaturesOne.com, and SimilacOrganic.com. Be sure to check the labels to see if the formula is iron-fortified, and check with your pediatrician to see if he or she recommends formula with or without iron for your baby.

Weaning Toward Food

Most experts agree that a child should be breast-fed at the minimum for six months, and longer (even as long as two years) has been suggested if it's comfortable for the mother. This allows the baby's digestive system to develop fully.

When you wean your baby, you can begin feeding him or her fruit or vegetable juice and then move on to strained vegetables and fruits. Try not to mix fruits and vegetables. Introduce one new food at a time, to see if your child is having discomfort with any type of new food. Consider feeding your baby only organic foods. Many companies are making organic baby food without sugar and artificial flavors now. If you're up for it, many moms use food processors to purée their own baby food.

Lettuce Explain

The **stomach teeth** are the molars. These teeth usually come in first, indicating the child is able to digest solid foods. The **eye teeth** are referred to as the canines. These are the pair of pointy teeth (top and bottom).

Nature's sign that your baby is ready for solid food is when his or her *eye* and *stomach teeth* come in. This indicates that the baby's stomach's digestive juices are flowing and he or she will be able to begin chewing and digesting a variety of starches and proteins.

Tofu-Touting Toddlers

When your toddler grows her stomach and eye teeth and is devouring solid foods, it's easy to have her eat what you eat. Just cut up a portion of your foods into tiny, bite-size pieces and let her feed herself. For picky kids, provide a variety of fresh fruits, vegetables, and meat-free protein foods so they can choose what they like. As long as they're wholesome foods, your toddler will get what she needs.

Toddlers need more calorie-dense foods for their growing bodies, and less fiber. Bulky foods such as salads and raw plant foods can fill up a child's tiny stomach before he meets all his caloric needs. Be sure to have denser foods such as bananas, avocados, and nut and seed butters available.

A good food guide pyramid for the toddler (from the top down) includes the following:

> 1 teaspoon vegetable oil
>
> 3 small to medium-size fruits
>
> 1 cup raw veggies and ¹/₂ cup cooked (equivalent to the recommended two servings of daily vegetables)
>
> 1 cup rice milk or soy milk
>
> 1 tablespoon nut butter or nuts
>
> 1 cup cooked beans
>
> 1 cup cooked grains or pasta
>
> 1 or 2 cups cereal
>
> 1 or 2 slices whole-grain bread

Veggie Soup for the Soul

Some tests indicate that kids' tastes have a lot more to do with their mental conditioning than not. Blind taste tests showed that most students liked soy-based burgers. Then the students tasted the same burgers but were told they were soy. The kids gave the same burgers the thumbs-down!

Seems like an awful lot for a tiny stomach, doesn't it? Let me give you a sample menu for the day to help you visualize what all this food would look like in a given day:

> *First thing in morning:* 1 banana
>
> *Breakfast:* 1 cup slow cooked grains with raisins and 1 cup rice milk
>
> *Snack:* apple and carrot pieces
>
> *Lunch:* 1 small baked potato topped with sprouts and olive oil
>
> *Snack:* whole-grain toast with nut butter
>
> *Dinner:* 1 cup veggie chili

As you can see, it's rather easy. You shouldn't have to calculate anything, but just feed your child what you have. But do be sure he gets more dense foods and less bulky foods, and most of all, avoid feeding sugary snacks and too many refined carbs, which leads to poor health.

Veggie Soup for the Soul _____

If you need another good reason to avoid processed foods, eat organic, and drink clean water, consider this fact: vegetarian moms tend to have substantially fewer environmental toxins in their breast milk, due to eating more clean, organic foods. Remember, toxins are stored in fatty tissue, such as in the breasts. These toxins can be passed to baby when breast-feeding.

The Teenage Vegetarian

Teens do very well on a vegetarian diet as long as they avoid eating junk foods too often. A vegetarian diet helps keep the hormones steady, reduces constipation and acne troubles, and can help keep maintain ideal weight.

Don't be alarmed if your vegetarian teen experiences a slower puberty onset. Give them until age 21 to reach growth maturity. Animal products contain natural and synthetic hormones and can speed a child into menstruation and puberty earlier than vegetarian kids. Many holistic practitioners believe this is really the more natural way to develop anyway. Who needs periods and wildly fluctuating hormones when trying to learn prealgebra?

Be sure your child is getting enough calories. Dense foods are better for growing bodies, and a growing child needs a little extra protein, calcium, iron, vitamin B_{12}, and vitamin D to grow properly. And provide a range of foods for your teenager to choose from. If you're a nonvegetarian parent, follow the guidelines in this book for cooking, shopping, and providing veggie snacks for your vegetarian child. Give the recipes in this book a try—maybe make a veggie meal once a week for the whole family—or invite your teen to make it. If you're already a vegetarian, continue to set a good example for your child in your eating habits and dining choices. Help your teen choose the right foods while at school, or buy him foods to pack for a lunch that will be the envy of all his schoolmates.

Steer Clear _____

Anyone can be a sickly, overweight, toxic vegetarian if they choose junk foods as their staples. *Vegetarianism* should be used as a term to describe health consciousness, not just an absence of meat.

And whether you're a vegetarian yourself or not, consider talking to your child about visiting a registered nutritional consultant or dietician who specializes in vegetarian nutrition for more information about this diet. Teens often are more willing to take advice from another authority who is not a parent. If your teen sees that the practitioner is there to help him or her be healthy and feel good, your teen will be more likely to heed the advice.

Sprouts of Info

Chinese women who develop later also seem to have less breast cancer than those who begin menstruation earlier. If you're concerned about your child's physical maturity, be patient. Realize that your children's peers may be developing unnaturally early because of a chemical- and fat-laden diet. Always seek your pediatrician's advice if you have any concerns.

Argh, Hormones!!!

Hormones are messengers that constantly send signals through the body to regulate sex drive, digestion, moods, sleep, reproductive cycles, growth, and maturity. Hormonal balance is also involved with fat distribution. The human body contains hormones, and that goes double, it seems, for teenagers!

The hormones given to factory-farmed animals, from cows to pigs to poultry, to make them larger or produce more meat or milk, are another reason for growing kids to avoid animal products. Consider the healthful choice your kids are making by going vegetarian. As a parent, you should be happy to know that you'll probably have a calmer household while your child goes through his or her adolescence without being manipulated artificially by external factors such as the hormones in meat and dairy products.

Consider this: the human female's pituitary gland creates hormones that circulate throughout her body to control the production of breast milk. The same holds true for other animals that produce milk, including cows. These hormones are found not only in their milk, but in muscle tissue as well. And that's not all: hormones are found not in only the muscles and fat of animal flesh, but in eggs, milk, cheese, yogurt, sour cream, ice cream—all milk-based products. When you or your teenager ingests these foods, you also ingest those extra hormones. Another great reason to go for organic, hormone-free dairy products if you eat dairy.

Maybe you've already witnessed for yourself that it takes only a small dose of hormones, such as steroids, estrogen replacement, birth control pills, or cortisone, to create a dramatic change in the body. And because hormones affect how you feel, you can imagine how even a small amount of residual hormones ingested through dairy products and eggs could make a dramatic difference in your teen's moods. An imbalance of hormones in your body can …

Steer Clear

Cow's milk contains hormones that are secreted by the cow's pituitary gland. These hormones are not necessarily destroyed through the pasteurization and homogenization process.

- Create accelerated maturity in young children or adolescents.

- Aggravate or increase sexual maturity in adolescence.

- Cause excessive hair growth.

- Cause abnormal or excessive facial whiskers or hair in both sexes.

- Add to feelings of depression.

- Cause feelings of aggression.

- Cause overly emotional feelings.

Especially with growing children who are already going through natural hormonal changes, why would anyone want to add to the discomfort by feeding them excess hormones?

The Least You Need to Know

- Vegetarians can get everything they need for a healthy pregnancy and subsequent breast-feeding. Just be sure to increase your caloric intake by eating denser foods.

- Nursing is the best way to feed your infant and is suggested for at least the first six months of the child's life. Beyond that, raising a child as a vegetarian can give him or her health benefits for years to come.

- A growing child needs a little extra protein, calcium, iron, vitamin B_{12}, and vitamin D to grow properly.

- Traces of hormones and antibiotics exist in dairy products and eggs, which can lead to hormonal imbalances and immune system difficulties of your own when you eat them.

Nonchicken Nuggets

Spicy, and mildly nutty, crunchy on the outside, and tender on the inside, these wheat-meat–based veggie nuggets are excellent finger food for dipping and snacking or as part of a main meal served alongside vegetables or a salad.

1½ cups unbleached white flour

4 TB. nutritional yeast flakes

1 tsp. freshly ground black pepper

1 tsp. garlic powder

1 tsp. dried parsley flakes

½ tsp. onion powder

4 TB. Dijon mustard

½ cup water

1 lb. pkg. seitan, cut in nugget sizes

2 cups vegetable oil

Serves: 4		
Prep time: 10 minutes		
Cook time: 10 minutes		
Serving size: 1 cup		

1. In a deep bowl, mix together flour, nutritional yeast flakes, pepper, garlic powder, parsley flakes, and onion powder.

2. In a separate bowl, whisk Dijon mustard with water. Add ⅓ cup flour mixture, and stir until batter thickens.

3. Mix seitan chunks into batter. When seitan is fully coated, mix into flour mixture and stir to coat all sides.

4. In a deep skillet, heat vegetable oil over high heat. When oil is hot, add battered and floured seitan cubes, and fry until crispy golden brown. Use a spicy mustard or sweet and sour sauce for dipping if desired.

Variation: Instead of seitan, you could use White Wave Chicken Style Meat of Wheat or firm tofu, frozen and then thawed. (Read more about seitan in Chapter 3.)

Sprouts of Info

Snack tip: leftover nuggets are great cold from the fridge, too.

No one will bawk at these
Nonchicken Nuggets!

Tempeh Sloppy Joes

Saucy, chunky, and sloppy! These meat-free sloppy joes—chopped tempeh in a warm tomato sauce spiced with onion, sweet red and green bell peppers, a hint of cloves, and a twang of apple cider vinegar—are delicious and fun to eat.

1 TB. olive oil	1 TB. apple cider vinegar
1 lb. tempeh, diced/crumbled	1 (6-oz.) can tomato paste
1 cup chopped onion	2 TB. Dijon mustard
½ cup chopped green bell pepper	½ tsp. ground cloves
½ cup chopped red bell pepper	4 sesame seed hamburger buns
1 TB. firmly packed brown sugar	

Serves: 4
Prep time: 10 minutes
Cook time: 30 minutes
Serving size: 1 sandwich

1. In a large skillet over medium heat, heat olive oil. Combine tempeh, onion, and green and red bell peppers. Cook until tempeh is heated through or browned and peppers and onions are tender.

2. Stir in brown sugar, vinegar, tomato paste, Dijon mustard, and cloves. Reduce heat to low, cover, and simmer for about 30 minutes. Serve on hamburger buns.

Sprouts of Info

Not a big fan of tempeh? You can substitute any variety of meatless ground beef substitutes or textured vegetable protein for the tempeh in this recipe.

Macaroni and Tomato Cheese

Your family will love this cheesy, creamy, tomato-y macaroni with two types of organic cheeses, garlic, and oregano and dices of crunchy red bell pepper.

Serves: 2
Prep time: 10 minutes
Cook time: 10 minutes
Serving size: 1 cup

1 TB. olive oil

1 shallot, finely chopped

2 garlic cloves, crushed

1 (15-oz.) can chopped tomatoes, drained

1 TB. dried oregano

½ cup chopped red bell pepper

8 oz. elbow macaroni

1 TB. butter

1½ cups grated cheddar or soy cheese

1 cup grated Parmesan or soy cheese

Freshly ground black pepper (optional)

1. Heat olive oil in a skillet over medium heat. Add shallot and garlic, and sauté for 1 minute. Add tomatoes, oregano, and bell pepper, and cook, stirring, for 10 minutes.

2. Meanwhile, in a saucepan, boil macaroni in water for 8 to 10 minutes. Drain well.

3. Return macaroni to hot saucepan, add butter, and mix until melted. Mix in cheddar and Parmesan cheeses. Add tomato sauce and mix. Season with black pepper, if desired. Serve immediately.

Veggie Soup for the Soul

Traditional macaroni and cheese leaves a lot to be desired, nutrition-wise. This tomato and cheese version adds more nutrition, thanks to the tomatoes, garlic, oregano, and red bell peppers. Among other nutrients, tomatoes are rich in lycopene, which supports good eyesight. Red bell peppers and oregano contain antioxidant properties. And garlic is a good protector for the immune system.

Veggie Bean Chili

Dark, rich, and creamy kidney beans; pungent black beans; sweet golden corn kernels; and tender hominy set this veggie chili apart in texture and variety of taste. Sweet, semi-crunchy green bell peppers, onions, garlic, and cumin burst with flavor while heat from the chili powder and chopped green chiles stimulate the taste buds.

3 TB. olive oil

1 large yellow onion, sliced

3 garlic cloves, minced

1 green bell pepper, ribs and seeds removed, and diced

1 to 2 TB. canned diced green chiles, drained

1 TB. chili powder

1 TB. ground cumin

2 tsp. dried oregano

⅛ tsp. cayenne

2 bay leaves

1 (15-oz.) can red kidney beans

1 (15-oz.) can black beans

1 (15-oz.) can *hominy*

1 (28-oz.) can tomatoes, chopped

½ cup sweet yellow corn, fresh or frozen and thawed

Freshly ground black pepper

½ cup water

1 lb. tempeh, crumbled, or TVP or other ground beef substitute

Serves: 4-6
Prep time: 25 minutes
Cook time: 30 minutes
Serving size: 1 bowl

1. In a large soup pot, over medium-high heat, heat olive oil. Add onion, garlic, bell pepper, green chiles, chili powder, cumin, oregano, cayenne, and bay leaves. Sauté until softened, about 10 minutes.

2. Add kidney beans, black beans, hominy, tomatoes, corn, black pepper, and water. Bring to a boil. Reduce heat to low, and simmer 30 minutes.

3. Add crumbled tempeh, and heat through. (If using TVP, you might need to add more water.) Taste, remove and discard bay leaves, and adjust seasonings.

Lettuce Explain

Hominy is a type of corn sometimes referred to as *posole*, especially in the southwest. Ground up hominy makes the traditional southern hot breakfast dish known as grits. It can be further processed and ground into a powder to make cornstarch.

Part 4

What's for Dinner?

It's the question probably every mother has heard: "What's for dinner?"
You've turned to the right place. In Part 4, I share more than 20 recipes
for really good dinner dishes, including dark leafy greens; grains; beans;
cruciferous, health-promoting veggies; and good old comfort food meals.
Within each chapter in Part 4, you learn the benefits of each of these types
of foods, which I hope makes you feel good about choosing, using, preparing, and eating them. And just wait until you taste them!

Chapter 14

Clean, Lean, Healthful Greens

In This Chapter

◆ The importance of iron in the diet

◆ The nutritional benefits of arugula, watercress, spinach, and other greens

◆ Great main-dish recipes using greens

By now you should know the importance of eating greens, but that doesn't mean eating just salads from now on. A variety of green leafy vegetables are available that, when mixed with grains and/or cheeses, make delicious main courses. Besides being delicious, low in calories, and almost free of net carbs, greens pack a ton of minerals that help you build a healthy, energetic, strong body.

You should also know that you need vitamins and minerals to stay alive. Vitamins nourish your body and keep you vital, but they can't do their job without minerals. Minerals are the activators that help the vitamins get to work where they need to be in your body. You need both. How you feed your body these necessary mineral elements can vary from person to person. Getting your nutrients is easy when you eat green foods, as you'll see in this chapter.

The Importance of Iron

The mineral iron is a blood element, meaning it's one of the main constituents of animal and human blood. Meat-eaters get iron from red meat, as animal flesh is rich in red blood cells. Vegetarians get iron by ingesting chlorophyll, or the "blood" of green plants. How does iron get into the plant in the first place? Here's how: iron is an element found in dirt, which is also full of all the other minerals and trace minerals you can think of—calcium, copper, nickel, magnesium, and so on. In dirt, iron is in an inorganic form—nails are made with this type of iron. When a plant's roots absorb iron and process it (along with other nutrients in the soil), it becomes a version of iron our bodies can biochemically process. Neat trick, huh?

Generally, products enriched with iron and most iron supplements are made from synthetics and other nonliving materials. It's difficult to get rid of this type of iron once it's in the body, and extra iron can build up in the liver and tissues and cause irreversible damage. Iron also promotes the growth of infectious bacteria, so don't use supplements indiscriminately! Iron supplements can make you constipated, too. Overall, synthetic iron supplements may not be the best way to get iron.

Your body is better able to utilize natural forms of iron from food and herbs. This might be why plant sources of iron aren't as easily absorbed as iron from meat; perhaps it's a natural protective mechanism to keep us from ingesting too much iron. Plant sources of iron are much safer, so vegetarians are generally protected from getting an iron overload in their diets.

> **Sprouts of Info**
>
> Vitamin C helps the body absorb iron, so eating foods rich in vitamin C along with your iron-rich meals helps increase your iron absorption. So go ahead and add a slice of tomato to your veggie sandwich!

Some symptoms of an iron deficiency include the following:

- Anemia
- Breathing difficulty
- Bruising easily
- Constipation
- Depression
- Dizziness
- Fatigue

- Headaches

- Heart palpitations

- Heartburn

- Slow wound healing

Hopefully, you don't have any of these symptoms, but if you do and are diagnosed with iron deficiency, see your natural health consultant and consider taking in some extra plant sources of iron, along with vitamin C to help you utilize it more effectively. (See the "Common Elements Lacking in Most American Diets" table in Chapter 1 to find some good vegetarian sources and herbal supplements for this mineral.)

Veggie Soup for the Soul

An iron deficiency isn't necessarily a concern with folks who eat a variety of vegetarian foods, but some people—especially pregnant women, those who tend toward anemia, or those with a tendency toward a low blood count—should be aware of this important mineral and how eating greens supplies it in the diet.

Wonderful Watercress

At the end of this chapter, I've included some of my favorite dark leafy greens recipes. One of these greens is watercress, an aquatic plant rich in vitamins A and C, which makes it an excellent antioxidant and cancer fighter. Watercress is in the cabbage family, along with cabbage, mustard greens, kale, collard greens, and turnip greens. Like other dark greens, watercress contains iron and calcium.

Fatigue often accompanies low blood iron levels, so building the blood helps boost energy. In addition, the calcium in watercress and other leafy greens is necessary for strong structural, nervous, and circulatory systems.

Awesome Arugula

Arugula (pronounced *uh-roo-guh-luh*) is also known as rocket, sea rocket, or dame's rocket in Italy and other European countries. (So if you're in Italy and see rocket salad on the menu, go for it!) Arugula is from the mustard family and, just like mustard, contains a spicy flavor—the baby arugula and the buds can taste almost hot! This is no lame green, and you might be surprised how much arugula can spice up a pizza and tantalize your taste buds!

Arugula is also rich in iron and calcium, B_6, and copper, and it's high in fiber, too. You can eat it raw (as in the following Arugula "Rocket" Pizza recipe), in salads, or cooked. In fact, you can use arugula in place of watercress for the Mouthwatering Watercress Pie recipe at the end of this chapter.

Super Spinach

Spinach is another great-tasting green you can eat raw or cooked. Spinach is one of the best dietary sources of lutein, a nutrient that promotes good eyesight and helps prevent macular degeneration and cataracts. Spinach also is rich in folic acid, an important B vitamin that's also critical in preventing birth defects, especially of the brain and spinal cord. Folic acid also may help prevent cervical dysplasia.

Sprouts of Info

If you're not crazy about cooked spinach, try squeezing some fresh lemon juice over it to counteract its strong flavor (see more on acquiring tastes in Chapter 2). To change up the flavor a bit, you can also add a sprinkle of capsicum and toss cooked spinach with some toasted pine nuts for a great side dish.

The Least You Need to Know

◆ Dark leafy greens are a great source of fiber, iron, calcium, and chlorophyll, which all contribute to good health.

◆ Watercress is an aquatic plant rich in antioxidant properties, which are known for helping prevent cancer.

◆ Arugula, with its unique spicy flavor, is a delicious way to get your greens.

◆ Spinach is one of the richest sources of lutein, a phytochemical that protects eyesight.

Arugula "Rocket" Pizza

This delicious raw topping pizza allows the full flavor of spicy, raw arugula leaves, rich, quality Parmesan shavings, spicy olive oil, ripe Roma tomato slices, and fresh basil to shine on a crispy, homemade pizza crust.

1 (.25-oz.) pkg. active dry yeast

¼ tsp. sugar

¾ cup 110°F water

1¾ cups all-purpose flour

½ tsp. salt

Organic Roma tomatoes, thinly sliced

Fresh chopped basil leaves

Extra-virgin olive oil

Freshly ground black pepper

Fresh, organic arugula, washed and dried (baby leaves optional)

Shaved slices Parmesan cheese

Serves: 4
Prep time: 15 minutes
Cook time: 8 to 12 minutes
Serving size: 2 slices

1. Preheat the oven to 500°F. Lightly grease a 12-inch pizza pan.

2. In a small bowl, mix yeast and sugar in water. Allow it to sit for about 8 minutes. (Yeast feeds on sugar, and the time it sits begins to activate yeast.)

3. In a separate bowl, combine flour and salt. Add yeast mixture flour and mix well. Roll dough on a floured surface, and knead for about 2 minutes. Form dough into smooth ball, put back in the bowl, cover, and let it sit in a warm place for 15 minutes.

4. Press dough into a 12-inch circle or rectangle, depending on the shape of your pan. Stretch dough to the edges of the pan. Bake for 8 to 12 minutes or until edges are golden brown.

5. Remove dough from the oven and let cool for a couple minutes.

6. Arrange tomato slices on crust. Sprinkle basil on top. Drizzle olive oil over crust and tomatoes. Grind some black pepper over pizza. Tear arugula into bite-size pieces (or use whole baby leaves) and arrange on top. Top off with Parmesan cheese shavings, and serve fresh!

Sprouts of Info

Baking flour changes the amino acid lysine (found in bread-type foods like pizza crust) into pronyl-lysine, which activates enzymes that *inactivate* free radicals! It also helps sweeten and darken bread's crust.

Mouthwatering Watercress Pie

This dense creamy pie made with tart watercress, sharp cheddar cheese, fresh garlic, and crunchy water chestnuts is baked in a whole-wheat crust.

Serves: 4
Prep time: 20 minutes
Cook time: 20 minutes
Serving size: 4

¾ **cup whole-wheat flour**

¼ **tsp. salt**

½ **cup butter or soy margarine, at room temperature**

3 **TB. cold water**

2 **bunches fresh watercress, washed in cold water and drained**

2 **garlic cloves, crushed**

¼ **cup diced red onion**

4 **TB. sharp cheddar cheese, grated**

4 **TB. plain yogurt**

1 **(6-oz.) can sliced water chestnuts, drained**

½ **tsp. paprika**

1. Preheat the oven to 350°F.

2. Sift flour into a large bowl, and add salt. Mix ⅓ cup butter into flour until mixture resembles breadcrumbs. Stir in cold water to make dough.

3. Roll out dough onto a floured surface and lay into 4 individual tart pie pans or a 9-inch pie pan. Poke some holes in crust with a fork.

4. Cut and discard stems from watercress.

5. Heat remaining butter in a frying pan over medium heat. Add garlic and onion, and sauté for about 1 minute. Add watercress and cook another 1 or 2 minutes or until watercress is wilted.

6. Remove the pan from heat and stir in cheese, yogurt, water chestnuts, and paprika. Spoon mixture into the uncooked pie dough and bake for 20 minutes or until filling is firm.

7. Turn out the individual tarts onto a plate, or if you made the large version, slice and serve. This pie is excellent served with a fresh green salad and a glass of red wine.

Sprouts of Info

Water chestnuts are vegetables, not nuts. They are the tubular root of an aquatic growing plant, mostly produced in Asia. They have no fat and are high in fiber and potassium, but also are high in carbohydrates.

Spinach and Cheese Pie

Cheesy, tart, lemony-flavored spinach and feta fill this pie with crunchy water chestnuts, seasoned with fresh garlic, and a hint of spicy cayenne pepper cooked in a crisp, golden brown rice crust.

2½ **cups cooked brown rice**

2 TB. butter or soy margarine, melted

Egg replacer equal to 1 egg, premixed

3 TB. all-purpose flour

1 TB. fresh minced parsley

Freshly ground black pepper

2 bunches fresh organic spinach

1 TB. olive oil

1 cup diced red onion

2 garlic cloves, minced

¼ **cup fresh minced parsley**

1 tsp. fresh minced dill

1 tsp. dried oregano

1 cup crumbled feta cheese

¾ **cup soy milk**

Dash cayenne

Lemon slices

Serves: 4+		
Prep time: 15 to 20 minutes		
Cook time: 30 to 40 minutes		
Serving size: 1 slice		

1. Preheat the oven to 350°F. Butter a 9-inch pie pan.

2. In a medium bowl, combine cooked rice with melted butter, egg replacer mix, 1 tablespoon flour, parsley, and pepper. Mix well with a fork. Gently pat mixture into the prepared pie pan, pressing against the edges and the bottom of the pan. Bake for 30 to 40 minutes or until evenly browned.

3. While crust bakes, chop stems off fresh spinach and rinse spinach with cold water. Put wet leaves in a saucepan with a tight-fitting lid, heat on medium-high heat, and steam leaves for 2 or 3 minutes or until leaves are wilted. Drain leaves in a colander, and press out all liquid with the back of a wooden spoon. Chop spinach coarsely and set aside.

4. In a large nonstick skillet, over medium-high heat, heat olive oil. Add onion and garlic, and sauté until softened.

5. In a medium bowl, combine spinach, onion, garlic, parsley, dill, oregano, feta, remaining 2 tablespoons flour, soy milk, pepper, and cayenne. Mix well, pour into prepared rice crust, and pat down evenly. Bake until filling is browned and set—about 30 minutes.

6. Serve with lemon wedges. Squeezing a bit of fresh lemon juice over the spinach gives it a nice, zesty, refreshing taste.

Steer Clear

Be sure you press out all the water you can from freshly steamed or thawed spinach before adding it to the rest of your ingredients, or you'll have runny pie. If the ingredients still seem too runny before putting them into the crust, mix in a few teaspoons of arrowroot powder to give the mix a more sticky consistency.

Spinach and Feta Pie will quickly become a family favorite.

Spinach and Artichoke Bake

Rich, cheesy pungent spinach, tangy artichoke hearts, and savory feta cheese casserole blend perfectly with chewy, nutty-tasting whole wheat kernels and lend interesting texture and flavor.

2 bunches spinach, washed, well drained, and chopped	2 TB. slivered fresh basil or 2 tsp. dried
2 TB. butter	1 tsp. dried oregano
2 shallots, diced	Freshly ground black pepper
2 garlic cloves, minced	1½ cups cooked wheat kernels
1 cup artichoke hearts, drained and chopped	1 cup crumbled feta cheese
1 tsp. grated *lemon zest*	¼ cup grated Parmesan cheese
4 TB. fresh lemon juice	

> *Serves: 4*
>
> **Prep time:** 15 minutes
> **Cook time:** 30 minutes
> **Serving size:** about 1¼ cups

1. Preheat the oven to 350°F. Grease a 2-quart casserole dish.

2. Rinse chopped spinach with cold water. Put wet leaves in a saucepan with tight-fitting lid, heat on medium-high heat, and steam leaves for about 2 or 3 minutes or until leaves are wilted. Drain spinach in a colander, and press out all liquid with the back of a wooden spoon.

3. In a large skillet, melt butter over medium-high heat. Add shallots and garlic, and sauté until softened. Stir in spinach, chopped artichoke hearts, lemon zest, lemon juice, basil, oregano, and black pepper, and mix well. Stir in cooked wheat kernels and feta cheese.

4. Pour mixture into the prepared casserole dish. Top with Parmesan cheese, and bake for 30 minutes or until browned and heated through.

Lettuce Explain

Lemon zest is the concentrated, essential oils from the lemon peel. use a zester to scrape the top of the skin of a washed lemon.

Chapter 15

The Mighty Bean

In This Chapter

- Why beans are good for you
- Bean? Legume? What's the difference?
- Gas-prevention tips
- Hearty, bean-y recipes

You remember that rhyme, don't you? *Beans, beans, good for your heart, the more you eat, the more you …* I don't remember the rest of it. But seriously, could there be any truth to that silly little rhyme about beans? Are they good for your heart?

Let me spill the beans on the general benefits of legumes:

- They provide a good source of fiber.
- They are satisfying and can fill you up.
- They are versatile and can be mashed to make great meat substitutes.
- They are low in fat.
- They taste good.
- They go with just about anything.

- They provide a low-fat dietary source of protein.

- Added to rice, they provide a complete protein.

- In general, they are richer in calcium than meat.

You know that lowering your intake of dietary fat and increasing dietary fiber is good, not only for your intestinal tract, but for heart health, too. And you probably know that you do need protein to maintain and rebuild muscle tissue, and the heart is a muscle. Beans and legumes provide protein. Given all that, I'd say that beans and legumes really are good for the heart! The more you eat them, the more you … have a healthy heart!

Well-Rounded Proteins

In Chapter 1, I talked about protein and told you how a well-rounded, varied diet contains all the protein your body needs. Although most beans (with the exception of soybeans) provide an incomplete protein, you get what you need as long as you eat some type of vegetable or other type of grain on the same day to complete the protein. Keep in mind that it's hard not to get enough protein with a varied diet! As long as you're not eating the same food over and over and over, the plant kingdom takes care of all your protein needs.

Sprouts of Info

To prepare dried beans: rinse dried beans thoroughly, and remove any tiny pebbles and broken beans. Put them in a container (a slow cooker works great) and add water to cover. Soak at least 6 to 8 hours to bring them to life. Now they're ready to cook up in chili, rice and beans, or other dishes.

Beans can work as a replacement for meat in many meals and are great garnished with vegetables or thrown in stews, chili, and casseroles.

Beans or Legumes?

The words *legumes* and *beans* are used interchangeably. Legumes, beans, and peas are technically any of a large number of plants belonging to the *Leguminosae* family. The fruit is a seedpod.

Legumes live symbiotically with bacteria on their roots. The bacteria are able to convert nitrogen into compounds that feed the plant. Farmers often use legume plants to improve the soil's nitrogen content. Some popular legumes include peas, lima beans, soybeans, lentils, kidneys, garbanzos, navy beans, pinto beans, and black beans.

The legume category also includes peanuts, but because most of us categorize peanuts as nuts, that's where we're going to leave them. (It's like a tomato technically being a fruit instead of a vegetable. Maybe so, but most of us think of and use it like a vegetable!)

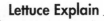

Lettuce Explain

The terms *legume* or *bean* describe a plant that has edible pods and seeds that are generally eaten cooked.

Tootin' Your Own Horn

The outside of the bean contains a sugar substance called *hemicellulose*, which is chiefly responsible for causing the gas so commonly associated with beans. To get rid of this coating on dried beans, spill off the water after you soak them and rinse them well again with fresh water before cooking them. If this doesn't work, try some of the following tricks.

Swallowing a food enzyme or two before consuming beans helps many people digest them better. An enzyme supplement may contain varying mixtures of enzymes, including amylase, glucoamylase, and invertase. These help break down the carbohydrates in beans, which helps break down the cellulose in the legume's cell wall. Ask your herbalist, your natural health-care provider, or the specialist at the store where you purchase supplements for help choosing the best food enzyme for you.

Traditional Hawaiian cooks add a slice of raw ginger to the pot of beans to help eliminate gas.

Add a drop or two of Beano to the pot of beans before you eat them. Beano is a commercial product found in most health food stores and supermarkets that eliminates the gas-producing effects of beans.

Try chopping a large carrot into a few pieces and add it to the beans while they cook and then throw away the carrot before eating the beans. The carrot sucks up the gaseous properties of the beans.

Steer Clear

Do not use the Beano product if you have a penicillin allergy.

Some people simply don't experience any gassy effects from beans. Many find that the problem goes away, or at least lessens, as they add more whole foods to their diets and start to eat beans more often.

The Least You Need to Know

- Beans are a fibrous, protein-rich food that can serve as the main course of a vegetarian meal.

- Beans and rice make a complete protein.

- Soaking and rinsing dried beans before cooking can help break down the outer coating, which is largely responsible for causing gas.

- Beans are naturally low in fat.

Bean and Mango Enchilada Bake

Spicy firm black beans, sweet chunks of mango, golden corn, tender-crisp sweet yellow onion, creamy, melted goat and ricotta cheeses—all baked in layers of enchilada sauce–soaked corn tortillas.

2 TB. olive oil

1 large yellow onion, diced

1 garlic clove, minced

½ tsp. ground cumin

1 tsp. dried basil

1 (28-oz.) can enchilada sauce

¼ cup tomato paste

Freshly ground black pepper

1½ cups black beans, cooked or canned and drained

1 mango, peeled and diced

½ cup chopped whole scallions

3 TB. minced fresh cilantro

½ cup corn kernels

1 cup goat cheese, crumbled

1½ cups ricotta cheese

1 TB. fresh lime juice

2 tsp. chili powder

12 corn tortillas

1 avocado, sliced

Corn chips

Serves: 8		
Prep time: 20 minutes		
Cook time: 25 to 30 minutes		
Serving size: 2 enchiladas		

1. Preheat the oven to 375°F.

2. In a large nonstick skillet, heat olive oil over medium-high heat. Add onion, garlic, cumin, and basil, and sauté until softened, about 5 minutes.

3. Add enchilada sauce, tomato paste, and black pepper. Bring to a boil, reduce heat to low, and simmer for 15 minutes, stirring occasionally.

4. In a large bowl, mix together cooked beans, mango, scallions, 2 tablespoons cilantro, corn, goat cheese, ricotta cheese, lime juice, and chili powder. Season with black pepper.

5. Pour 1 cup enchilada sauce into a 9×13-inch baking dish. Place 6 tortillas on top of sauce in dish. Spoon in enchilada filling, and cover with remaining tortillas. Pour rest of sauce over top.

6. Bake for 25 minutes or until hot and bubbly. Garnish with slices of avocado and remaining 1 tablespoon cilantro. Serve with corn chips.

Add a simple salad to the Bean and Mango Enchilada Bake, and dinner's ready!

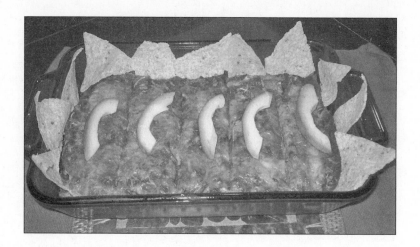

Lentil Loaf

This crumbly, nutty, and hearty lentil loaf peppered with fresh parsley, sharp cheddar, and chopped button mushrooms makes an excellent meatloaf substitute. Serve with mashed potatoes and steamed greens for an American-style family meal.

1 TB. butter, softened

2 TB. dried breadcrumbs

1 cup lentils

1 (15-oz.) can vegetable broth

1 bay leaf

2 cups grated sharp cheddar cheese

½ cup yellow onion, chopped

4½ oz. button mushrooms, finely chopped

1 carrot, shredded

1½ cups fresh whole-wheat breadcrumbs

2 TB. chopped fresh parsley

2 TB. tamari

Freshly ground black pepper

1 TB. fresh squeezed lemon juice

Egg replacer equal to 2 eggs, premixed

Sprigs fresh Italian parsley

Serves: 6
Prep time: 30 minutes
Cook time: 1 hour
Serving size: 1 slice

1. Preheat the oven to 375°F. Line the bottom of a loaf pan with baking parchment. Grease the pan with butter, and sprinkle with dried breadcrumbs.

2. In a saucepan over high heat, bring lentils, broth, and bay leaf to a boil. Cover and simmer for 15 to 20 minutes or until liquid is absorbed and lentils have softened. Discard bay leaf.

3. Stir cheese, onion, mushrooms, carrot, breadcrumbs, and parsley into lentils, and season with tamari and pepper. Add lemon juice and egg replacer to bind together all ingredients. Add more egg replacer (premixed), if needed.

4. Pour mixture into the prepared loaf pan, and smooth over the top with a rubber spatula. Bake uncovered for 1 hour or until golden.

5. Loosen loaf with a spatula and turn out onto a warmed serving plate and slice into thick serving slices. Garnish with parsley. Serve with mashed potatoes and steamed collard greens or any of your favorite veggies.

Sprouts of Info

This recipe is also excellent with veggie gravy on top. See the recipe for veggie gravy with the Tofu Pot Pie in Chapter 17.

Kidney Bean–Garlic Butter Patties

Here, soft kidney beans, leeks, and celery paté surround a garlic butter breadcrumb coating and are fried to a golden brown.

Serves: 2 to 4
Prep time: 25 minutes
Cook time: 7 to 10 minutes
Serving size: 1 or 2 patties

8 TB. butter

3 garlic cloves, crushed

2 TB. chopped fresh parsley

1¼ cups can red kidney beans, drained

1¼ cups breadcrumbs

2 TB. butter

1 leek, white part only, chopped

1 celery stalk, chopped

Salt and freshly ground black pepper

Egg replacer equal to 1 egg, premixed

Vegetable oil

1. In a medium bowl, combine butter, garlic, and 1 tablespoon parsley. Place garlic butter mix on a sheet of wax paper, and form it into something that resembles a stick of butter. Chill in refrigerator.

2. Mash beans in a mixing bowl, and stir in ¾ cup breadcrumbs.

3. Melt butter in a frying pan over medium-high heat. Add leek and celery, and sauté for 3 or 4 minutes.

4. Add bean mixture to the pan together with remaining 1 tablespoon parsley, season with salt and pepper, and mix well. Remove from heat and leave to cool slightly.

5. Shape bean mixture into 4 equal-size patties.

6. Slice garlic butter in quarters, and place a slice in the center of each bean patty. Mould bean mixture around garlic butter to encase it completely. Dip each bean patty into egg-replacer mix to coat, and then roll in remaining breadcrumbs.

7. Heat a little vegetable oil in a frying pan, add the bean patties, and fry for 7 to 10 minutes or until golden, turning once.

Black Bean, Pumpkin, and Jalapeño Ravioli

Puréed black beans, cinnamon spiced pumpkin, and hot jalapeños make for a spicy hot, creamy, and filling ravioli.

2 TB. fresh minced parsley

1 (6-oz.) can diced jalapeños, drained

1 (15-oz.) can cooked black beans, drained

6 TB. grated Parmesan cheese, plus more for garnish

½ tsp. ground allspice

Pinch ground cardamom

1 (15-oz.) can pumpkin purée

2 lb. pasta sheets

1 (25-oz.) jar marinara sauce (your favorite)

Serves: 2 to 4
Prep time: 25 minutes
Cook time: 6 to 8 minutes
Serving size: 3 to 6 raviolis

1. In a food processor or in a blender, purée parsley, jalapeños, ½ black beans, 6 tablespoons Parmesan cheese, allspice, and cardamom. Add pumpkin purée, and mix thoroughly. Fold in rest of black beans.

2. Lay 1 pasta sheet on a chopping board. (Keep the rest from drying by spraying with water occasionally or laying a wet cloth on top.) Spoon about 1 tablespoon filling about 1 inch apart along the bottom edge of pasta sheet. Fold pasta sheet over filling, and cut out each ravioli with a ravioli cutter (or any cookie cutter or a juice can). Be sure the edges are sealed well. Set aside cut ravioli and cover with damp cloth. Repeat until all filling is used.

3. In a small saucepan, warm marinara sauce over medium-low heat.

4. In large saucepan, bring 4 quarts water to a rolling boil. Add ravioli and boil until *al dente*, about 6 to 8 minutes.

5. Transfer ravioli to a warm serving plate, add marinara sauce over top, and serve. Garnish with additional grated Parmesan cheese and a sliced jalepeño, if desired.

Your friends and family will want the recipe for these Black Bean and Jalapeño Raviolis.

Chapter 16

Cancer-Preventing Cruciferous Vegetables

In This Chapter

- Lower your cancer risks
- Lower your toxin exposure
- The pros of vegetables
- Recipes with crunchy, cruciferous vegetables

As a full-time vegetarian, you should be happy to know that, compared to meat-eaters, your risk for developing chronic diseases like high blood pressure, heart disease, kidney failure, osteoporosis, and cancer is decreased by a whopping 40 percent! This chapter explains why and how vegetarians are generally at lower risk for cancer than meat-eaters, and what other factors besides eating your vegetables are important in achieving and maintaining health. And of course, I include a few recipes that can help make disease prevention a yummy experience!

Lowering Cancer Risks

Being vegetarian and living the typical vegetarian lifestyle does prove to lower the risk of developing cancer. Let's talk a little bit about why.

Free radicals are one reason. In Chapter 5, I talked about free radicals—unstable atoms or groups of atoms with an unpaired electron found naturally in everyone's body. Free radicals are byproducts of digestion and other normal body processes, and contribute to aging, inflammation, and most disease processes.

Veggie Soup for the Soul

Free radicals are produced when we eat, so it's thought that eating less could also mean a longer life. Also, when we eat natural foods—those more in their whole, natural state—the body and mind aren't as tempted to overeat. (When's the last time you gorged on apples?) And when the body is well nourished with natural foods, you won't get that full-but-unsatisfied feeling that triggers you to eat more, even when you've had a sufficient amount of calories.

You can think of free radicals as little Tasmanian devils on a rampage inside your body. They can and do destroy or damage anything they come into contact with, including other cells and even your genes. Excess free radicals are created by many lifestyle and dietary choices, and also things you can't control, like exposure to toxins in the air. When you increase your exposure to things that cause free radicals, the damage they can do increases and can cause health problems, including cancer.

Lettuce Explain

Antioxidants are free radical scavengers that fight off and destroy questionable or unstable cells that can cause cancer. Antioxidants are found naturally in fruits and vegetables, grains, and herbs, and can be taken in supplement form.

Antioxidants are compounds referred to as "free radical scavengers." Abundant in fresh fruits and vegetables, antioxidants tame free radicals. The main antioxidants that help fight off free radicals and the damage they do include the following:

- Beta carotene
- Chromium
- Magnesium
- Selenium
- Vitamin A

- Vitamin C
- Vitamin D
- Vitamin E
- Vitamin K
- Zinc

Let's take a look at the high-risk factors associated with cancer:

- Smoking
- Low-fiber diet
- Chronic constipation
- High-fat diet
- Obesity
- Alcohol abuse
- Low-antioxidant diet
- Excessive exposure to chemicals

Smoking is the only factor in this list that isn't directly related to food, but one thing they all have in common is that they cause or allow lots of free radicals to be produced in the body. Cancer risks related to smoking are fairly obvious because each cigarette contains about 2,000 chemicals that go directly into your system with every puff. But how and why do these other factors increase the risks? Read on.

More Fiber, Less Fat

A diet low in fiber can lead to constipation, and in Chapter 5, I discuss the problems associated with a slow colon transit time. Meat, in particular, goes through the digestive system more slowly than vegetarian foods, and the meat and other processed food products left in the colon for long periods have time to release toxins and free radicals, which are believed to increase your cancer risk.

Sprouts of Info

Your daily intake of dietary fat should not exceed 20 percent of your total calories for the day. In addition, getting at least 25 grams of dietary fiber in your diet daily can decrease your risk of colon and other cancers.

Fat intake and obesity are often related and are both factors in causing cancer and other illnesses. Excess dietary fat not burned as energy soon turns into stored fat in your tissues and arterial walls. Your body stores a lot of toxins in your fat cells, including pesticide residues; pollutants you eat, breathe, and drink; and food colorings, preservatives, and many other chemicals used in foods and medicines.

Caution: Toxins

Exposure to toxic or otherwise unnatural chemicals increases your risk of cancer. These chemicals can come from foods and environmental chemicals found in the air you breathe. Chemicals such as pesticides, car exhaust, industrial air pollution of all sorts, house-cleaning products, cosmetics, radiation, industrial materials, and gases from paints and dry-cleaning, carpet, and construction materials can all increase your chances of getting cancer. They can also overburden your liver, which can then lead to other sensitivities and illnesses.

> **Sprouts of Info**
>
> By choosing organic foods, you can limit your chemical intake more effectively than a nonvegetarian.

Unfortunately, it's almost impossible to avoid being exposed to chemicals on a daily basis, so it's a good idea to limit the chemicals you do have control over by making wise choices in the foods you eat. Choose naturally grown foods organically produced. (See more about choosing foods wisely in Chapter 3.)

Watch What You Drink

Although moderate alcohol consumption has been shown to be beneficial, heavy consumption has the opposite effect. Heavy consumption of alcohol depletes the body of many vitamins and minerals, leading to malnutrition, and it leaves the body more susceptible to illnesses and degenerative conditions of the liver, pancreas, kidneys, and immune system.

Vegetarians vs. Meat-Eaters

Now that you understand which choices increase your risks for cancer and other diseases, let's see why the vegetarian who eats for health could be at lower risk. (If you happen to be a vegetarian who lives on junk food, potato chips, chocolate, and soda pop, however, then all bets are off.) Generally, vegetarians …

◆ *Eat a diet high in fiber.* Fruit, vegetables, grains, and legumes contain more fiber than meat and other animal products.

◆ *Are not constipated* because their diet contains plenty of fiber, which keeps the colon moving toxins on through and helps exercise and strengthen the bowels.

◆ *Have a fairly low-fat diet* due to the low fat content of most vegetarian foods.

◆ *Are leaner than meat-eaters* because vegetarians eat plenty of fiber and keep high-fat animal products to a minimum. Both of these factors are key to maintaining a healthy weight.

◆ *Are not smokers or heavy drinkers.* Because many vegetarians are fairly health conscious, vegetarians who smoke cigarettes and drink heavily are not found in abundance.

◆ *Get plenty of antioxidants* that fight free radical damage from a diet loaded with fresh fruits and vegetables, whole grains, raw nuts, seeds, beans, and legumes.

◆ *Choose their fruits and vegetables wisely* because these foods are the main course in most vegetarian meals.

◆ *Stay hydrated.* Many vegetarians also drink filtered water to filter out exposure to chemicals in tap water. Also, fresh fruit and veggies are high-water-content foods. Keeping the body hydrated fends off constipation, wrinkles, kidney stress, and a number of other health problems.

Veggie Soup for the Soul

Many vegetarians choose organic foods over commercially grown crops to limit chemical exposure and to make a positive contribution toward the health of the environment.

◆ *Exercise,* which prevents constipation by exercising the bowel, improves circulation for cardiopulmonary health, and brings out endorphins for a better attitude. And we all know how we think affects our immunity and how we feel!

All these factors are in direct opposition to the high risk factors associated with cancer. As a result, vegetarians are among those least likely to get cancer.

Benefits of Cruciferous Veggies

Researchers have found several compounds in *cruciferous vegetables* that are considered cancer preventatives and even inhibitors. A study announced at the American Association of Cancer Research in 2006 showed that a compound in the cruciferous veggie broccoli slowed cancerous prostate tumor growth in mice. Another study reported that antioxidants released when chewing cruciferous veggies reduced the number and size of colon polyps in mice.

Lettuce Explain

Cruciferous vegetables are from a huge family called *Cruciferae* or *Brassicaceae*. The family is also referred to as the mustard or cabbage family. Cruciferous vegetables include broccoli, Brussels sprouts, cauliflower, cabbage, kale, rutabaga, seakale, turnips, radishes, kohlrabi, rapeseed (canola), mustard, horseradish, wasabi, and watercress.

So not only do vegetables create fiber to help keep the colon free from excess free radicals and provide nutrients to feed your body, but scientists are finding that many of the naturally occurring compounds in vegetables actually fight, prevent, and maybe even cure cancer!

The following recipes are by no means the only cruciferous-centered meals in this book, but I've chosen a few of the more mildly flavored cruciferous veggies to show you how tasty they can be. Feel free to venture to include them in your diet more often and maybe even experiment with other cruciferous vegetables.

The Least You Need to Know

◆ Vegetarians generally have a lower risk for cancer because their diet and lifestyle let them avoid many high risk factors.

◆ Vegetarians lower their toxic chemical intake by avoiding meat and choosing more organic, whole foods.

◆ Cruciferous vegetables contain compounds proven to help prevent cancer and many other life-threatening diseases.

Veggie Spring Rolls

Fried or baked, the crunchy veggie spring rolls burst with hot, sweet, and spicy seasonings and feature crunchy, shredded green and red cabbage, carrots, tender bamboo shoots, soft green peas, diced onion, ginger, garlic, and fresh cilantro.

½ cup shredded green cabbage

½ cup shredded red cabbage

¼ cup finely diced onion

2 cups grated carrots

5 scallions, including tops, finely sliced

½ cup green peas

8 garlic cloves, minced (about 2½ TB.)

2 cups chopped fresh cilantro, including stems

1 cup thinly sliced bamboo shoots

4 TB. tamari

5 TB. maple syrup

1½ tsp. freshly ground black pepper

12 (3½-in.) square wonton or egg roll wrappers

Spicy mustard or wasabi

Serves: 6 to 12		
Prep time: 20 minutes		
Cook time: 15 minutes		
Serving size: 1 or 2 rolls		

1. Preheat the oven to 375°F. Spray a cookie sheet with olive oil.

2. Combine green cabbage, red cabbage, onion, carrot, scallions, peas, garlic, cilantro, and bamboo shoots in a large mixing bowl.

3. In a separate bowl, whisk together tamari, maple syrup, and pepper, and add to vegetable mix. Mix well.

4. Spray a large skillet with olive oil, add vegetable mixture, and sauté over medium-high heat until vegetables are tender, about 4 minutes. Set aside to cool.

5. Remove spring roll wrappers from the package and cover with a damp cloth. Place 1 wrapper on a flat surface with a pointed edge toward you. Place about ⅓ cup filling in the center of wrapper, fold the point up and over filling, tuck underneath, roll the sides in toward the middle, and roll tightly to the opposite point. Moisten edges with water to seal. Place rolls on the prepared cookie sheet. Bake on one side for 15 minutes, turn, and bake on the other side for another 15 minutes until golden brown and crunchy.

6. Serve with spicy mustard or wasabi.

Sprouts of Info

Freeze excess spring rolls in a freezer bag. Spring rolls can be eaten as a snack, as a meal if served with a salad, or as a nice addition to any stir-fry recipe (see Chapter 22).

Veggie Spring Rolls are a satisfying way to eat cancer-preventing cabbage.

Broccoli and Wheat Kernel Casserole

This cheese-free—but cheesy (thanks to the nutritional yeast flakes)—nutty-flavored casserole features fresh tender-crisp broccoli florets, spiked with garlic and onion flavors over puffy, chewy wheat kernels and is baked to bubbly perfection.

1 bunch fresh broccoli, cut into florets, or 1 (10-oz.) pkg. frozen florets

2 cups wheat kernels, cooked

½ cup (1 stick) butter

½ cup unbleached all-purpose flour

3½ cups boiling water

1 TB. tamari

2½ tsp. garlic powder

2½ tsp. onion powder

Pinch turmeric

1 cup nutritional yeast flakes

Freshly ground black pepper

Pinch paprika

Serves: 4 to 6
Prep time: 20 to 25 minutes
Cook time: 15 to 20 minutes
Serving size: 1 cup

1. Preheat the oven to 350°F.

2. Place steamer (with cover) over a pot filled with 1½ to 2 cups water. Put on high heat to boil. When water is boiling, add broccoli florets, cover, and steam for 3 to 6 minutes until bright green and crisp-tender.

3. Spread cooked wheat kernels over the bottom of a 9×13 baking dish. Sprinkle broccoli over top, and set aside.

4. Melt butter in a medium skillet over low heat. When butter is melted, increase heat to medium and whisk in flour until mixture is smooth and bubbly. Whisk in boiling water, tamari, garlic powder, onion powder, and turmeric, and cook until thick and bubbling. Whisk in nutritional yeast flakes and season with pepper. Pour sauce over broccoli and kernels, sprinkle with paprika, and bake for 15 to 20 minutes.

5. Remove from the oven and place under the broiler on high for a few minutes until top is browned and crusty.

Steer Clear

When steaming veggies, be careful to add just enough water to efficiently steam them. Too much water takes too long to boil and lengthens the time it takes to begin steaming; too little water evaporates before the steaming is finished. Note that root veggies take much longer to steam, while softer veggies take the shortest length of time.

Cauliflower Cheese Pie

Seasoned cauliflower florets and sharp cheddar cheese fill this pie baked in a crisp shredded potato crust, sprinkled with paprika, and baked until firm and golden on top.

Serves: 4-6
Prep time: 35 minutes
Cook time: 35 to 40 minutes
Serving size: 1 cup

2 cups shredded russet potatoes, rinsed and drained

¼ cup chopped onion

Egg replacer equal to 2 eggs, premixed, plus egg replacer equal to 2 eggs, premixed

1 tsp. salt

1 TB. all-purpose flour

1½ TB. olive oil

1 TB. vegetable oil

1 medium onion, chopped

2 cloves garlic, minced

½ tsp. dried thyme

Salt and freshly ground black pepper

½ tsp. dried basil

1 head cauliflower, coarsely chopped

1½ cups shredded cheddar cheese

¼ cup soy milk

¼ tsp. paprika

1. Preheat the oven to 400°F. Grease a shallow 9-inch baking dish or pie pan.

2. Using cheese cloth or paper towels, squeeze extra liquid from rinsed, shredded potatoes.

3. In a medium-size mixing bowl, combine potatoes, grated onion, egg replacer equal to 1 egg, salt, and flour. Transfer mixture to the prepared pie pan, and pat down with a rubber spatula. Bake for 30 minutes.

4. Brush crust with olive oil, or spray if using spray olive oil, and bake for another 10 minutes. Remove crust from the oven, and reduce the oven temperature to 350°F.

5. In a large frying pan over medium heat, heat vegetable oil until hot. Add chopped onion, garlic, thyme, salt, pepper, and basil. Sauté for 8 to 10 minutes. Stir cauliflower into the pan, and cook for 7 or 9 minutes.

6. Spread ½ cheese onto potato crust. Spoon vegetables on top of cheese, and sprinkle remaining cheese over sautéed vegetables.

7. Combine soy milk and prepared egg replacer equal to 2 eggs in a small bowl, and pour over vegetables and cheese. Sprinkle paprika over mixture. Bake for 35 to 40 minutes or until top of pie is slightly browned.

Veggie Soup for the Soul

Cauliflower comes in different colors. Purple cauliflower is rich in anthocyanin, a group of antioxidants also found in purple cabbage and red wine. A hybrid orange cauliflower contains about 25 times more vitamin A than the white variety. Green cauliflower is also available. Purple and orange cauliflower are more commonly found in European countries like Italy. All cauliflower contains a property known as Indole-3-Carbinol, which serves to buffer excess estrogen. Excess estrogen promotes some cancers, so again, eat plenty of crunchy cruciferous veggies and stay well!

Shredded Brussels Sprouts with Fakin' Bacon

Tender, shredded Brussels sprouts are tossed with toasted pine nuts and crumbled, crispy tofu-bacon in this dish seasoned with freshly ground black pepper.

Serves: 4
Prep time: 35 minutes
Cook time: 10 to 15 minutes
Serving size: 1 cup

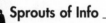

Sprouts of Info

Freezing and then thawing tofu produces a more fibrous texture and allows the salty flavorings to penetrate more thoroughly.

½ **lb. firm tofu (smoked flavor optional), frozen and thawed**

1 **TB. nutritional yeast flakes**

1 **TB. water**

2 **TB. maple syrup**

2 **TB. tamari**

1 **tsp. onion powder**

½ **tsp. garlic powder**

2 **TB. plus ¼ cup butter**

⅔ **cup pine nuts, toasted**

2 **lb. Brussels sprouts, washed, cored, and shredded**

3 **minced scallions**

Freshly ground black pepper

1. Slice thawed tofu into thin slices.

2. In a medium bowl, stir together nutritional yeast flakes, water, maple syrup, tamari, onion powder, and garlic powder. Add tofu slices, and marinate for at least 10 minutes.

3. Heat 2 tablespoons butter in a large skillet over medium-high heat. Add marinated tofu, and fry until crisp, turning once, about 5 minutes. Crumble and set aside.

4. Melt remaining ¼ cup butter in a skillet over medium heat. Add Brussels sprouts and scallions, and season with pepper. Cook until sprouts are wilted and tender, 10 to 15 minutes. Stir in ½ pound crumbled tofu (i.e., fake bacon) just before serving.

Comfort Foods

In This Chapter

- ◆ Why we eat for comfort
- ◆ How dietary fat makes us feel satisfied
- ◆ Why textures give us comfort
- ◆ Filling, warm, creamy, comfort food recipes

You probably have some foods you'd call "comfort foods"—those foods you crave when you're happy, sad, or ill. In this chapter, I give you some comfort food recipes that can give you comfort when you eat them, and without a lot of fat and with no meat. These foods are rich, warm, creamy, and hearty, and give you the same feeling of security and comfort as a plush robe and soft warm slippers on a cold day. In this way, comfort foods are truly medicinal—not only for the body, but for the mind and soul.

Food and Your Mood

Stress and anxiety affect you physically and can make it harder for your body to digest foods properly. But stress is a part of modern life, and we all handle it in different ways, depending on our upbringing, our hard-wiring, our biochemistry, and our character. One thing we all have in common, though, is the need to feed our stress with *something*. Therefore, to keep control of weight and health, it's important to be mindful when you feel hungry. Think about whether you're eating because you're truly hungry or whether you're trying to feed a need other than nourishment.

If you're very stressed or emotionally upset, it's important that you get your nutrients, but it's just as important to not overload your stomach with unnecessary eating or unhealthful foods. By all means, steer clear of stimulants like sugar and caffeine, which can only aggravate already frazzled nerves and further deplete nutrient stores.

Veggie Soup for the Soul

When stress calls for chocolate, remember that chocolate is rich in magnesium. Magnesium is a muscle relaxer, so consider supplementing to lessen cravings. Also, chocolate is rich and creamy and contains fat, which can make you feel comforted. Go ahead and indulge, but try to eat it *after* a meal so the sugar is absorbed more slowly and doesn't spike your blood sugar—which adds more stress to your body. Or consider chocolates sweetened with natural ingredients like xylitol or stevia that won't interfere with your blood sugar.

Your body also uses up more of the B-complex vitamins under stress. Foods that help calm and are easy to digest are your best bets if you must eat when stressed. Think soups, stews, and creamy smoothies. Stick with drinking only pure water or a hot herb tea (noncaffeinated, of course!). And when you get home from your stressful day, take the time to slowly enjoy one of the comforting meals from the recipes in this chapter.

Creamy, Fatty Happiness

Some biochemical reasons exist for why many of us use food when we feel down or stressed. Much of it has to do with how foods, like refined carbohydrates such as cakes, pasta, and candy, give us a quick energy boost. These foods also stimulate the thyroid gland and boost your body's release of mood-enhancing neurotransmitters like *serotonin*.

Lettuce Explain

Serotonin is a hormone that makes us feel at ease and happy. Too much or too little serotonin can make our moods unbalanced.

Some people connect certain food textures such as creaminess with feeling certain feelings like security. And when we're anxious, the thing we strive for the most is to feel secure. That's why ice cream tends to be one of the things people grab after a break-up with their lover. I believe it also partly comes from deep-seated memories of being fed milk or formula as an infant. Whether breast-fed or not, someone who loved you was holding you comfortingly, making you feel secure and feeding you something warm and creamy.

Dietary fat and protein also stimulate the satiation signal to your stomach. So if you find yourself gorging on a big bowl of mashed potatoes after a fight with your boss, add a pat of butter or some olive oil before you burst!

Now on to some of my favorite comfort food meals. Most of these meals have lengthy prep times, but the payoff is sooo comforting!

The Least You Need to Know

- ◆ Comfort foods are generally creamy or rich foods that make you feel better.

- ◆ Refined carbohydrates can stimulate the feel-good neurotransmitter serotonin.

- ◆ Dietary fat makes you feel satiated, so adding a little olive oil to your bread when you do decide to eat refined carbs may help you slow down and not overeat.

- ◆ Stress reduces the effectiveness of your digestion, so consider foods like soup if you must eat when stressed. Or better yet, wait until you're calm before eating.

Southwest Potato Medley

Here, hot baked potato wedges topped with a garlic seasoned tofu purée with black beans, salsa, golden corn, and sweet red bell pepper are garnished with sour cream and fresh cilantro.

Serves: 4
Prep time: 10 minutes
Cook time: 9 minutes
Serving size: 1½ cups

1 lb. pkg. soft, water-packed tofu

1 tsp. finely chopped garlic

2 tsp. butter

1 tsp. chili powder

1 cup salsa

½ cup frozen corn kernels, thawed

1 large red bell pepper, ribs and seeds removed, and chopped

1 (15-oz.) can black beans, drained

4 medium hot baked potatoes, each cut into 4 wedges

Paprika (optional)

Fresh chopped cilantro

Sour cream (optional)

Sprouts of Info

The potato peel contains a high amount of potassium. Potassium affects the heart and all muscles of the body, allowing the sending of all nerve impulses in humans and animals.

1. In a food processor or a blender, blend tofu and garlic until smooth.

2. Melt butter in a large skillet over medium-high heat. Add chili powder, salsa, corn, red bell pepper, and black beans, and sauté until vegetables are tender.

3. Add tofu mixture to the skillet, and stir constantly until heated through.

4. Sprinkle potato wedges with paprika (if desired). Spoon vegetable mixture over potato wedges, and garnish with cilantro and sour cream (if using).

Vegan Gravy

Savory, creamy, rich, buttery brown gravy—your diners won't know it's vegan.

½ cup olive oil

3 to 6 cloves garlic, minced

2 or 3 slices onion, finely chopped

½ cup all-purpose flour

4 tsp. nutritional yeast flakes

4 TB. tamari

2 cups soy milk

¼ tsp. freshly ground black pepper

½ tsp. dried sage

Arrowroot powder or cornstarch (optional)

Yield: 1 quart
Prep time: 5 minutes
Cook time: 10 minutes

1. Heat olive oil in a small saucepan over medium heat. Add garlic and onion, and sauté until onion is soft.

2. Add flour, nutritional yeast flakes, and tamari to make a paste. Gradually add soy milk, stirring constantly with a wire whisk. Bring gravy to a boil on medium to medium-high heat, stirring constantly—gravy will thicken as it boils. Add pepper and sage. Taste and add extra tamari, if desired.

3. Wisk in 1 or 2 tablespoons cornstarch or arrowroot powder to thicken, if needed.

> **Sprouts of Info**
>
> Use this vegan gravy recipe for biscuits and gravy, with Thanksgiving tofurkey, over mashed potatoes or lentil loaf, or anywhere you want gravy! *Please note:* this gravy is *not* a low-fat food. Each serving has about ⅔ tablespoon oil.

Voussaka (Vegetarian Moussaka)

A medley of tastes meld in this feel-good hearty dish. Tender slices of eggplant, potatoes, tomatoes, and nutty lentils mix with layers of feta and mozzarella cheeses seasoned with onion, garlic, parsley, and hints of nutmeg.

Serves: 6 to 8	
Prep time: 45 minutes	
Cook time: 90 minutes	
Serving size: 1 large piece	

1 eggplant, washed, peeled, and thinly sliced

2 TB. salt 1 TB. olive oil

1 large zucchini, thinly sliced

2 russet potatoes, thinly sliced

1 onion, sliced

1 clove garlic, chopped

1 TB. apple cider vinegar

1 (15-oz.) can whole peeled tomatoes, chopped

½ (15-oz.) can lentils, drained and juice reserved

1 tsp. dried oregano

2 TB. chopped fresh parsley

1 cup crumbled feta cheese

1½ TB. butter

2 TB. all-purpose flour

1¼ cups rice or soy milk

Freshly ground black pepper

Pinch ground nutmeg

Egg replacer equal to 1 egg, premixed

⅔ cup shredded, low-moisture, part-skim mozzarella

1. Put eggplant slices on several layers of paper towels and sprinkle evenly with salt. Set aside for 30 minutes. After 30 minutes, put more paper towels over top of eggplant and squeeze or press down to absorb moisture from eggplant. (Salt helps draw out moisture from eggplant.)

2. Preheat the oven to 375°F.

3. Heat olive oil in a large skillet over medium-high heat. (Use more oil as needed to brown vegetables, but avoid frying in too much oil and making them soggy.) Add eggplant and zucchini slices, and lightly brown on both sides; drain. Add more oil if necessary, and brown potato slices; drain.

4. Add onion and garlic to the skillet, and sauté until lightly browned. Pour in vinegar. Stir in tomatoes, lentils, ½ juice from lentils, oregano, and parsley. Cover, reduce heat to medium-low, and simmer 15 minutes.

5. In a 9×13-inch casserole dish, layer eggplant, zucchini, potatoes, onions, and feta. Pour tomato mixture over vegetables, and repeat layering. Cover with aluminum foil, bake for 25 minutes, and remove from the oven.

6. Meanwhile, in a small saucepan, combine butter, flour, and rice or soy milk. Bring to a slow boil, whisking constantly until thick and smooth. Season with pepper, and add nutmeg. Remove from heat, cool for 5 minutes, and stir in egg replacer.

7. Pour sauce over vegetables, finishing with shredded mozzarella on top. Return to the oven and bake, uncovered, for another 25 to 30 minutes.

Sprouts of Info

Putting salt on eggplant pulls out the moisture from the eggplant, leaving it with a more firm and less slimy texture—which, in my opinion, makes any eggplant dish much better!

Voussaka is a vegetarian version of moussaka, a Middle Eastern dish that traditionally contains lamb or other meat. The preparation is lengthy, but for something very different, filling, and delicious, it's well worth the time!

Sheppard's Potato Pie

Creamy mashed potatoes seasoned with butter, cream, sage, thyme, marjoram, paprika, salt, and celery seed complement the mixture of chopped tempeh, scallions, onions, celery, and green peas and are baked to a golden crust.

Serves: 4 to 6
Prep time: 40 minutes
Cook time: 45 minutes
Serving size: 1½ cups

8 to 10 small potatoes, cut into 2-in. cubes

1 stalk celery, chopped

1 bay leaf

1 large garlic clove, peeled and minced

½ cup plus 3 TB. butter

1 (8-oz.) pkg. tempeh, chopped

1 medium onion, finely chopped

1 shallot, finely chopped

½ cup finely chopped celery

½ cup green peas

¼ cup minced scallions

8 cups ½-in. whole-grain bread cubes, preferably stale

2 tsp. ground sage

½ tsp. dried marjoram

½ tsp. dried thyme

½ tsp. celery seed

¼ tsp. paprika

½ tsp. salt

Freshly ground black pepper

1 TB. fresh minced parsley

1 (15-oz.) can vegetable broth

¼ cup heavy cream

Vegan Gravy (recipe later in this chapter)

1. Place potatoes in large kettle of cold water. Add celery, bay leaf, and garlic, and bring to a boil. Cover and simmer for 20 to 30 minutes or until potatoes are tender enough to break apart with a fork.

2. While potatoes are cooking, melt ½ cup butter in a large, heavy saucepan over medium-high heat. Add tempeh, onion, shallot, celery, peas, and scallions, and sauté until vegetables begin to soften. Add bread cubes, sage, marjoram, thyme, celery seed, paprika, parsley, salt, and pepper, and mix well. Add vegetable broth, and mix well. Reduce heat to *very* low, cover, and steam, stirring frequently, for 15 minutes.

3. Preheat the oven to 375°F.

4. In a small skillet, melt remaining 3 tablespoons butter and add cream. Heat until hot, but do not boil.

5. Remove and discard bay leaf from potatoes. Place potatoes in food processor or mash by hand, mixing in butter-cream mixture. Season with salt and pepper, and whip thoroughly.

6. Place stuffing in an ovenproof casserole, and top with mashed potato topping. Bake for 30 to 45 minutes or until potatoes have formed a golden crust. Serve with Vegan Gravy.

Steer Clear

Mashed potatoes make an excellent comfort food, but eat them only on occasion. Cooked potatoes especially are full of starch, and the extra carbohydrates have the same effect on the body as too many sweets and can make you pack on the pounds.

Tofu Pot Pie

Savory cubes of firm tofu swim in a thick, hearty gravy with chunks of tender carrots, potatoes, celery, broccoli, green beans, onions, all baked in a tender whole-wheat piecrust.

Serves: 6
Prep time: 30 minutes
Cook time: 1 hour
Serving size: 1 slice

2 cups all-purpose flour

1 tsp. salt

⅔ cup butter

6 to 8 TB. cold water

2 TB. nutritional yeast flakes

¼ tsp. freshly ground black pepper

2 TB. garlic powder

2 TB. dried oregano

½ lb. firm tofu, marinated in tamari and cut into bite-size cubes

2 TB. olive oil

1 onion, chopped

1 clove garlic, minced

2 large carrots, diced

2 potatoes, diced

2 stalks celery, sliced ¼-in. wide

2 cups broccoli florets

1 cup fresh green beans, trimmed and snapped into ½-in. pieces

3 cups vegetable broth

3 cups Vegan Gravy (recipe later in this chapter)

1. In the bowl of a food processor mix flour and salt with butter. Mix in cold water, and stir until mixture forms a ball. Divide ball in half.

2. Using a rolling pin, roll 1 ball and fit it into the bottom and sides of a round pie dish. Set aside other ½ of dough to use later for top of pie.

3. Preheat the oven to 425°F.

4. In a large resealable plastic bag, add nutritional yeast flakes, pepper, garlic powder, and oregano. Add tofu cubes, and shake until tofu is covered. Arrange tofu cubes on a nonstick cookie sheet, and bake for about 20 minutes or until browned. Set aside.

5. Heat olive oil in a large skillet or saucepan over medium high heat. Add onion and garlic, and cook for 3 to 5 minutes, stirring frequently. Stir in carrots, potatoes, and celery. Stir in broccoli, green beans, and vegetable broth. Bring to a boil, reduce heat cover and simmer. Cook until vegetables are tender, and broth is about evaporated. Season with salt or tamari and pepper.

7. Place cooked veggies in a large mixing bowl and add gravy. Taste and adjust seasonings. Add cooked tofu cubes, and mix gently with fork.

8. Pour filling into pastry-lined dish. Roll out remaining dough, arrange over filling, seal and flute the edges, and poke a few holes in the top crust. Bake for 30 minutes or until crust is brown.

Veggie Soup for the Soul

Amy's Kitchen brand offers individual-size organic veggie tofu pot pies that take about 5 minutes to cook in a microwave and are very tasty. Look for them in the freezer section.

18

Grains for Your Brain

In This Chapter

◆ The nutritional benefits of grains

◆ Learn why grains warm the body

◆ Tips for preparing grains to bring them to life

◆ Grain-glorifying recipes

All grains—wheat, oats, barley, and others you might not have heard of—share many of the same benefits, like providing fiber and nutrients that nourish the brain and nervous system. In this chapter, I share with you some specifics about certain grains, including the ones that are gluten free—which is important to allergy sufferers and anyone with Celiac disease (the inability to digest gluten). I encourage you to experiment substituting different grains with all the recipes included at the end of this chapter.

The Health Benefits of Grains

Grains are a staple food of the vegetarian diet. They provide starch, roughage, energy, and nutrients if they're prepared properly and eaten in a balanced manner. Plus, grains come in so many varieties that it would be difficult for you *not* to find a few you enjoy!

Whole grains ...

- Provide many of the B vitamins.

- Are higher in protein, vitamin E, zinc, phosphorus, and phytonutrients than their refined, enriched counterparts.

- Are rich in magnesium and calcium.

- Provide fire or heat (energy) for the body.

- Contain enzymes when prepared properly.

- Are low in fat and help fill you up.

- Taste good and go with almost any meal.

- Are inexpensive.

Lettuce Explain

Whole grains are the most nutritious form of grain and contain many vitamins, minerals, and, when cooked correctly, natural enzymes. A whole grain is in its unprocessed state.

In agricultural terms, grains are considered a cereal crop. And sorry, but Froot Loops and even our beloved Cheerios are not considered *whole grains*. These cereals are made *from* whole grains but are refined into a product that must then be enriched with the nutrients stripped out during the refining process.

Dietician Beth DiLuglio concisely describes whole grains as follows: "Whole grain is literally that: the whole of the grain, without the tougher outer hull removed. Whole-grain products are made from the bran, the germ, and the endosperm. Refined grains are made only from the endosperm." Whole grains can include wheat berries, barley, quinoa, oats, rye, rice, bulgur, and millet. You can purchase these grains in their whole, raw, uncooked state and, with a little preparation, bring them to life to provide your body with satisfying nourishment.

Warming Up

When you eat beans and grains, you're eating starches. Starches make the body warmer. I suggest to my clients that eating should follow nature as closely as possible and should be varied according to the season and your activity levels. For instance, if you live in a place where you have four seasons, you need foods that generate more heat in the winter to help you stay warm.

Have you ever noticed that you usually feel like eating lighter fare in the summer months? That's because heat has a tendency to suppress your appetite, so you fill up more easily on water-packed foods such as raw fresh fruits and raw and cooked vegetables, and eat fewer starches and proteins. This type of diet provides many essential minerals and also helps keep you cooler during hot months.

If you're an active athlete performing lots of cardio, your body burns more sugar for energy and you need more grains for fuel than an inactive person. Grains eaten with greens or other nonstarchy vegetables make the best food combinations. But eating grains with other more refined starches like bread or mashed potatoes can leave you feeling sluggish. Try limiting your starch servings to only one per meal to keep your energy levels up.

> **Steer Clear**
>
> Consider eating brown rice or wild rice instead of polished (hulled) white rice. Polishing rice removes B vitamins and other nutrients. The hull of the rice kernel contains thiamine (B_1), an important nutrient in preventing the disease beriberi, which is characterized by a weakened heart, nerve and muscle degeneration, and edema.

Too, Too Refined

For a healthful diet, avoid loading up on *refined grain* products, such as boxed cereal, breads, muffins, cookies, and pasta. When a grain is in its whole state, it contains enzymes, vitamins, minerals, roughage, and other nutrients that are completely lost when they are processed.

The process of taking a wheat kernel, for example, and grinding it down to a powdered flour, mixing it with other ingredients, and finally cooking it at high temperatures to make bread turns the grain into a denatured, processed food. Granted, the manufacturers of bread products enrich the bread with synthetic vitamins, but the grain still loses a lot of its intrinsic nutritional value.

> **Lettuce Explain**
>
> **Refined grains** are less nutritious than whole grains because of the grinding and heating process. Examples of refined grain products are rolled oats and all refined flours.

I'm not telling you to give up bread, but don't assume a slice or two of white bread meets your whole grain requirements for the day. Be sure to get some variety, and take care that some of the grains you eat are whole and live.

Sprouts of Info

A 2005 study published in the *American Heart Journal* that showed that postmenopausal women with cardiovascular disease who ate at least six servings of whole grains each week had slowed progression of atherosclerosis and less narrowing of the diameter of the arterial passageways, known as stenosis.

It's Alive!

When grains are cooked slowly with low heat (a very simple procedure I explain shortly), the grain comes out of its dormant state and releases enzymes that signal it to grow. The grain literally comes alive! This activates other nutrients, so when you eat grain in its live state, you eat its life-nourishing properties, too. Don't believe me? Do your own test: prepare some grain the way I suggest and then plant a few kernels. If done correctly, the kernel will grow into a plant. Now *that's* live food!

Here's the simplest way to prepare live grains. Before you start, be sure you have a quality thermos bottle.

1. Rinse your favorite grain (mine is wheat berries) with tepid water.

2. Soak the rinsed grain in pure or distilled water for 10 to 15 hours. It's best to soak in a dish or jar other than plastic.

3. Pour some boiling water into the thermos, let it warm up for about 5 minutes, and empty it.

4. Fill the thermos about ⅓ full of the soaked grain. Fill the rest of the thermos with more boiling water.

5. Flip the thermos around a bit to get all the grains exposed to the hot water, and set it in a warm area for 8 to 10 hours.

Sprouts of Info

If you soak whole grains before you leave for work in the morning and then slow cook them overnight in a thermos, you'll have breakfast waiting for you when you wake up!

When you get up in the morning, empty the contents into a bowl and garnish however you like. The kernels will be warm, puffed up, and popped open. You can turn these grains into a sweet breakfast cereal or a hearty meal, depending on the toppings you add.

Bulking Up on Grains

Many grains have varying tastes and benefits that can make your diet more interesting and healthful. I encourage you to incorporate a variety of the following grains into your diet. Have fun experimenting!

Quinoa (pronounced *KEEN-wah*) is getting more recognition these days. It provides a hefty supply of protein, minerals, and vitamins. Quinoa has a mild, nutty flavor and is somewhat crunchy when prepared. Unlike most cooked grains, quinoa is non-acid-forming. It can be used in place of rice or added to stews and casseroles.

Sprouts of Info

You can find grains in the bulk sections in most health food stores, and many are also individually packaged. When buying in bulk, be sure to ask for cooking instructions if they aren't provided (sometimes you'll need to copy them off the bin yourself). As a rule of thumb, most grains are cooked by adding double the amount of water, bringing to a boil, and simmering covered for anywhere from 20 to 60 minutes.

Rice comes in many varieties besides plain white, including basmati, brown basmati, jasmine, wild, long grain, short grain, and brown. Brown rice is generally the heartier rice; basmati and jasmine are more buttery and sweet tasting; wild rice has its own unique flavor. Always choose rice with hulls over polished rice.

Barley is rich in nutrients that feed the brain. It can be purchased in bulk and slow cooked to eat as a cereal or added to soups and casseroles. Barley is high in selenium and a good source of phosphorus, copper, and manganese. Barley has been studied for its effect on lowering high cholesterol, and it also plays a role in the growth of beneficial bacteria in the intestines, which is good for digestion and immunity.

Wheat berries are whole, raw berries that are crushed into cracked wheat. Cracked wheat is found in 3 grades of coarseness: fine, medium, and coarse. I have used wheat berries in place of rice in recipes where I wanted a little bit chewier, thicker texture. Cook wheat berries like you would rice—in water and simmered on low, covered, for about 45 to 60 minutes. You can cook a bigger batch of berries, cool them, and store them in freezer bags in the fridge or freezer for use later in soups, stews, salads, and other dishes calling for rice or grain.

Bulgur is partially hulled whole-wheat kernels that are soaked, steamed, dried, and crushed. Bulgur is more expensive than whole-wheat kernels because of the processing involved. However, bulgur is more tender than cracked wheat, making it easier to digest, and it also has a nice taste and slightly chewy texture. Bulgur also has a much longer storage life than cracked wheat. I've substituted bulgur for ground beef in some recipes.

Millet is a highly nutritious grain and one of the few grains that's gluten free and also non-acid-forming. Millet is one of the least allergenic grains and one of the most digestible. (Easily digested foods means less energy output, which may help slow aging.) Millet has a sweet and nutty flavor and is high in fiber, B-complex vitamins, iron, potassium, magnesium, and niacin. Millet is also great slow cooked or sprouted and used in sandwiches or salads.

Sprouts of Info

Millet makes delicious cooked cereal and, like most grains, works well in casseroles, soups, stews, and stuffing. It can be used as a side dish or served under sautéed vegetables or with beans. The grain mixes well with any seasonings commonly used in rice dishes, and for interesting taste and texture variations, it can be combined with quinoa or brown or basmati rice.

Buckwheat, although commonly thought of as a grain, is actually a fruit seed. However, it can be used like most other grains in most dishes, ground as flour, and eaten as a cereal. It is a non-acid-forming food and is easy to digest. Buckwheat is high in flavonoids and magnesium, making it a heart-healthy food.

The Least You Need to Know

◆ Grains are best in their whole state, slow cooked to retain their enzymes and release the most nutritional value.

◆ Whole grains all contain valuable B vitamins that nourish the brain and nervous system.

◆ Grains are an inexpensive, low-fat, high-fiber, mineral-rich food.

◆ Cooked grains are a starchy food high in carbohydrates, so limit cooked grains if you're trying to reduce your carb intake and in the summer, when you don't want to generate a lot of heat in your body.

Asparagus and Cream Cheese Risotto

This creamy but textured mix of hearty brown rice, sweet cream cheese, and Asiago cheese, with fresh asparagus, red bell peppers, and green peas, make the most of leftover rice.

1 TB. extra-virgin olive oil	1 cup frozen peas, thawed
1 medium onion, diced	4 oz. reduced-fat cream cheese
2 cups cooked brown rice	
4 cloves garlic, chopped	½ cup grated Asiago cheese, plus more for topping (optional)
1 (15-oz.) can vegetable broth	
1 lb. asparagus, trimmed and cut into ¼-in. pieces	¼ cup minced chives
1 red bell pepper, ribs and seeds removed, and chopped	

Serves: 4
Prep time: 15 minutes
Cook time: 40 minutes
Serving size: 1½ cups

1. Heat olive oil in a large nonstick skillet over medium-low heat. Sautée onion until onion is soft and just beginning to brown, 4 to 6 minutes. Add rice and garlic, and cook until garlic is fragrant, 30 seconds to 1 minute. Add broth and bring to a boil. Cover, reduce heat to a simmer, and cook for 5 minutes.

2. Remove cover and spread asparagus and bell pepper on top of simmering rice—do not stir into rice mixture. Replace cover and continue simmering, adjusting the heat if necessary, until liquid is almost absorbed and asparagus is bright green but still crisp, about 5 minutes.

3. Add peas and cream cheese, and stir until mixture is creamy and cheese is incorporated. Return to a simmer, and continue cooking until liquid has evaporated and asparagus is tender, about 5 minutes more. Stir in ½ cup Asiago, and serve topped with chives and additional grated Asiago cheese (if using).

Variation: Substitute any vegetables you like for the asparagus and bell pepper.

Veggie Soup for the Soul

Risotto is a tasty way to use leftover cooked rice. It can be a side dish served alongside a protein source, such as Quorn, or as a meal itself served with a salad. Also consider baking this risotto or any of the other grain dishes in this chapter in a large green or red bell pepper, a hollowed zucchini, or a squash.

Barley Zucchini Bake

This light-tasting casserole is full of puffed, tender barley baked with pine nuts, scallions, onion, and zucchini.

Serves: 6
Prep time: 10 minutes
Cook time: 1 hour, 15 minutes
Serving size: 1½ cups

¼ cup butter

1 medium onion, diced

1 cup uncooked pearl barley

½ cup pine nuts

2 scallions, thinly sliced

½ cup sliced fresh zucchini

½ cup chopped fresh parsley

¼ tsp. salt

⅛ tsp. freshly ground black pepper

2 (15-oz.) cans vegetable broth

1. Preheat the oven to 350°F.

2. Melt butter in a skillet over medium-high heat. Stir in onion, barley, and pine nuts. Cook and stir until barley is lightly browned. Mix in scallions, zucchini, and parsley, and season with salt and pepper. Transfer mixture to a 2-quart casserole dish, and stir in vegetable broth.

3. Bake 1 hour, 15 minutes or until liquid has been absorbed and barley is tender.

Sprouts of Info

Pearl barley needs no presoaking and usually cooks within 30 to 45 minutes. Quick barley cooks in 10 to 12 minutes. When cooking barley, use twice as much liquid as the barley measure. About 1½ cups cooked barley enhances 2 quarts soup or stew.

Millet, Cheese, and Walnut-Stuffed Peppers

Nutty, cheesy, and creamy millet is mixed with a hint of Dijon and tender walnut pieces and fill green and red bell pepper halves.

3 large green bell peppers, tops and seeds removed

3 large red bell peppers, tops and seeds removed

4 cups cooked millet

1 cup shredded Monterey Jack cheese

½ cup shredded Asiago cheese

½ cup fresh minced parsley

⅔ cup minced scallions

⅔ cup corn kernels

1 cup raw walnuts, chopped

2 TB. Dijon mustard

Freshly ground black pepper

1 tsp. cayenne

¼ cup shredded Parmesan cheese (optional)

Serves: 6 to 12
Prep time: 10 minutes
Cook time: 30 to 35 minutes
Serving size: 1 stuffed bell pepper

1. Preheat the oven to 350°F.

2. In a large steamer, bring 2 cups water to a boil. Add green and red bell peppers, cover, and steam until just tender, about 5 minutes. Remove the pan from heat, and set aside to cool.

3. In a medium bowl, combine millet, Monterey Jack cheese, Asiago cheese, parsley, scallions, corn, walnuts, Dijon mustard, black pepper, and cayenne. Spoon mixture into peppers.

4. Arrange filled peppers in a shallow baking dish. Add about ½ inch of water to bottom of dish to prevent burning. Bake for 30 to 35 minutes or until filling is hot.

5. Add shredded Parmesan to top of peppers (if using), and place under broiler briefly to brown cheese.

Sprouts of Info _____

To cook millet, use 3 cups water for every 1 cup dried millet. Boil water, add millet, cover and lower heat to low, and simmer for about 45 minutes. Cooked this way, the cooked grain is similar to a mashed potato texture. To get 4 cups cooked millet for this recipe, use 1½ cups dried millet to 4½ cups water.

Millet, Cheese, and Walnut–Stuffed Peppers.

Quinoa with Arugula, Feta, and Water Chestnuts

Spicy arugula, crunchy water chestnuts, and creamy, salty feta cheese meld with grainy, nutty-flavored quinoa.

2 cups vegetable stock	1 cup chopped tomatoes
1 cup quinoa, rinsed and drained	¼ cup slivered fresh basil or 2 tsp. dried
1 bunch fresh arugula chopped	1 (6-oz.) can sliced water chestnuts, drained
2 TB. extra-virgin olive oil	1 tsp. grated lemon zest
2 garlic cloves, minced	½ cup crumbled feta cheese
½ cup diced onion	Freshly ground black pepper

Serves: 6
Prep time: 10 minutes
Cook time: 30 minutes
Serving size: 1 cup

1. In a medium saucepan with a tight-fitting lid, bring stock to a boil. Add quinoa and return to a boil. Cover, reduce heat to low, and simmer 15 minutes until all liquid has been absorbed. Remove from heat and let sit, covered for 10 minutes.

2. Wash arugula well, removing the stems. With water still clinging to leaves, place arugula in a medium saucepan with a tight-fitting lid. Turn heat to medium-high, and steam arugula until leaves are wilted, 2 to 3 minutes. Drain in a colander, and press out all liquid with the back of a wooden spoon. Chop arugula coarsely, and set aside.

3. In a large skillet, heat olive oil over medium-high heat. When oil is hot, add garlic and onion, and sauté until softened, about 5 minutes. Add tomatoes and cook for 5 minutes. Add arugula, basil, water chestnuts, prepared quinoa, lemon zest, feta cheese, and black pepper. Mix well and cook until heated through. Taste, and adjust seasonings.

Sprouts of Info

This quinoa and arugula dish can be eaten as a side with a meat substitute such as a Quorn cutlet, or served as a meal along with a salad.

Part 5
International Main Dishes

Fortunately for vegetarians, much of the non-Western world consists mostly of vegetarian foods and dishes. The staples of Indian, Mexican, Italian, Asian, Middle Eastern, and Mediterranean cuisines are filled with beans, legumes, grains, vegetables, noodles, and tofu.

With the recipes in Part 5, you expand your tastes and enjoy the bountiful flavors of the world—beyond just substituting meat replacements for steak dinners. Each of the following chapters offers some interesting tidbits about the particular ingredients and/or philosophies of the regions, along with many vegetarian versions of ethnic dishes. This part is also where you get tips on traveling vegetarian style, wok-cooking hints, and lessons about refined carbs and how to keep them in balance. *Bon appétit!*

Chapter

19

Mexican-Style Meals with a Veggie Twist

In This Chapter

◆ The health benefits of hot peppers

◆ Proper hot chile pepper handling

◆ Substitution tips for strict vegetarians

◆ Veggie-friendly Mexican-style recipes

Vegetarians can't go too wrong with Mexican foods because the staples of typical Mexican fare include mostly vegetarian foods such as beans, rice, tortillas, corn chips, salsas, peppers, cheese, avocados, and peppers. Assembling these ingredients in delicious ways is easy.

Now let's spice up your taste buds a bit by learning some of the things that make hot peppers so good for you and also some foods you can have nearby if you happen to touch or bite into a too-hot pepper! And of course, at the end of the chapter, you'll find several of my favorite Mexican-type vegetarian meals. So let's fire it up and get cooking. *¿Sonido bien?*

Hot Stuff!

Chile peppers are a fruit and part of the nightshade family, which also includes toma-toes, eggplants, potatoes, and your more heat-friendly sweet green and red bell pep-pers. Fresh chile peppers are an excellent source of vitamin C, B vitamins, magnesium, potassium, and calcium, and are considered good food for your circulatory system.

Chile peppers also contain capsaicin, the chemical (actually an antioxidant) that gives them their hot-to-your-tongue sensation. Capsaicin is an oil of the hot pepper, making its burning sensation fiercer than a water-soluble chemical, which can simply be rinsed off. However, because of its powerful properties, this naturally occurring chemical has been studied and used historically for its therapeutic benefits. Found in capsicum or cayenne peppers, capsaicin has been used in topical products and taken internally in some preparations to ease joint pain such as arthritis. Capsaicin has also been reported to boost metabolism; therefore, many weight-loss remedies include a dash of cayenne or capsicum powder.

> **Steer Clear**
>
> When handling fresh jalapeños or any other hot chile peppers, wear latex or rub-ber gloves to be safe. Also be sure to not accidentally touch your skin or rub your eyes with your gloves after handling peppers. If you do come in contact with peppers, wash your hands with something containing fat, oil, or alcohol; try whole milk, cream, or a grease-cutting soap. The burning chemicals won't wash away with water.

Capsicum/cayenne powder has many uses besides just making Mexican foods taste good. Herbalists recommend it to assist in curing stomach ulcers. The heat from the pepper stimulates the stomach to produce more mucus lining to cover and protect it from the pepper heat, curing the ulcer.

> **Sprouts of Info**
>
> Is capsaicin a double-edged sword? It tells your brain that you're in pain by triggering the release of a neu-rotransmitter (Substance P), but it also stimulates the release of endorphins, which are chemicals that promote euphoria! How's that for hurting so good?

Both liquid and powdered capsicum can be used in several different emergency situations, so you might consider keeping some in your vehicle or taking with you camping or on other adventures. You can place a few drops under the tongue of someone having a heart attack or going into shock to help remedy the situation and stabilize blood pressure. For self-defense, you could blow a handful of the powder into an attacker's eyes. Capsicum powder can also be sprinkled in socks or gloves to help warm the feet and hands. Or spray it on the back of the throat to relieve sore throat pain.

Cool the Burn

The substance in peppers that burns isn't water soluble, so don't go reaching for a big glass of ice water to cool your burning tongue. Instead, consider dairy products. Dairy products contain casein, a protein that chemically reacts with capsaicin to quench the burn. So be prepared and serve a side of organic sour cream or plain low-fat yogurt with your spicy enchiladas.

For vegetarians who don't do dairy, try avocado, a fat-containing food. Or try chewing some fresh cilantro, which contains its own essential oil that might help counterbalance the heat. Parsley and cilantro always make excellent garnish for almost any dish anyway, and the chlorophyll in their green leaves helps refresh your burrito breath.

Some tell me that eating rice and sometimes downing a beer (alcohol) works well, too.

Meatless Mexican Fiestas

The recipes at the end of this chapter are my own creative twists on Mexican dishes, and most of them are not something you'll find on a typical Mexican restaurant menu. But believe me, they are delicious and healthful, and I know you'll find yourself making them over and over again. First, though, I want to give you some typical meal ideas for vegetarians dining on Mexican fare:

◆ Veggie burritos topped with melted cheese, salsa, and sour cream, with a side of Spanish brown rice and vegetarian refried beans

◆ Enchilada combo (one cheese and onion; one cheese, spinach, and water chestnut; one cheese) sautéed mixed veggies covered with red enchilada sauce, served with Spanish brown rice and side of black beans

◆ Bean and bulgur tacos with diced tomatoes, onion, shredded lettuce, shredded cheese, avocado, and dollop of plain or vanilla yogurt or sour cream

> **Sprouts of Info**
>
> These meal suggestions are lacto vegetarian, so vegans or strict vegetarians will want to either replace the dairy items (I offer suggestions later) or just eliminate the dairy products completely.

- Guacamole tostadas, beans, and rice

- Taco salad—hold the beef—with three types of beans, cheese, shredded lettuce, onion, corn, salsa, and jalapeños; topped with sour cream, guacamole, and black olives; served in a large taco shell

- For an appetizer or as a meal: nachos with the same ingredients used in the taco salad

- Bowl of vegetarian chili with TVP for the meatlike texture of your liking, served with a wedge of green pepper corn bread

Steer Clear

If you aren't making your own refried beans from scratch, be sure to read the labels on the canned beans you purchase, because canned refried beans typically contain lard (animal fat). To avoid the lard, look for cans clearly labeled "vegetarian." You can also purchase dried refried bean flakes, which you can whip up in a flash simply by adding water.

Here are some replacement items for strict vegetarians:

- Soy cheese

- Tofu cheese

- Soy-based sour cream

- Guacamole instead of sour cream

And for you lacto vegetarians watching your fat intake, try these subs:

- Low-fat, partly skim-milk cheeses

- Plain or vanilla low-fat yogurt in place of sour cream (Try the vanilla mixed with salsa—yum.)

The Least You Need to Know

- Always wear rubber or latex gloves when handling fresh jalapeños or other hot peppers to avoid getting serious burns.

- Casein, the protein found in dairy products, is the main natural remedy used to counteract pepper burns.

- Capsicum can create a sense of euphoria, boost metabolism, promote proper circulation, and reduce pain.

- In an emergency situation, capsicum liquid or powder placed under the tongue of a shock or heart attack victim may help stabilize them.

Tofu Tamale Bake

This delicious mix of red kidney beans, firm tofu cubes, golden corn, onion, and diced green bell pepper is mixed in a fiery tomato base and topped with a thick, sweet, buttery, crumbly corn bread–like top crust.

3 TB. olive oil

1 large onion, diced

3 garlic cloves, minced

1 large green bell pepper, ribs and seeds removed, and diced

1 lb. firm tofu, cut into ¼-in. cubes

1 TB. chili powder

1 tsp. ground cumin

1 tsp. dried oregano

Freshly ground black pepper

Dash cayenne

1 (28-oz.) can crushed tomatoes

1 (15-oz.) can red kidney beans, drained

1 cup frozen corn kernels, thawed

½ cup pine nuts

2 TB. chopped fresh cilantro

1 (6-oz.) can diced green chilies

1½ cups yellow cornmeal

2 tsp. baking powder

3 TB. butter, melted

½ cup soy milk

½ cup water

Egg replacer equal to 1 beaten egg, premixed

1 cup grated Monterey Jack cheese

Sour cream (optional)

Serves: 8	
Prep time: 20 minutes	
Cook time: 45 minutes	
Serving size: 1 piece	

1. Preheat the oven to 350°F. Lightly grease a casserole dish.

2. In a large, deep nonstick pot, heat olive oil over medium-high heat. Add onion, garlic, bell pepper, tofu, chili powder, cumin, oregano, black pepper, and cayenne, and sauté until tofu is browned.

3. Add tomatoes and bring to a boil. Reduce heat to low. Add kidney beans, corn, pine nuts, cilantro, and green chilies, and simmer 5 minutes. Transfer mixture to the prepared casserole dish.

4. In a medium bowl, combine cornmeal and baking powder, and mix well. Add butter, soy milk, water, and egg replacer, and stir just until combined. Add grated cheese, and mix well. Pour over bean mixture in the pan, spreading the top smooth.

5. Bake 45 minutes or until golden brown. Top with sour cream (if using).

Steer Clear

When ordering tamales in restaurants, be sure to clarify with the waitperson if the tamales are vegetarian, as they traditionally contain pork.

Zucchini and Bean Burritos

Here, crunchy and tender seasoned zucchini, carrots, sweet red bell peppers, and onion, are spiced with garlic, cumin, oregano, and chili powder and mixed with veggie refried pintos, all rolled in a whole-wheat tortilla and covered with melted cheeses.

Serves: 6

Prep time: 20 minutes
Cook time: 25 minutes
Serving size: 1 burrito

---

2 TB. olive oil	½ tsp. ground cumin
1 large yellow onion, sliced	½ tsp. oregano
2 garlic cloves, minced	1 (15-oz.) can vegetarian refried beans
2 medium carrots, peeled and julienned	1 cup grated Monterey Jack cheese
1 large red bell pepper, ribs and seeds removed, and julienned	1 cup grated cheddar cheese
1 cup frozen corn kernels, thawed	6 (10-in.) burrito-size whole-wheat flour tortillas
4 medium zucchini, cut in ½-in. slices	Sour cream
1 (6-oz.) can diced green chilies	Guacamole
1 tsp. chili powder	Sunflower seeds
	Salsa

Sprouts of Info

Spanish rice goes great as a side to any Mexican-type meal. To make quick, healthful Spanish rice, simply mix your favorite salsa with cooked brown rice.

1. Preheat the oven to 350°F.

2. In a large skillet with a lid, heat olive oil over medium-high heat. Add onion, garlic, and carrots, and sauté until carrots begin to get tender. Add bell pepper, corn, zucchini, chilies, chili powder, cumin, and oregano, and toss to coat veggies with spices. Cover and cook until veggies are tender, about 10 minutes. (Add a splash of water to steam, if needed.) Uncover and boil away any excess liquid.

3. Reduce heat to low, and stir in refried beans until thoroughly mixed and warmed. Fold in ½ of Monterey Jack and cheddar cheeses. Spoon mixture into flour tortillas, roll up, and arrange in a 9×12 baking pan. Top with remaining cheese.

4. Bake until top cheese is melted and contents are hot, about 10 minutes. Top with sour cream, guacamole, sunflower seeds, and salsa for garnish, and serve with corn chips and salsa on the side.

Tempting Tempeh Tacos

Your family will love these tacos, filled with chunks of nutty tempeh spiced with peppers, onions, chili powder, garlic, black pepper, and cumin, topped with shredded lettuce, diced tomatoes, fresh cilantro, sour cream, shredded cheese, and sliced avocado.

3 TB. olive oil

1 large onion, diced

1 (6-oz.) can diced green chilies

1 medium red bell pepper, ribs and seeds removed, and diced

2 tsp. ground cumin

2 tsp. dried oregano

2 tsp. chili powder

1 (8-oz.) pkg. tempeh, diced

Freshly ground black pepper

6 regular-size taco shells

1 tomato, diced

2 cups shredded romaine lettuce

2 ripe avocados, sliced

1 cup sour cream or vanilla soy yogurt

½ cup shredded cheddar cheese

2 TB. chopped fresh cilantro

½ cup salsa

Serves: 3	
Prep time: 8 minutes	
Cook time: 10 minutes	
Serving size: 2 tacos	

1. In a large skillet, heat olive oil over medium-high heat. Add onion, chilies, bell pepper, cumin, oregano, and chili powder, and sauté until onion begins to soften, about 3 minutes.

2. Add diced tempeh, and cook until lightly browned, about 5 minutes. Season with black pepper.

3. Spoon ⅛ of tempeh mixture into each taco shell. Top with tomatoes, lettuce, avocados, sour cream, cheese, cilantro, and salsa, and serve.

Veggie Soup for the Soul

This tempeh taco filling is also excellent for making a taco salad. Simply use a taco salad crust, fill with crunchy Romaine lettuce leaves, add the tempeh taco filling, and top with sour cream and salsa.

Tempting Tempeh Tacos—
I think the name says it all!

Eggless Chile Relleno Bake

Mild green chilies and chewy, bubbling Monterey Jack and cottage cheeses burst with Mexican hot spices in this bake.

8 canned whole green chilies	½ cup soy milk
2 cups cottage cheese	Freshly ground black pepper
1½ cups grated Monterey Jack cheese	¼ tsp. garlic powder
	2 TB. chopped fresh cilantro
1 tsp. dried oregano	3 TB. thinly sliced scallions
Dash cayenne	
Egg replacer equal to 4 eggs, premixed	

Serves: 6
Prep time: 30 minutes
Cook time: 35 minutes
Serving size: 1 large piece

1. Preheat the oven to 375°F. Spray a 9-inch square Pyrex pan with olive oil spray. Arrange chilies in a single layer in the bottom of the pan.

2. In a medium bowl, mix cottage cheese, grated cheese, oregano, and cayenne. Spread mixture over chilies in pan.

3. In a medium bowl, whisk together egg replacer, soy milk, black pepper, and garlic powder until fluffy. Pour over chile and cheese in pan.

4. Bake, uncovered, for 35 minutes or until golden brown. Sprinkle cilantro and scallions over top for garnish, and serve.

Veggie Soup for the Soul

Here's a quick and delicious green salsa recipe: add ½ cup chopped fresh cilantro, ½ cup fresh basil, ½ cup chopped scallions, 2 garlic cloves, ⅓ cup balsamic vinegar, 1 cup olive oil to a blender and blend until the mixture reaches the desired consistency. (Makes about 2 cups.) This salsa can be used to spice up just about any food, from veggies to tofu to cheesy enchiladas.

Italian *Pasta*bilities!

In This Chapter

◆ Some good things about wine

◆ Balancing carbohydrates

◆ Why you shouldn't eat too much pasta

◆ Delicious Italian-style vegetarian recipes

For most people, the thought of Italian food conjures up the intoxicating smells of oregano, provolone cheese, simmering tomato sauces, hints of wafting garlic, and fresh-baked baguettes, along with red-checkered table-cloths and accordion music playing in the background. How romantic, our image of Italian foods! And how delicious! This chapter includes some yummy Italian-style recipes and shows you how *not* to get plump on too much pasta.

Now *That's* Italian!

Hey, you lacto ovo vegetarians, listen up! You can still eat most Italian foods as they are. Just think of all the yummy, cheesy (and fattening) possibilities:

- Fettuccini Alfredo

- Cheese pizza with vegetarian toppings

- Cheese ravioli

- Vegetarian lasagna

- Spaghetti with marinara sauce

- Vegetarian manicotti

Steer Clear

Most pastas are made with egg, so opt for eggless pastas if you don't eat eggs. You can find spinach and other vegetable pastas made without eggs in most stores. Be sure to read your labels.

What do you get if you are dairy and egg free, or even a vegan? There's still plenty to choose from right off the menu, such as these favorites:

- Eggless angel hair pasta tossed with garlic, olive oil, and roasted pine nuts

- Eggless spaghetti noodles with meatless marinara sauce

- Eggless pasta salad

- Pasta primavera (made with eggless noodles)

Or you can replace the cheeses in some of the popular Italian dishes with the following:

- Shredded soy cheeses for mozzarella

- Crumbled soft tofu for ricotta cheese

- Soy-based Alfredo sauce

You can make things more interesting for everyone by considering the additions and substitutions in the following table.

Instead of ...	Try Adding or Substituting ...
Spaghetti with meatless sauce	tofu balls or falafel balls
Plain cheese or strict vegetarian lasagna	eggplant Parmesan or five-vegetable lasagna
Marinara sauce	pesto sauce

Instead of ...	Try Adding or Substituting ...
Meatless marinara	TVP
Any spaghetti or pasta dish	veggies, pine nuts, or chopped tofu cubes added to the sauce while heating

Wine and Dine, and You'll Be Fine

If you drink alcohol, red wine goes great with most Italian dishes. And you'll be happy to know that there's a naturally occurring substance in wine and cheese, *pyruvate*, that may help make red wine good for you! In the book *The Pyruvate Phenomenon: The Facts, the Benefits, the Unanswered Questions*, author David Prokop reports that researchers have studied the effects of supplementing with pyruvate and have found that it may benefit humans. It acts as an antioxidant and can be useful in weight loss, with diabetes control, in endurance, and in heart health.

However, science also shows that pyruvate causes lactic acid to build up in the muscles. Obviously, more research needs to be done on this substance before supplementing with it or counting on it as a health benefit of wine.

Another substance found in wine, resveratrol, is being studied for its blood cholesterol–lowering effects and its possible affect on weight loss. There are still more studies to be done on this one, too.

In the meantime, of course, alcohol should always be consumed in moderation because too much of it can negate the positive effects of your overall healthful diet and lifestyle. So in moderation, enjoy your meal and your glass of wine, and as the Italians say, *salute!*

Lettuce Explain

Pyruvate is a naturally occurring substance in the body that's also found in apples, red wine, and cheeses.

Sprouts of Info

For the nondrinker, remember that most of the benefits found in wine come from the grape, so you can always sip grape juice for the same nutrients!

Pros and Cons of Carbs

Pasta is great, but ...

When eaten, refined carbohydrates like pasta, rolls, bread, muffins, cookies, cakes, pies, and other flour-based products almost immediately turn to sugar in the body. This makes your insulin levels shoot up, increases blood sugar problems, creates mucus production in your digestive track that inhibits your absorption, leads to diabetes, and also makes you fat! Need I say more about why you should balance out your diet and go for refined products less often?

Those who swear by high-protein diets are right about the refined carbohydrates and starches causing obesity and poor health. And those who blame all the weight problems on meat and animal consumption are also right. Both of these diets, in excess, are imbalanced; neither is close to nature; and both cause the health problems people suffer from today. No wonder so many people are trying diet after diet and still winding up fat! The key to some of these diets is that they usually incorporate some food-combining principals either on purpose or accidentally, which naturally affects weight metabolism. The true, lasting answer lies in the middle.

Hungry vegetarians who don't want to gain weight can fill up on beans; fatty fruits such as avocados; fruits that goes through your system slower, like bananas; and nuts and seeds, like a handful or two of raw cashews.

Athletes who have high cardio demands for long lengths of time, such as long-distance runners and bicyclists, actually need a high amount of carbs to survive. They burn sugar constantly; some fitness experts would call them "sugar burners." Loading up on refined carbohydrates like pasta and garlic bread on a regular basis for these folks is okay because they burn the sugar before it has time to convert to extra weight and blood sugar imbalance. However, the average person should enjoy pasta dishes only occasionally, to avoid unwanted weight gain. But don't fret—you can do some things to get away with pasta more often.

Adding vegetables to your pasta helps slow the sugar absorption, as the veggies add fiber, as in my vegetarian lasagna recipe. Having a salad before your meal adds even more fiber.

For those of you who have weight concerns or who have totally skipped Italian foods because of a low-carb diet, I've included a low-calorie, low-carb alternative for spaghetti and meatballs—see my Spaghetti Squash with Falafel Balls recipe at the end of this chapter. In fact, $^1/_2$ cup cooked spaghetti squash contains only 5 total carbs and 1 gram fiber, making it a total of only 4 *net carbs!*

Lettuce Explain

Net carbs are the amount of carbohydrate a given food has per serving, minus the amount of fiber it has per serving.

The Least You Need to Know

- Many pastas are made with egg, so if you're not an ovo vegetarian, choose eggless pastas.

- Eating excessive carbohydrates causes blood sugar irregularities and most likely causes weight gain.

- Low-carb dieters can eat spaghetti squash in place of spaghetti noodles.

- Adding vegetables to your pasta and eating a salad beforehand or with the meal helps balance the high-carbohydrate effect.

Pineapple, Onion, and Green Chili Calzone

A calzone with sweet pineapple chunks, yellow onion, and spicy green chilis are smothered in marinara sauce and melted mozzarella, surrounded by a homemade, tomato-flavored whole-wheat crust.

Serves: 6	
Prep time: 1 hour, 15 minutes	
Cook time: 30 minutes	
Serving size: 1 calzone	

3½ cups flour

2 tsp. easy-blend dried yeast

1 tsp. granulated sugar

1⅓ cups vegetable broth

¼ cup crushed tomatoes

1 TB. vegetable oil

1 onion, chopped

5½ oz. can pineapple, chopped

1 (5-oz.) can diced green chilies

1 TB. chopped fresh parsley

1 TB. tomato paste

¼ tsp. ground cumin

1 TB. dried oregano

1 tsp. garlic powder, or 2 minced garlic cloves

Freshly ground black pepper

½ cup shredded mozzarella cheese

3 TB. butter, melted

Quick Marinara Sauce (recipe follows), or store bought

1. In a large mixing bowl, add flour, yeast, and sugar. Mix in vegetable broth and tomatoes.

2. Turn out dough onto a lightly floured surface and knead for about 10 minutes. Place dough in a clean, lightly oiled bowl and leave to rise in a warm place for 1 hour or until dough is doubled in size.

3. Meanwhile, heat vegetable oil in a frying pan over medium-high heat. Add onion and sauté for 2 or 3 minutes. Add pineapple, green chilies, parsley, tomato paste, cumin, oregano, garlic, and pepper. Stir to combine.

4. Preheat the oven to 425°F. Lightly grease a baking sheet.

5. Divide risen dough into 6 equal portions, and roll each onto a floured surface, forming 5- to 6-inch circles. Spoon ⅙ of filling onto ½ of each dough circle, and top with cheese.

6. Fold dough over to encase filling, pressing down edges with the tines of a fork. Using a pastry brush, brush top and edges of each calzone lightly with butter.

7. Put calzone on a lightly greased baking sheet and bake 25 to 30 minutes or until puffed and golden. Serve with heated marinara sauce on top or on the side.

Veggie Soup for the Soul

For Quick Marinara Sauce, bring to a boil in a saucepan: 1 (28-oz.) can crushed tomatoes, 2 tablespoons dried oregano, 1 tablespoon dried basil, 2 dried bay leaves, 2 tablespoons red wine, and 3 crushed garlic cloves. Season with fresh ground pepper. Stir, cover, and simmer until ready to eat.

For a filling Italian-style lunch, you can't go wrong with a Pineapple, Onion, and Green Chili Calzone.

Vegetarian Lasagna

Scrumptious veggie lasagna with spinach noodles is loaded with chunks of fresh, tender, crisp organic broccoli, zucchini, carrots, and onions and baked in delicious oregano-seasoned tomato sauce with Monterey Jack, ricotta, and Parmesan cheeses.

Serves: 6 to 8
Prep time: 15 minutes
Cook time: 30 minutes
Serving size: 1 large piece

10 spinach lasagna noodles

½ cup chopped onion

1 TB. olive oil

1 cup raw grated organic carrots

2 cups organic broccoli florets

2 cups ½-in. thick slices organic zucchini

1 (15-oz.) can tomato sauce

1 (6-oz.) can tomato paste

1½ tsp. dried oregano

2 cups cream-style cottage cheese

1 lb. sliced Monterey Jack cheese

¼ cup grated Parmesan cheese

1. Preheat the oven to 375°F. Butter a 13×9×2-inch casserole pan.

2. Place noodles in a deep pot of boiling water, and cook for 8 to 10 minutes. Drain noodles and cool in a single layer on a piece of wax paper.

3. In a large skillet over medium-high heat, sauté onion in olive oil until onion is soft. Add carrots, broccoli, and zucchini, and cook until crisp-tender. Stir in tomato sauce, tomato paste, and oregano.

4. Layer ½ each of noodles, cottage cheese, and sauce mixture, and ⅓ of Monterey Jack cheese slices in the prepared pan. Repeat, placing remaining ⅓ of cheese slices on top. Sprinkle top with Parmesan cheese.

5. Bake for 30 minutes or until hot and bubbly.

 Veggie Soup for the Soul _____

Wining and dining? Many who produce and consume organic wines swear they don't suffer hangovers after drinking it.

Pine Nut Manicotti

Cheesy manicotti noodles with toasted pine nuts and fresh parsley are smothered in seasoned marinara sauce and cooked until bubbling over and browned on top.

14 pieces manicotti noodles, uncooked

1¾ cups part-skim ricotta cheese

2 cups shredded mozzarella cheese

¼ cup freshly grated Parmesan cheese

½ cup pine nuts, toasted

2 TB. chopped fresh parsley

¼ tsp. freshly ground black pepper

3 cups spaghetti sauce

Serves: 6 to 8
Prep time: 15 minutes
Cook time: 40 minutes
Serving size: 2 manicotti

1. Preheat the oven to 350°F.

2. Place noodles in a deep pot of boiling water, and cook for 8 to 10 minutes. Drain noodles and cool in a single layer on a piece of wax paper.

3. In a large bowl, stir together ricotta cheese, mozzarella cheese, Parmesan cheese, pine nuts, parsley, and pepper. Spoon mixture into cooled pasta tubes.

4. Spread a thin layer of spaghetti sauce on the bottom of a 13×9×2-inch baking dish, and arrange filled pasta in a single layer over sauce. Pour remaining sauce over pasta, cover with foil, and bake for 40 minutes. Remove the foil, and bake for 15 minutes longer or until hot and bubbly.

Sprouts of Info

Toasting pine nuts or sunflower seeds gives them a nuttier flavor and crunchier texture. To toast, place nuts in a single layer in a skillet over medium-high heat (no oil necessary). Stir constantly with a spatula, wooden is preferred, until nuts are browned, about 1 minute. Or scatter nuts on a cookie sheet and broil, turning occasionally until lightly browned all over. Let cool and store refrigerated.

Bow Tie Pasta with Sunflower Seeds and Blue Cheese

Assorted colored bow tie pastas mixed with chunks of broccoli, red bell pepper, and fresh basil and brought together with pungent blue cheese crumbles, sweet cream cheese, and crunchy toasted sunflower seeds make this delightful pasta dish great as a main meal or attractive side dish.

Serves: 4
Prep time: 5 minutes
Cook time: 10 to 13 minutes
Serving size: 1 cup

1½ cups bow tie pasta, uncooked

1 large red bell pepper, ribs and seeds removed, and chopped

⅔ cup broccoli florets

1 cup whipped cream cheese

¼ cup soy milk

1 TB. chopped fresh basil

3 oz. blue cheese, crumbled

Salt and freshly ground black pepper

1 cup sunflower seeds, toasted

Sprigs fresh basil

1. Place noodles in a deep pot of boiling water, and cook for 8 to 10 minutes.

2. Meanwhile, steam bell pepper and broccoli a few minutes or until broccoli turns bright green.

3. Heat cream cheese in a saucepan over medium-low heat, stirring constantly. Stir in soy milk and basil, and cook for 2 or 3 minutes. Stir in blue cheese, and season with salt and pepper.

4. Drain pasta and add broccoli and bell pepper to the pan. Pour cheese mixture over pasta and broccoli. Add sunflower seeds, and toss gently to mix. Garnish with fresh basil sprigs, and serve with a green salad.

Sprouts of Info

Look for fresh herbs in the refrigerated produce section of your grocery store.

Spaghetti Squash with Falafel Balls

Delicious, tender-crunchy thick strings of spaghetti squash are topped with spicy, nutty-tasting fried falafel balls and zingy marinara sauce.

1 spaghetti squash

1 (10-oz.) box falafel mix or about 1½ cups

1 (28-oz.) jar (2 cups) your favorite spaghetti sauce (or Quick Marinara Sauce, recipe earlier in this chapter)

Grated Parmesan cheese (optional)

Serves: 2
Prep time: 5 minutes
Cook time: 40 to 45 minutes
Serving size: ½ spaghetti squash

1. Preheat the oven to 450°F. Add about ½ inch of water to a cookie sheet or a 9×13 pan.

2. Cut spaghetti squash in ½ lengthwise. Scoop out and discard the seeds. Place both squash halves face down (exposed side down) on the water-covered cookie sheet or pan, and bake for 40 to 45 minutes.

3. Meanwhile, prepare falafel balls according to package directions (or see Chapter 10 on how to prepare falafel balls). Set aside.

4. Warm about 2 cups your favorite spaghetti sauce in a saucepan over medium-low heat.

5. When squash is done—most of the water should have evaporated—remove from oven. Use an oven mitt to hold squash with one hand, and use a wide-toothed fork to scrape out contents onto a plate or dish. The squash should come out in spaghettilike strings and be somewhat crisp. Cook less for crisper, and longer for squishier!

6. Add falafel balls and spaghetti sauce to squash, and top with Parmesan cheese. *Bon appétit!*

Veggie Soup for the Soul _____

The traditional vegetable spaghetti squash originated in Mexico/Central America, where it's typically grown as a winter squash. It's a healthful, delicious, low-calorie substitute for spaghetti pasta. The flesh is very low in calories; is high in fiber, folic acid, and potassium; contains a small amount of vitamin A; and is very low in sodium.

Chapter 21

Flavors of India

In This Chapter

- ◆ Indian philosophies
- ◆ Oh la la!: exotic spices
- ◆ A quick tour of Indian dishes
- ◆ Flavorful vegetarian Indian recipes

If you've never tried Indian food, you are in for some real vegetarian treats! Many people from this part of the world abstain from eating meat for a variety of reasons, so you'll find a plethora of creative, interesting meatless choices in this cuisine. India is also a land of spices, so you'll find many interesting aromatic flavors.

This chapter covers just a little about vegetarian philosophies, introduces you to some interesting spices, and ends with some of my favorite Indian dishes.

What Would Gandhi Eat?

Great social philosophers—and vegetarians—Mahatma Gandhi and George Bernard Shaw both professed the philosophical side of vegetarianism. Their cruelty-free diets supported their nonviolent messages by extending their belief systems to their dinner plates.

Every decision you make has a consequence. Although most meat-eaters are not killing any animals personally, their choice to eat meat means they have contributed to the taking of a life to satisfy their tastes. So even limiting meat consumption can make a difference.

Vegetarians who are sincerely heartfelt about animal suffering can have a happier heart knowing that every day the vegetarian diet makes a difference by saving many animals from abuse, suffering, and slaughter. Vegetarians know that they're naturally living a more kind, compassionate life.

I am not condemning meat-eaters for their choices. It's important to remember that vegetarianism, just like religion and spirituality, is a personal choice. This Bible verse sums up what I mean:

> The man who eats everything must not look down on him who does not, and the man who does not eat everything must not condemn the man who does, for God has accepted him. (Romans 14:3)

Hinduism—Ya'll Come Back Now

Some religions, such as Hinduism and Buddhism, abstain from eating meat partly because of a belief in reincarnation. Certain sects believe that all life is sacred and that our souls reincarnate, or continue to come back to Earth, to learn lessons. Because any human's departed soul might come back in the body of an animal, animals should be shown respect. Consuming animal flesh is therefore off-limits.

Sprouts of Info

To read more about the Buddhist perspective on vegetarianism, check out *To Cherish All Life: A Buddhist View of Animal Slaughter and Meat Eating* by Philip Kapleau (Rochester Zen Center, 1981).

According to Vedic scriptures, it's considered sinful to kill cows or eat their flesh. The scriptures warn that the sinful human who eats the flesh of cows will be reborn and killed as many times as there are hairs on the body of the slaughtered animal. The Vedic scriptures also explain that wars are a direct consequence of the slaughter and eating of innocent animals.

Overall, Buddhists and Hindus show reverence for all life. As the Christians follow the commandment "Love thy neighbor," the Hindu's Unity of Life Doctrine would add to that precept, "Love thy neighbor, and every living creature is thy neighbor."

Karma-Free Cooking

India is a land of colorful textiles and spicy foods. Indian dishes are often mostly vegetarian fare and include foods such as basmati rice, peas, carrots, lentils, cauliflower, spinach, eggplant, tomatoes, potatoes, a variety of spices, and a popular spice mixture known as *curry*.

Curry originated in India and is used to flavor many Asian foods. It is a pungent mixture containing up to 20 spices and herbs, turmeric chief among them. Other ingredients can include sesame seeds, cloves, cardamom, fennel, nutmeg, red pepper, black pepper, coriander, saffron, and pimento. Curry is generally found in powder form but also comes in pastes and liquids.

If you decide to make Indian food at home, you'll surely tempt your family and friends with the mouthwatering aromas emanating from your kitchen. And unlike some foods that smell better than they taste, Indian dishes taste even better than they smell. In fact, my husband decided he could give up meat altogether after I introduced him to what is now our favorite Indian restaurant in New York. I remember him waving his fork over a plateful of food, enthusiastically exclaiming, "If I can eat like this every day, why in the world would I eat meat?"

> **Lettuce Explain**
>
> **Curry** is a pungent seasoning mixture, containing up to 20 spices and herbs, that is used to flavor many Indian and Asian foods. A chief ingredient is turmeric, which gives it its distinctive yellow color.

Let me introduce you to some ingredients you'll need to prepare and season your homemade Indian dishes. You should be able to find all of these ingredients at Indian specialty shops, health food stores, or gourmet food stores:

Garam masala (gah-RAHM mah-SAH-lah) is a mixture of spices, predominately ground cumin, ground coriander, and ginger. You can find many variations. *Garam* means "warm" or "hot."

Curry powder is a mixture of spices, usually yellow or gold in color. It usually includes turmeric, cumin, coriander, fennel seed, and fenugreek.

Asafetida or *hing*, a potent-smelling spice, is derived from the resin of the dried sap of the asafetida plants. It's also used medicinally as a digestive aid. For fruitarians and others who don't believe in killing the entire plant for eating, root vegetables are forbidden; therefore, this onion and garlic substitute is a lifesaver!

> **Veggie Soup for the Soul**
>
> Curry powder is an English invention made of a mix of spices from India taken back to England to try to reproduce the flavors of Indian foods.

Ghee, or clarified butter, is a substitute for cooking oil. To make it, butter is melted and allowed to settle, at which time the dairy solids are left in the bottom of the pan. The fat solids are the ghee. It doesn't smoke or burn at high temperatures and can be used for deep-frying.

Filo are thin sheets of pastry, usually found frozen.

What's for Dinner?

Here are some items you might see on an Indian dinner menu but not be familiar with. I've explained them as best I can, but you still should try them all to enjoy all the flavors!

Dahl, meaning "lentil" in Hindi, is a soupy mixture usually with a bean (lentil or mung) base and might also include chopped vegetables. It can be eaten alone or served over rice.

Kofta balls are deep-fried, meatlike balls, usually made from a mixture of garbanzo bean flour, cauliflower, cabbage, and spices.

Chutney is a chunky vegetable- or fruit-based relish.

Paneer (or *panir*) are cheese cubes.

Samosas are fried pastries stuffed with cauliflower and peas.

Aloo samosas are fried pastries stuffed with potatoes and peas.

Naan is similar to flatbread, usually warmed.

Pakoras are various vegetables dipped in a garbanzo bean batter and deep-fried.

Subjis are cooked vegetables served with cheese.

> **Sprouts of Info**
>
> Indian food goes great with garlic naan. To make your own, butter some flatbread, chop some fresh garlic onto it, and broil for a few minutes to melt the butter.

Basmati rice is the general staple served with Indian food. This fragrant rice is perfect alone, but you can also add peas, cashews, and some curry spice to fancy it up a bit.

Now that you can see how many choices you have when choosing Indian foods, *curry up and cook*—I'm getting hungry!

The Least You Need to Know

- Ghee is a processed butter used for deep-frying in Indian dishes.

- Asafetida or hing is a spice that can be used as a replacement for onion or garlic.

- Naan is an Indian-style flatbread, usually served warm.

- Curry powder is an English invention, created by using some of the main spices of Indian foods.

Paneerless Saag Paneer

Aromatic bursts of cloves, cinnamon, ginger, cumin, and more flavor this spicy hot spinach purée. Chunks of firm, chewy tofu are served over fragrant, brown basmati rice in this high-protein, low-fat dish.

Serves: 4
Prep time: 40 minutes
Cook time: 40 minutes
Serving size: 1½ cups

4 cups water

2 cups brown basmati rice, uncooked

½ lb. firm tofu, cut into bite-size cubes

Pinch cumin seed

1 cinnamon stick

3 bay leaves

2 whole cloves

1 tsp. fresh grated ginger

1 clove of fresh pressed garlic

1 tsp. freshly ground black pepper

2 tsp. turmeric

1 tsp. ground coriander

½ tsp. garam masala

2 TB. olive oil

1 large onion, chopped

1 small fresh tomato, sliced

½ lb. fresh spinach, rinsed and chopped

1 cup (½ pt.) whipping cream

1 tsp. tomato paste

1 small bunch fresh cilantro leaves, chopped

1. Bring water and rice to a boil. When rice comes to a full boil, reduce heat to low and cover. Cook for 40 minutes for moister rice and 45 minutes for drier rice. (If using white basmati or jasmine rice, cut the cooking time in half.)

2. Preheat the oven to 375°F. Grease or spray a cookie sheet with olive oil.

3. Spread tofu cubes onto the prepared cookie sheet and bake for approximately 10 minutes. Turn over tofu with a spatula and bake for about 10 more minutes. Your goal is to slightly brown the tofu, giving it a firmer texture. Remove tofu from the oven and set aside.

4. In a small bowl, combine cumin, cinnamon stick, bay leaves, whole cloves, ginger, garlic, and pepper.

5. In a separate small bowl, combine turmeric, coriander, and garam masala.

6. Ten minutes before rice is done cooking, add vegetable oil to a large saucepan over high heat. Add onion and sauté until lightly browned. Reduce heat to medium-high, add cumin spice mixture and tomato slices to the saucepan, and mix well. Add spinach and gently fold into pan—do this fairly quickly. Spinach will wilt and shrivel as it heats.

7. When spinach changes to a dark green, add turmeric spice mixture and stir well. Add cream, tomato paste, fresh cilantro, and tofu cubes, and mix well.

8. Increase heat to high until cream boils, stirring constantly to avoid scorching. Boil mixture for approximately 1½ minutes and then serve over rice immediately.

Sprouts of Info

You can store opened tofu in the refrigerator in a closed container, covered with water. It will keep for several days if you change the water every day or two. If the tofu smells spoiled, discard it. If you won't be using the tofu within a week, you can freeze it, although freezing changes it to more of a fibrous texture. Never refreeze tofu after thawing it.

This is a vegan version of traditional saag paneer. In India, saag *means "spinach," and* paneer *is "cheese cubes." This recipe uses tofu cubes instead of cheese.*

Samosas

Pastry-type crusts surround spicy and aromatically flavored potato, cauliflower, and green pea mash. These appetizers burst with flavors of black mustard seed, cumin, coriander, garlic, turmeric, and sweet garam masala.

Serves: 8 (makes 24)
Prep time: 20 minutes
Cook time: 15 to 20 minutes
Serving size: 3 samosas

2 cups cauliflower, cut into small pieces

1 cup peas

⅓ cup plus 3 TB. ghee, plus more for deep-frying

1 tsp. black mustard seeds

1 tsp. cumin seeds

½ tsp. turmeric

¼ tsp. garlic

1 TB. garam masala

1 tsp. coriander powder

2 cups whole-wheat flour

1. Using a steamer over a pot of boiling water, cover and steam cauliflower and peas until soft.

2. In a frying pan, melt 3 tablespoons ghee. Add black mustard seeds, and cumin seeds. When seeds begin to crackle, add turmeric and garlic. Add steamed cauliflower, peas, turmeric, garlic, garam masala, and coriander. Mash vegetables with a fork or blend in a food processor and cook over medium heat until you have a thick paste.

3. In a large bowl, combine flour with ⅓ cup ghee. Add enough water to make a rollable dough. Divide dough into 12 balls. With a rolling pin, flatten each ball into a 5-inch circle. Cut the circles in half, and spoon 1 tablespoon stuffing on one side of each half. Fold dough over stuffing, and seal the edges, making little pockets. Seal samosas tightly enough to hold together when frying.

4. In a skillet over medium heat, heat a small amount of ghee. Add samosas and fry for 15 to 20 minutes, turning over occasionally, until both sides are browned.

Veggie Soup for the Soul

In India and Pakistan, samosas are a common snack and are generally served with various types of chutneys such as mango or mint. If ordering samosas in a restaurant, be sure to ask for vegetarian, as some samosas have meat fillings.

Indian-Style Cauliflower with Potatoes

Soft, cooked cauliflower, potatoes, and green beans are spiced with an aromatic blend of Indian spices, including garlic, ginger, cumin, paprika, turmeric, garam masala, and fresh cilantro.

1 TB. vegetable oil	**½ tsp. ground turmeric**
1 tsp. cumin seeds	**½ tsp. paprika**
1 tsp. minced garlic	**1 tsp. ground cumin**
1 tsp. ginger paste	**½ tsp. garam masala**
2 medium russet potatoes, peeled and cubed	**1 small head cauliflower, chopped into florets**
1 cup green beans, chopped	**1 tsp. chopped fresh cilantro**

Serves: 4	
Prep time: 15 minutes	
Cook time: 20 minutes	
Serving size: 1 cup	

1. Heat vegetable oil in a medium skillet over medium heat. Stir in cumin seeds, garlic, and ginger paste, and cook until garlic is lightly browned.

2. Add potatoes and green beans, and season with turmeric, paprika, ground cumin, and garam masala. Cover and continue cooking 5 to 7 minutes, stirring occasionally.

3. Mix cauliflower and cilantro into the saucepan, reduce the heat to low, and cover. Cook for 10 minutes, stirring occasionally, or until potatoes and cauliflower are tender.

Veggie Soup for the Soul

Turmeric is used in many Indian dishes. It's a member of the ginger family and has a bitter taste and yellowish color. Historically, turmeric has been used medicinally as an antibacterial, and more recently, the active substance contained in turmeric, curcumin, is being researched intensely for its potential anti-cancer properties. In fact, the National Institute of Health currently has several clinical trials underway to study the possibilities of using curcumin in the treatment of colorectal and pancreatic cancer, Alzheimer's disease, and multiple myeloma.

Spicy Potato and Cabbage

Indian-spiced soft potato chunks and shredded cabbage fill this hearty dish.

Serves: 4
Prep time: 10 minutes
Cook time: 20 minutes
Serving size: 1 cup

4 TB. ghee

1 TB. black mustard seeds

1 small jalapeño, finely diced

¼ tsp. turmeric

3 large russet potatoes, cut into bite-size cubes

1 TB. ground coriander

1 TB. or the juice of 1 wedge fresh lemon

1. In a large skillet, heat ghee, mustard seeds, jalapeño, and turmeric. When mustard seeds start to crackle, add potatoes. Stir for 7 minutes on medium heat.

2. Add cabbage and cook for 15 more minutes until cabbage and potatoes are both tender.

3. Add ground coriander. Sprinkle with lemon juice. Serve hot.

Sprouts of Info

If you can't find ghee or clarified butter, don't fret. You can use whatever vegetable oil available to you, such as olive, coconut, or grapeseed. See more information about cooking oils in Chapter 22.

Chapter 22

A Taste of Asia

In This Chapter

- ◆ Tips for choosing and maintaining a wok
- ◆ Healthful hints for cooking with oils
- ◆ Great stir-fry accompaniments
- ◆ Asian-inspired stir-fry recipes

Asia has had a great influence on Western diets. The foods from countries such as Japan, Korea, China, Vietnam, and Taiwan all share similar staples: rice, vegetables, and soy—perfect foods for vegetarians. You should have no trouble finding all sorts of Asian foods to fill your plate—and your stomach.

This chapter gives you information about some of the oils, ingredients, and tools you can use to whip up some great stir-fries at home—and hopefully stirs up your appetite to try some of the following recipes!

It's an Asian Art

Vegetable stir-fries are delicious and healthful, especially when paired with the traditional serve-withs of steamed or fried rice. I sometimes like to use eggless pastas or different steamed grains like wheat kernels, too.

Veggie Soup for the Soul _____

The Japanese diet has traditionally centered on vegetables, rice, and some fish. Researchers used to think genetics kept Japanese people at low risk for heart disease, cancer, and obesity—all of which are prevalent in the Western world. However, they found that when Japanese people change their diets from traditional to more Westernized fare, they begin to develop the same diet-related ailments as Westerners.

Vegetarian spring rolls make a great accompaniment to any stir-fry, as do noodle and vegetable broths. (See Chapter 16 for my Veggie Spring Rolls recipe. I have them in that chapter because of the cancer-fighting cruciferous cabbage used as one of the main ingredients in the rolls.) And for a little more satisfying power, you can add a high-protein source like tofu or tempeh to your stir-fries.

You can use tempura batter to cover tofu or vegetables for deep-frying. Traditional tempura batter is made with egg and flour, but instead, you can use the same eggless, spicy batter I use to make Nonchicken Nuggets in Chapter 13, which uses flour, nutritional yeast flakes, mustard, and water; cook these separately and serve with your stir-fry veggies. You can also leave out the onion, parsley, and garlic in the batter recipe so you don't get overpowering or conflicting flavors.

Lettuce Explain _____

Tamari is a lower-sodium version of soy sauce. It's a dark brown, salty liquid made from fermented soybeans and used as a flavoring agent, especially in Asian foods.

To make stir-fries, you also need some soy sauce or tamari for flavoring. _Tamari_ is a low-sodium version of soy sauce made from fermented soy beans. For a hot dipping sauce for tempura-battered veggies or spring rolls, try spicy mustard, found in powder form with other spices. It also makes an excellent dip for a veggie spring roll and can be used therapeutically to help clear out stuffed sinuses. Wasabi is another fiery-hot dip made from horseradish, so eat it with caution. Seaweeds, pickled plums, and picked radishes are some other vegetarian favorites to accompany an Asian-style meal.

Wok 101

Although not absolutely necessary to cook stir-fries, a wok comes in handy and can help you make your stir-fries easier and more traditionally. Woks come in many choices of finish and a couple shapes. They're generally relatively inexpensive.

What Shape Wok?

Whether it's a flat- or round-bottom wok (which I talk about more in a second), a wok's overall shape lessens the amount of oil needed to cook with, helps keep vegetables in the pan while stirring, creates more even cooking, and helps distribute heat more evenly.

Woks have flat or round bottoms. Flat-bottom woks work on all cooking surfaces, but round-bottom woks aren't as amicable. Your stove might determine what type of wok is best for you.

Electric, flat-surface cooking stoves require a flat-bottom wok; otherwise, you might find your vegetables wobbling right out of the wok and onto the stove! Plus, all that sliding around could scratch or damage the surface of a glass stove top, and the intense heat created in the apex of the wok could reflect the heat and damage an electric burner.

Round-bottom woks work well on gas stove tops, as most of them fit perfectly on the gas grill top. Many round-bottom woks come with a circular stand so you can remove your gas topper and/or place the stand right over the top and then place the wok on it.

> **Veggie Soup for the Soul**
>
> Flat-bottom woks look similar to a skillet, have a long skillet handle, and most of the time have a handle on the other side for lifting with both hands. Traditional round-bottom woks have handles on both sides and no long skillet handle.

A Seasoned Finish

As with all cookware, inside wok finishes vary from aluminum, copper, and Teflon, to stainless steel. The most popular—and my choice for health—is the carbon-steel finish. I recommend against the nonstick/Teflon finishes and copper and aluminum. With all cookware, at least some of the finish is transferred into the food, so why potentially add metals or man-made, nonstick substances into your additive-free organic food?

Let's assume you'll use a wok with a carbon-steel finish. Here's how to get it ready for cooking and help make it last a lifetime:

1. Wash and scrub your wok with an abrasive scrubber (not abrasive *cleanser*), hot water, and cruelty-free dish soap. Rinse and dry the wok.

2. Put the dried wok over high heat, and tilt it back and forth until it changes in color—kind of a peacock coloring.

3. With a wad of paper towels and some coconut or olive oil, Wipe the entire inside wok surface with oil, being careful not to burn your fingers.

4. Put the wok back on the stove over medium-high heat for 8 to 10 minutes.

5. With another wad of paper towels, and being careful not to burn yourself, wipe the inside wok surface again. You should see a black residue on the paper towels. Repeat the oiling and wiping until you no longer get the black residue.

Your wok is now seasoned. From now on, never use an abrasive pad (or cleanser) on the inside surface. Just simply use dish detergent and a sponge to clean. Always rinse and dry your wok before putting it away to prevent rusting.

A Few More Stir-Fry Tips

A wooden spatula is a great tool to use for stir-frying, as it won't break your vegetables or scrape and damage your wok like a metal spatula would. Plus, it resists heat, unlike a rubber spatula would. Wood is also a natural material, making it a great choice for the health-conscious vegetarian.

Always try to use fresh vegetables for your stir-fry meals, as frozen veggies come out too soggy. If you're short on time, most grocery stores carry prewashed, precut assorted stir-fry veggies like broccoli, carrots, sweet peas, and cauliflower in the produce section. Add a handful of mung bean sprouts for some fresh crunch, and you're about 15 minutes away from a great stir-fry!

Keep some canned goods on hand to supplement your fresh veggies. Baby corn, bamboo shoots, and water chestnuts are good in stir-fries, and most of these items can be found in the ethnic food section of your grocery store.

Now You're Cooking with Oils

Part of what makes a stir-fry a stir-fry is the oil. I like the nutty taste of sesame oil, but you can try other flavors in an olive oil base such as garlic or ginger oil.

All oils begin to change their structure at high temperatures, making them potentially damaging to the body. That's why a healthful diet doesn't include a diet high in deep-fried foods! Although stir-frying heats the oils, it at least shortens the amount of time the oils are heated and also limits the quantity of oil you need.

To help you cook more healthfully, here are some tips you'll want to know for choosing and cooking with oils:

◆ Choose monounsaturated oils such as olive oil, peanut oil, coconut oil, high oleic sunflower oil, and high oleic safflower oil over hydrogenated or partially hydrogenated oils. Monounsaturated fats are higher in saturated fat content, which is why they're more stable at higher temperatures (remember the term *stubborn fat!*).

◆ Choose oils that say "high oleic" on the label. Oleic acid contains antioxidant properties that slow spoiling.

◆ Rinse your stir-fry veggies first and let a little water cling to them before you stir-fry. This reduces the amount of oil that soaks into the veggies.

◆ Choose organic oils because most toxins, such as pesticides, are fat-soluble—meaning stored in fat. Pesticides are concentrated in nonorganic oils.

◆ Never heat your oil until it smokes—it makes the oil damaging to your body and also reduces taste.

◆ Don't use flaxseed oil for cooking. Although it makes a great oil as a supplement or on a salad when used fresh, it goes *rancid* quickly and under very low heat.

◆ Purchase oils in small quantities to ensure freshness, and use within a couple months.

◆ To prolong oil shelf life, store in a dark, fairly cool place, especially if the oils are packaged in clear bottles. Store flax and sesame oils in the refrigerator. Olive and coconut oils need not be refrigerated.

◆ You can make your own flavored cooking oils by adding chopped or minced fresh garlic or ginger to a glass jar with olive oil. Shake well and let it sit for a few days in a cool, dark place.

Lettuce Explain

Rancid is a term used for an oil that has gone bad. Rancid oils are full of free radicals and are not healthful to consume. Not all oils smell bad when rancid, but if one does, dispose of it.

Veggie Soup for the Soul _____

Scientists have created a new cooking oil referenced as "functional oil" that contains a mix of flaxseed, coconut, and olive oils. In one study, use of the oil helped reduce cholesterol levels and helped the study participants lose a small amount of weight. Some say the oil may help reduce appetite, does not get stored as fat, and may help boost metabolism. Look for more news on functional oils in the future.

The Least You Need to Know

◆ In general, a traditional Asian diet is more healthful than the typical Western diet.

◆ Soy sauce, used to give stir-fries a salty flavor, is made from soy and high in sodium. Tamari is the lower-sodium version of soy sauce.

◆ Flat-bottom woks are better for electric ranges and work on gas stoves as well. All woks should be cleaned and seasoned before use.

◆ Monounsaturated oils and oils high in oleic acid are the best for cooking.

Sesame Tofu with Spinach Noodles

Nutty, floured, and fried tofu slices atop hearty spinach noodles are stir-fried with broccoli florettes, red bell pepper, and zucchini, and flavored with fresh ginger, garlic, and tamari and sprinkled with sesame seeds.

4 oz. spinach fettuccine noodles

1-in. square fresh ginger root, peeled

2 cloves garlic, peeled

4 TB. tamari

2 TB. water

1 lb. firm tofu, cut into about 16 (¼-in.) rectangular strips

⅓ cup sesame seeds

1 to 2 TB. Asian sesame oil

1 cup broccoli florets, rinsed and still wet

1 cup chopped red bell pepper

1 cup sliced zucchini

1 (6-oz.) can water chestnuts, sliced

Sesame seeds

Serves: 4 to 6	
Prep time: 10 minutes	
Cook time: 30 minutes	
Serving size: 2	

1. Preheat the oven to 350°F.

2. Bring 2 quarts water to a rolling boil. Add noodles, stir gently, and boil for 6 to 8 minutes or until pasta is tender or al dente. Do not overcook. Drain and set aside.

3. In a food processor or in a blender, chop ginger root and garlic. Add 2 tablespoons tamari and water, and blend.

4. Arrange tofu in a single layer on a cookie sheet. Pour ginger mix over tofu slices, and turn tofu so all slices are saturated. Bake tofu for about 15 minutes. After 15 minutes, remove from the oven, and sprinkle tofu with sesame seeds. Bake another 15 minutes or until tofu is browned and slightly crunchy.

6. In the meantime, heat sesame seed oil in a wok over medium-high heat. When hot, add broccoli, red bell pepper, zucchini, water chestnuts, and 2 tablespoons tamari, and stir-fry until broccoli is bright green and crisp-tender.

7. Add noodles to the wok, and stir to combine.

8. Serve noodle and vegetable mix on a plate and arrange browned tofu over noodles. Flavor with extra tamari sauce and a sprinkle of sesame seeds, if desired.

You'll love Sesame Tofu with Spinach Noodles served with Veggie Spring Rolls (recipe in Chapter 16).

Tempeh Peanut Stir-Fry with Brown Rice

Intense nutty flavors highlight this dish that includes tempeh, zucchini, red bell peppers, and peanuts stir-fried in peanut oil and flavored with ginger, garlic, sesame oil, tamari, and served over brown rice.

1 cup short-grain brown rice

2 TB. pure-pressed peanut oil

3 garlic cloves, minced

1 TB. finely minced fresh ginger

¼ cup shelled raw peanuts

4 medium zucchini, cut into ¼-in. circles

2 red bell peppers, ribs and seeds removed, and slivered

1 lb. tempeh, cut into ½-in. cubes

2 TB. tamari, plus more for flavoring

2 TB. dry sherry

2 TB. Asian sesame oil

1 TB. freshly squeezed lime juice

2 TB. minced scallions

2 TB. fresh minced cilantro

Butter (optional)

Serves: 2 to 3
Prep time: 20 minutes
Cook time: 15 minutes
Serving size: 1½ cup

1. Clean rice in a strainer under cool water to remove any rocks. Add rice and 2 cups water to a saucepan with a lid, and bring to a boil. Lower heat to a simmer, cover, and steam for approximately 40 minutes.

2. Just prior to rice being done, heat peanut oil in a wok over medium-high heat. When oil is hot, add garlic and ginger, and stir-fry, stirring constantly, for about 30 seconds.

3. Add peanuts, zucchini, red bell pepper, and tempeh to the wok, and stir-fry about 7 minutes or until vegetables are tender.

4. In a small bowl, combine tamari, sherry, sesame oil, lime juice, scallions, and cilantro. Pour mixture over tempeh and vegetables, and cook, stirring, until heated through. Taste, and adjust seasonings. Serve over brown rice flavored with tamari and butter, if desired.

Sprouts of Info

Raw peanuts and other nuts can usually be found in the produce section of most regular grocery stores, usually with shells on. And look for shelled, raw peanuts in the bulk section of your health food store.

Garlic Green Beans

Here, delicious, crisp fresh green beans are coated and stir-fried with a blend of chopped garlic and tamari.

Serves: 2
Prep time: 5 minutes
Cook time: 3 minutes
Serving size: about 1 cup

1 TB. coconut oil

6 cloves fresh garlic, chopped or crushed

1 lb. fresh whole green beans, stemmed washed, and drained

3 TB. tamari

½ tsp. arrowroot powder

1. Heat a wok (or a cast-iron skillet) over high heat. Add coconut oil when hot. Add garlic, and without letting garlic brown, stir to release garlic essence into oil and pan while it heats.

2. Add green beans to the wok, and stir gently to sear for 3 minutes.

3. In a small bowl, combine tamari and arrowroot powder. Add tamari mixture to the wok, and continue to stir, coating green beans, for 1 minute.

4. Remove beans from the wok, and serve with brown rice.

Sprouts of Info

Coconut oil contains high amounts of lauric acid and is one of the best oils to use at high heat because it resists going rancid. Coconut oil is pretty flavorless, however, so if you have a large amount to stir-fry, you might want to use this as your base oil for cooking and then add some flavored oil to season.

Veggie Fried Rice

This hearty brown rice is mixed with baby corns, bean sprouts, bamboo shoots, crunchy red cabbage, and celery; seasoned with sesame oil, ginger, tamari, and coriander; and sprinkled with nutty, toasted sesame seeds.

7 TB. Asian sesame oil

1 cup brown rice

2 cups water

1 tsp. grated fresh ginger

¼ tsp. hing or garlic

1 cup baby corns

1 small zucchini, chopped

¼ cup sliced water chestnuts

2 stalks celery, chopped

1 cup thinly sliced red cabbage

¼ lb. fresh bean sprouts

½ cup bamboo shoots

1 TB. tamari

4 TB. raw sesame seeds

1 TB. ground coriander

Serves: 2	
Prep time: 10 minutes	
Cook time: 45 minutes	
Serving size: 1 cup	

1. In a saucepan over low heat, heat 1 tablespoon sesame oil until hot. Add rice and fry for 30 seconds. Add water and bring to a boil. Cover and cook for 40 minutes. Set aside.

2. In wok over medium-high heat, heat 4 tablespoons sesame oil, ginger, and hing. Add baby corns, zucchini, water chestnuts, celery, and cabbage. Stir-fry 10 minutes or until cabbage is tender. Increase heat to high, add bean sprouts and bamboo shoots, and fry for 3 minutes. Stir in tamari. Empty fried vegetables into a bowl.

3. In the wok, heat remaining 2 tablespoons sesame oil over high heat. Add sesame seeds and fry for about 1 minute. Add rice and stir-fry for 2 more minutes. Sprinkle with ground coriander. Mix vegetables back in, and stir gently. Serve hot.

Sprouts of Info

Al dente in cooking means a way of cooking pasta and sometimes rice so it's firm but not hard. It's considered the ideal form of cooked pasta.

Chapter 23

Mediterranean-Style Delights

In This Chapter

◆ An introduction to some Mediterranean staples

◆ Understand what countries influence Mediterranean cuisine

◆ Family-style dining

◆ Delicious dishes from the Mediterranean

Maybe you've heard of the Mediterranean diet. It was created here in the West as a result of studies that showed people who live in that region of the world seem to have a low rate of chronic illness. It focuses on small, quality meals eaten *slowly*. The emphasis is not so much on restricting foods, but on taking time to prepare the food and enjoying the delight of the tastes, textures, and aromas, and even the company with whom you share your meals. You could say that the Mediterranean "diet" is more of a philosophy on eating.

Vegetarians especially can appreciate how much food and eating are engrained in our lifestyle and philosophies. Let's look at some of the delicious and interesting foods from this wide region and then I'll let you get on to enjoying the smells and tastes while cooking up a recipe in this chapter.

Ah, the Mediterranean ...

Understanding a region's food staples can give you a good idea about the climate and the geography, and even a sense about the lifestyles and culture of those who live there. Italians, for instance, amaze me with their creativity with the ways they can turn tomatoes, flour, and cheese into an unlimited number of different items and meals! So let's talk a bit more about the Mediterranean.

"The Mediterranean" is the land covering an area from western Spain to the Middle East and includes parts of Africa and Europe. Its culinary influence comes primarily from three main regions:

- Eastern Mediterranean, including the countries of Egypt, Israel, Turkey, and Greece

- Southern Europe, including Spain, France, and Italy

- North Africa, primarily Morocco

Mediterranean staples are another vegetarian food nirvana because most are veg-friendly:

- Olives and olive oil

- Vegetables such as cucumbers, tomatoes, onions, eggplant, and squashes

- Hearty beans, including lentils, chickpeas, and fava beans

- Pita bread

- Sheep and goat cheeses

- Savory fresh herbs like rosemary, oregano, dill, cilantro, basil, fennel, mint, and parsley

Veggie Soup for the Soul

The Mediterranean region surrounds the sea, so seafood is also a part of Mediterranean dishes, making this style of food an even broader culinary delight for pesco vegetarians.

Mediterranean and Middle Eastern fare share some ingredients with Indian foods, such as eggplant, garbanzo beans, and lentils, but they also include feta cheese, cucumbers, tomatoes, and olives. Just like anywhere else, Mediterranean meals emphasize the flavors of the region. Overall, Greek foods have a cool aromatic flavor due to the use of seasonings like mint, parsley, and cilantro.

Flavors of the Mediterranean

Mediterranean meals share a similarity with other non-Western cuisines in that, often, several dishes are served at a meal rather than one main dish, creating a variety of tastes and interest. In restaurants, this is called being served "family style." Instead of getting served your portion of rice, dolmas, and hummus on a plate, for example, big platters of each dish are brought out for the table to share.

After you experiment with these delicious Mediterranean foods, mix and match them to create a meal of your favorites:

Baba ghanoush is blended eggplant, usually flavored with lots of garlic. It's served chilled, sometimes with a little olive oil added, and often scooped up with pita bread.

Falafel is made from spices and garbanzo bean flour, shaped into balls and deep-fried until crunchy. They are often stuffed into pita pockets with salad fixings and tahini or hummus to make a delicious sandwich. They're also great added to a Greek salad.

Tabbouleh is mostly served as a side salad but can be added to any or all the foods mentioned in this chapter. Tabbouleh is a mix of bulgur, grain, parsley, and mint. It tastes cool, light, and refreshing.

Dolmas are grape leaves usually stuffed with *basmati* rice and spices such as parsley and dill. They are best chilled.

Greek salad is a combination of red onion, feta cheese, cucumber, tomatoes, and olives. The dressing is usually olive oil and vinegar with oregano. A traditional Greek salad does not include lettuce, but the American version does.

Lettuce Explain

Basmati is a variety of rice famous for its aromatic flavor and smell. Its name means "Queen of Fragrance" in Hindi. Basmati is available in brown or white.

Spanakopita is a filo pastry filled with layers of cooked spinach, egg (but not in my recipe!), feta cheese, and spices. You can make your own vegan version of this yummy entrée using egg replacer and replacing the feta with tofu or soy cheese. Beware if you're in a restaurant; this food is typically not suitable for a strict vegetarian.

Pita bread or flatbread. Pita bread is made without egg, but always check the package label when purchasing premade pita or flatbreads. Use these breads cut into wedges for dipping into baba ghanoush or hummus. Or use them to make sandwich wraps.

To make dolmas, place the filling in a grape leaf and wrap up the filling, similar to the way you would an egg roll.

Hummus is garbanzo beans ground into a smooth paste. It can be served plain or with spices such as garlic or capsicum for a change of flavor. Hummus is versatile; you can eat it as a dip or sandwich spread, a burrito filling, or a condiment in a falafel sandwich.

Sesame tahini is a creamy seed butter made from sesame seeds. It comes in a jar and is similar to nut butters, which is where you can find it in a market. If not, check your ethnic food aisle. Use it to add flavor and creaminess to your sandwiches, and as a salad dressing or condiment in any of these dishes.

Couscous is actually a pasta derived from durum semolina wheat but is usually found near the grains in the bulk section. This tiny, yellowish, granule-shape pasta is a staple in North African dishes and is very versatile. You can season it with your favorite vegetable broth and spices, or you can add garlic, chopped vegetables, some pine nuts, and a dab of olive oil to spruce it up.

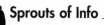

Sprouts of Info

By preparing meals from other countries that don't focus on meat, you will gradually change your ingrained beliefs about how meals are defined.

Tapenade served as a dip or spread is made from chopped black olives mixed with olive oil and sometimes with added spices or herbs like garlic and parsley.

This Middle Eastern plate contains hummus, tabbouleh salad, falafel balls, sliced tomatoes and cucumbers, pita slices, Ryvita crackers with crumbled feta cheese, and basmati rice. Other variations include baba ghanoush and dolmas.

The Least You Need to Know

◆ Mediterranean cuisine is influenced by the regions surrounding the Mediterranean Sea, including Greece, Morocco, Italy, Spain, and Lebanon, among others.

◆ Couscous is a versatile North African pasta that can be used like rice as a side dish or cold in salads or sandwiches.

◆ Cook several Mediterranean foods and serve them family style for a creative, fun, and delicious meal.

Tabbouleh Salad

This refreshing chilled side salad is made with chewy cooked bulgur wheat grains, chopped fresh parsley, tomato, cucumber, and fresh mint.

Serves: 4
Prep time: 5 minutes
Cook time: 15 minutes
Serving size: ¹/₂ cup

1 cup bulgur wheat

2 cups boiling water

2 TB. fresh lemon juice

1 TB. olive oil

6 TB. finely chopped fresh parsley

¾ cup finely chopped red onion

½ cup diced cucumber

3 TB. finely chopped fresh mint

1 large tomato, diced

Freshly ground black pepper

1. Add bulgur to medium-size mixing bowl, pour boiling water over bulgur, and allow to soak, covered, for 15 minutes.

2. Add lemon juice, olive oil, parsley, red onion, cucumber, mint, tomato, and pepper to bulgur, and mix well.

3. Cover and chill in refrigerator. Serve with falafel, hummus, baba ghanoush, and dolmas—or any variation of Middle Eastern fare.

Baba Ghanoush

This creamy, garlicky, rich dip made from pureed eggplant, sesame seed butter (tahini), tamari, and plenty of garlic is best served chilled.

2 organic, medium-size egg-plants, peeled

¼ cup fresh lemon juice

2 garlic cloves, peeled

1 TB. olive oil

1 cup plain yogurt

¼ cup tahini

1 TB. tamari

Serves: *4 to 6*		
Prep time: 10 minutes		
Cook time: 15 to 20 minutes		
Serving size: ¹/₂ to 1 cup		

1. Preheat the oven to 500°F.

2. Cut eggplants in half lengthwise. Bake on a cookie sheet for 15 to 20 minutes or until softish. Let cool.

3. Put fruit in a food processor. Add lemon juice, garlic, olive oil, and yogurt. Purée until smooth. Stir in tahini and tamari to taste.

4. Transfer mixture to a serving bowl, and keep refrigerated until ready to serve. Serve as part of a Mediterranean plate or as a dip for baby carrots or pita pocket wedges.

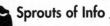 **Sprouts of Info**

Baba ghanoush makes an excellent dip for dipping warm pita triangles.

Dolmas (Stuffed Grape Leaves)

This is a mix of fragrant basmati rice, sweet currents, tender pine nuts, and tomato paste seasoned with a medley of aromatic herbs including mint, cinnamon, dill, allspice, and cumin—all wrapped in soft, dark green grape leaves and served chilled.

Serves: 8
Prep time: 30 minutes
Cook time: 10 minutes
Serving size: 4 dolmas

1½ cups uncooked brown basmati rice

3 cups water

1 TB. olive oil

1 large shallot, minced

2 TB. tomato paste

2 TB. dried currants, chopped

4 TB. pine nuts

1 TB. ground cinnamon

1 TB. dried mint

1 TB. dried dill weed

1 tsp. ground *allspice*

1 tsp. ground cumin

2 to 4 TB. fresh lemon juice

1 (8-oz. drained or 15-oz. in water) jar grape leaves, packed in water, separated, drained, and rinsed

1. In a medium saucepan over high heat, bring rice and water to a boil. Cover, reduce heat to low, and simmer for about 50 minutes.

2. While rice is cooking, heat olive oil in a large skillet over medium heat. Add shallot and sauté until tender. Remove from heat and stir in tomato paste, currants, pine nuts, cinnamon, mint leaves, dill weed, allspice, and cumin to make a paste.

3. When rice is done, fluff with fork, add to paste mixture, and mix thoroughly. Add lemon juice, mix, and taste and add more, if desired.

4. Rinse grape leaves in warm water, and drain and cut off any stems. Lay leaves out flat, and place 1 heaping tablespoon cooled rice mixture in the center of each leaf. Fold in the sides and then roll into a cigar shape, being sure to close all gaps to prevent leaves from bursting when steaming. Repeat with remaining leaves.

5. Place stuffed leaves in a steamer, and steam, covered, for about 10 minutes. Dolmas can be served warm, but typically they are served chilled. Store any leftovers in the refrigerator.

Lettuce Explain

Allspice, or Jamaica pepper, is made from the dark brown, dried berries of the pimiento tree, native to South America and the West Indies. It tastes like a combination of sweet and pungent spices, similar to nutmeg, cinnamon, and cloves. Allspice is used in savory recipes such as Middle Eastern fare and in desserts. Allspice contains vitamins A, B_1, B_2, and C, and also stimulates the gastrointestinal tract and may relieve intestinal gas and diarrhea.

Stuffed grape leaves, a.k.a. dolmas, make a great snack, are a hit at any party, and make a nice accompaniment to any Middle Eastern–style plate.

Chard Kopita Pie

Tender, cooked chard pie, complemented by three cheeses, and seasoned with spicy and sweet seasonings baked in buttery filo pasty sheets until crisp and flakey.

2 TB. olive oil

2 cups low-fat ricotta cheese

1 cup feta cheese

3 TB. freshly grated Parmesan cheese

Egg replacer equal to 3 eggs, premixed

½ tsp. ground nutmeg

¼ tsp. cayenne

¼ tsp. freshly ground black pepper

6 scallions, chopped

4 qt. or 16 cups chard leaves, rinsed, stemmed, and chopped

1 lb. pkg. filo sheets, thawed

½ cup plus 3 TB. melted butter

Sprouts of Info

The dish is an eggless, chard version of spanako-pita, which typically is a Greek pie filled with spinach, green onion, feta, and egg enclosed in layers of filo crust.

1. Preheat the oven to 375°F. Grease a 9×13 baking pan.

2. In a large bowl, combine ricotta, feta, Parmesan, egg replacer, nutmeg, cayenne, and black pepper.

3. In a large skillet, heat olive oil over medium-high heat. Add scallions and sauté until soft. Add chard leaves, cover, and cook a few minutes, stirring regularly, until wilted and tender. Add ricotta mixture and mix well.

4. Cut filo sheets in half to fit a 9×13 baking pan. Cover excess sheets loosely with a damp paper towel to keep them from drying out. Line the pan with 1 sheet of filo, and brush lightly with melted butter. Repeat this process for each sheet of filo until ½ filo has been used.

5. Spread chard-cheese mixture evenly over filo in the pan. Cover with a new sheet of filo, and brush with butter. Repeat with each sheet of remaining filo sheets. Brush top layer of filo completely with melted butter.

6. Bake 45 minutes or until top is golden brown. Cool slightly before serving.

Couscous Pita Sandwiches

These delicious lightly toasted pita sandwiches are filled with warm couscous, mixed vegetables, and toasted pine nuts, spiced with curry and cumin and balsamic vinegar.

2 cups water

1 cup refined couscous

1¼ cups mixed frozen veggies (corn, peas, carrots, broccoli)

1 tsp. ground cumin

½ tsp. curry powder

Freshly ground black pepper

¼ cup pine nuts, toasted

1 TB. olive oil

Whole-wheat pita pockets, sliced in half and lightly toasted

Shredded Monterey Jack cheese (optional)

Balsamic vinegar

Alfalfa sprouts or chopped lettuce

Serves: 4
Prep time: 5
Cook time: 5 to 6 minutes
Serving size: 1 stuffed pita pocket

1. In a medium saucepan over high heat, bring water to a boil. Add couscous and stir. Add frozen mixed veggies, cumin, curry powder, black pepper, pine nuts, and olive oil. Stir, and bring back to a boil. Turn off the heat, cover, and let sit for about 6 minutes.

2. Meanwhile, slice pita in half and lightly toast in the toaster. Place Monterey Jack cheese (if using) in pita pocket.

3. Uncover couscous, fluff with a fork, and spoon into toasted pita pocket halves. Drizzle balsamic vinegar into sandwich, top off with sprouts or lettuce, and serve.

Sprouts of Info

Couscous can be used as a hot side dish like rice, served with a protein, used as a cold salad, added to salads, or as shown here, used as a sandwich filling. Couscous makes a good filling for tortilla wraps as well.

Couscous is a versatile food that can be used as a side dish, as a salad, or even as a sandwich filling, as shown in the Couscous Pita Sandwich.

Part 6

Holidays and Entertaining

What do you do? You've been asked to host Thanksgiving dinner, but you're a vegetarian, and you can't bring yourself to cook the "traditional" Thanksgiving turkey. Or maybe you've been invited to a dinner party and wonder how best to tell the hostess you're vegetarian.

Welcome to Part 6, which I could have titled "Problem Solved!" Here you learn about hosting a party or going to one, and how best to share the great tastes of veggie fare with loved ones. Holiday feasts tips are covered, along with some great dishes and casseroles for hosting a big meal or dinner. And if you're hosting a barbecue or going to one, these chapters contain some great meatless grill recipes. I've also included some party food, dips, plates, and other foods that are sure to be a hit at your next get-together. And don't miss the romantic snacks for two to share—for much smaller parties! Enjoy!

Chapter 24

Barbecues, Vegetarian Style

In This Chapter

- ◆ What do vegetarians slap on the barbie?
- ◆ Grilling and BBQ hints
- ◆ Tasty hot dog and hamburger substitutes
- ◆ Fun BBQ and other picnic recipes

Ahh, summer. The fresh outdoors. The sun shining. The birds chirping. The sounds of children happily playing in the background. The smell of fresh tofu dogs frying on the grill. Wait … *huh?*

Typically, you don't think of barbecues as vegetarian events, but don't throw out that grill just yet! In this chapter, I give you several ideas for vegetarian foods delicious cooked on the backyard grill. Then we get into some yummy recipes, from Black Bean Burgers you can grill indoors or out, Eggless Potato Salad that's great any time of year, Tofu Veggie Kabobs, and more. So slap on your flip flops, grab a spatula, and let's get partying!

Vegetarian BBQ Tips

Of course vegetarian foods can be grilled, but they might not be the first foods thought of when it comes to firing up the coals. Let's see what we can do to change that way of thinking. Following are some delicious ways to cook vegetarian foods outdoors and the best ways to prepare them.

Meatless or vegan burgers of all types can be substituted for hamburgers and cooked on the grill in place of meat burgers. Boca burgers seem to have the best texture for grilling. They don't get too soggy after defrosting, like some frozen premade burgers that contain cheese. My favorites are Gardenburgers, and they come vegan style. (If you'd rather make your own, see my recipe for Black Bean Burgers at the end of this chapter.)

Cut vegetables such as zucchini, onion, yellow squash, and red bell peppers into bite-size pieces; place in aluminum foil; and add spices and a pat of butter, if you like. Place on the grill and cook until vegetables are slightly crunchy. (See my Marinated Grilled Veggies recipe later in this chapter.)

Corn on the cob can be wrapped in aluminum foil and thrown on the grill. Or you can soak the corn in water for 20 minutes or so, leaving the husks intact, and place it directly on the grill. Be sure to turn it a few times to ensure even cooking. (See my Horseradish Corn on the Cob recipe for something different.)

Tofu hot dogs, referred to commercially as Soy or Tofu Pups or Not Dogs, or Morningstar Farms Veggie Dogs can be cooked directly on the grill.

Tofu kabobs are good on the grill. Make them by cutting firm tofu into cubes, marinating the cubes in tamari sauce, and dipping them in a seasoned breadcrumb mixture. Add cubed green and red peppers, zucchini, and onions, alternating tofu and veggies on the skewers. Cook them directly on the grill, turning frequently, or cook them in aluminum foil. (See my Tofu Veggie Kabobs recipe.)

Sprouts of Info

If you've been invited to a barbecue, don't expect your host to have something vegetarian for you to eat. Take along something you can substitute for hamburgers or hot dogs, or you might wind up eating potato chips all afternoon.

Steer Clear

Stay away from baked beans unless you've made them yourself. Most baked beans, commercially prepared or not, contain lard (hardened animal fat). To be safe, make your own vegetarian version or seek out canned beans labeled "vegetarian" and/or Kosher.

If you're a strict vegetarian, make your own coleslaw with soy-based dressings. Most coleslaw is made with dairy products.

Bring along your own sprouted whole-wheat buns, but be sure to bring enough for everyone!

Bring a bag of alfalfa sprouts or organic leaf lettuce and tomatoes to top your veggie burger. Most toppings offered at parties include head lettuce and nonorganic vegetables. Head lettuce is typically void of most nutrients and high in pesticide residues.

Veggie Soup for the Soul

Because vegetarian dishes are more wholesome and tend to be interesting, enticing, and delicious, meat-eaters will also find them desirable. In my experience, most meat-eaters hog up vegetarian side dishes and high-quality breads quickly. For instance, I've brought sprouted whole-wheat buns for veggie burgers to a barbecue, and when I went to prepare my veggie burger, I found there were none left! However, there were still plenty of bleached white flour buns. Keep this in mind, and either bring your own personal serving or enough to feed everyone.

Thank Heavens for Little Grills

If you show up at a barbecue where the grill is being shared by meat-eaters and has been used to cook meat, you don't want to just slap your veggie victuals on there next to the steaks or hamburgers. Bleh. Use a piece of aluminum foil to wrap up your food or line the grill rack with, to protect your food from the animal grease remnants.

Or you can spend $25 to $30 on a portable little electric grill to take with you to non-vegetarian barbecues. If your barbecue is in a remote place like a campground, you can even get an adapter to power the grill via your car's cigarette lighter!

Electric grills can cook any or all of your vegetarian items, or you can dedicate their use solely to the vegetarians in your group. Not only do they come in handy in a mixed-diet group, but they make it possible to have grilled food anytime without having to fire up a barbecue! Most indoor grills have nonstick surfaces, making them fairly

Steer Clear

Wrapping food in aluminum foil before grilling it causes foods to steam in their own moisture, which can result in soggy food. It's better to simply lay down some foil on the grill as a protective surface when cooking items like veggie burgers.

easy to clean, but you can also get ones that have removable grills, which are safe to put in the dishwasher.

The Least You Need to Know

- Premade tofu dogs and meatless burgers make easy substitutes for traditional BBQ fare.

- Make the meat-eaters envious and show sophistication when you bring Tofu Veggie Kabobs and Horseradish Corn on the Cob to the grill.

- Health-conscious vegetarians are wise to bring their own healthful toppings and sides to barbecues. You can't go wrong with alfalfa sprouts, eggless mayonnaise, sprouted whole-grain buns, and organic lettuce and tomatoes.

- Small electric grills are handy for grilling vegetarian foods at a BBQ and can be used indoors for grilling anytime.

Tofu Veggie Kabobs

Skewers of tender, hot, and juicy grilled chunks of zucchini, red bell pepper, white onion, and creamy red potatoes, alternated with marinated, firm tofu cubes with hot, spicy mustard sauce on the side—delicious!

3 TB. mustard powder

2 TB. water

5 TB. tamari

1 tsp. fresh lime juice

4 red baby potatoes, washed

1½ lb. firm tofu, cut into 1½-in. cubes

¼ cup Asian sesame oil

2 TB. rice wine vinegar

1 TB. garlic powder

1 TB. dried oregano

1 TB. chopped fresh parsley

Pinch cayenne

1 red bell pepper, seeds and ribs removed, and cut into large, bite-size chunks

1 large white onion, cut into large, bite-size chunks

2 small zucchini, sliced into ¼-in. rounds

8 (8-in.) bamboo skewers, soaked in water 15 minutes

Serves: 4
Prep time: 10 minutes
Cook time: 7 to 10 minutes
Serving size: 2 kabobs

1. In a small bowl, combine dried hot mustard, water, 4 tablespoons tamari, and lime juice until well blended. Set hot mustard sauce aside.

2. Microwave or steam baby potatoes until slightly tender, about 3 or 4 minutes. (Baby potatoes should be about bite size, but if they are too big, chop to bite-size chunks.)

3. Place tofu cubes in a large bowl, add remaining 1 tablespoon tamari, sesame oil, rice wine vinegar, garlic powder, oregano, parsley, and cayenne. Toss until tofu cubes are thoroughly coated. Add red bell pepper, onion, potatoes, and zucchini chunks, and marinate at room temperature for at least 15 minutes.

4. Thread marinated tofu on skewers, alternating with bell peppers, onion, potatoes, and zucchini.

5. Arrange skewers on a hot grill, and cook until browned, about 7 to 10 minutes per side, brushing with leftover tamari marinade during cooking. Brush with hot mustard sauce just before serving.

Sprouts of Info

Soaking bamboo skewers in water before using on the grill helps saturate the wood and makes them more resistant to burning on the hot grill.

Horseradish Corn on the Cob

Try this dish—golden corn on cob grilled on the barbee and spiked with a hot, horseradish and mustard sauce—for your next backyard party.

Serves: 8
Prep time: 15 minutes
Cook time: 45 minutes
Serving size: 1 cob

½ cup butter, softened

½ tsp. salt

¼ tsp. freshly ground black pepper

1 TB. chopped fresh parsley

2 TB. prepared Dijon-style mustard

2 tsp. prepared horseradish

8 ears corn, husked and cleaned

1. In a small bowl, combine butter, salt, pepper, parsley, Dijon mustard, and horseradish. Mix well.

2. Spread about 1 tablespoon horseradish mixture evenly over each ear of corn. Wrap ears in heavy-duty aluminum foil, and seal well.

3. Place corn on the hot grill, and cook for about 20 minutes, turning occasionally, until corn is juicy and tender.

Sprouts of Info

To grill regular corn on the cob, soak unhusked corn in water for 30 minutes before grilling and then put directly on grill. For an even smokier flavor, do not soak the corn. For a distinctly smoky, caramelized flavor, shuck the corn, brush it lightly with oil, and then grill it.

Marinated Grilled Veggies

This is a colorful assortment of grilled zucchini, red and yellow sweet peppers, squash, plump cherry tomatoes, and red onions marinated in a spice and tamari soy sauce, grilled until crisp tender.

½ cup zucchini chunks

½ cup red bell pepper chunks

½ cup sliced yellow bell pepper chunks

½ cup yellow squash chunks

½ cup red onion chunks

16 cherry tomatoes

½ cup olive oil

½ cup tamari

½ cup lemon juice

½ clove garlic, crushed

Serves: 3 or 4	
Prep time: 15 minutes	
Cook time: 15 minutes	
Serving size: 1 cup	

1. Place zucchini, red bell pepper, yellow bell pepper, squash, red onion, and tomatoes in a large bowl.

2. In a small bowl, mix together olive oil, tamari, lemon juice, and garlic. Pour over vegetables. Cover bowl, and marinate in the refrigerator for 30 minutes.

3. Wrap vegetables in aluminum foil, pour leftover marinade over veggies and grill for 12 to 15 minutes or until tender.

Sprouts of Info

For crunchier and smoked veggies, place the veggies directly on the grill or in grill baskets. Check your BBQ and outdoor supply stores and catalogs.

Eggless Potato Salad

This creamy and cool potato salad is made using chunks of potatoes, red onion, and celery with uplifting and refreshing flavors of smooth eggless mayo, stone ground mustard, dill, black pepper, and fresh cilantro.

Serves: 4 to 6
Prep time: 3 to 5 minutes
Cook time: 10 minutes
Serving size: 1 to 1½ cups

2 large red skinned potatoes (or your favorite)

¼ cup eggless mayonnaise

2 TB. stone-ground mustard

1 TB. white wine vinegar

⅓ cup diced red onion

½ cup chopped celery

1 TB. chopped fresh cilantro

1 TB. dried dill

Freshly ground black pepper

Pinch paprika

1. Chop potatoes into bite-size pieces. Add to a medium saucepan over high heat, and add enough water to cover potatoes. Boil until potatoes are tender, about 10 minutes.

2. In a medium bowl, combine eggless mayonnaise, mustard, vinegar, onion, celery, cilantro, dill, and pepper. Mix well.

3. Fold potatoes into mayo mixture, and toss until fully covered. Sprinkle paprika on top, and serve chilled.

Eggless Potato Salad makes a delicious side dish for a picnic or barbecue.

Black Bean Burgers

Hearty, thick, rich, this black bean patty is spiced with garlic, onion, and cheesy-flavored nutritional yeast. Cook it on the grill or fry it in a skillet and serve on a whole-wheat bun with all your favorite hamburger toppings.

1 (15-oz.) can vegetarian black beans, drained

Olive oil

1 large onion, chopped finely

1 tsp. nutritional yeast flakes

⅔ cup shredded carrot

1½ cups whole-wheat breadcrumbs

Egg replacer equal to 1 egg, premixed

1 tsp. freshly ground black pepper

Serves: 6
Prep time: 8 minutes
Cook time: 10 minutes
Serving size: 1 burger

1. Empty beans into a large mixing bowl, and mash with a potato masher or fork.

2. Heat about 1 tablespoon olive oil in a large skillet over medium-high heat, and sauté onion for 3 or 4 minutes or until softened.

3. Add onion, yeast flakes, carrot, breadcrumbs, egg replacer, and pepper to beans, and mix to combine. (Mixture will be some-what dry but will form good patties if pressed firmly.)

4. With wet hands, form mixture into six hamburger-size patties approximately 3½ inches in diameter. Grill on the hot grill for about 3 or 4 minutes per side or until heated through, or fry in skillet for same.

Sprouts of Info

You can serve these black bean burgers as you would a hamburger, on a fluffy sesame seed bun, with Veganaise (a delicious eggless mayo), mustard, ketchup, red onion, and lettuce. Or try them on toasted buns with just slices of Swiss cheese and a couple tablespoons of homemade guacamole.

Black Bean Burgers are equally delicious grilled as fried in a skillet.

Barbecue Sauce

You'll love this tangy, sweet, and spicy vegetarian barbecue sauce.

3 TB. tomato paste

2 TB. honey

2 TB. red wine vinegar

2 TB. vegetarian
Worcestershire sauce

1 tsp. celery salt

¼ tsp. chili powder

Dash hot red pepper sauce

Serves: 1 or 2
Prep time: 5 minutes
Serving size: 1 or 2 table-spoons

1. In a small bowl, combine tomato paste, honey, vinegar, Worcestershire sauce, celery salt, chili powder, and red pepper sauce until well blended.

2. Use to top Black Bean Burgers, kabobs, corn on the cob, or even a grilled Quorn cutlet!

Sprouts of Info

If you can't find vegetarian Worcestershire sauce at your local health food store, try VeganGoods.com, where they sell Wizard brand organic, vegan/vegetarian Worcestershire sauce, along with many other vegan goodies.

Chapter 25

Holiday Feasts and Casseroles

In This Chapter

- ◆ Holiday meals your whole family will enjoy
- ◆ Dealing with a meat-centered family
- ◆ Great ideas for a turkey-free Thanksgiving
- ◆ Delicious holiday dish recipes

Holidays are a time usually spent with family and friends—and that includes mealtime. More than likely, you'll be in the minority as a vegetarian. So until the rest of the world catches up, this chapter helps by giving you some tips on getting through the holidays happily—and not hungrily! And even better, it includes some delicious dishes that are sure be appreciated by more than just the vegetarians.

What Do Vegetarians Eat for Thanksgiving?

Here's a phenomenon long-time vegetarians are all too familiar with—and if you're new to vegetarianism, you'll soon hear it, too. Invariably, shortly before each upcoming holiday, someone will say something to the effect of, "You're a vegetarian? So what do you eat for Thanksgiving?" (Often this is followed by "Tofu turkey?" and peals of laughter.)

But rather than laughing off their question or getting annoyed with them, stop and think for a moment. Remember the time when you might have asked a vegetarian the same question. Consider this inevitable question your chance to reflect on how far you've shifted your own thinking about food. After all, you've gone from thinking of your meals as needing to be centered around animal flesh to knowing your diet is better, for you and the world, chock-full of a daily variety of earthly delights. And as far as Thanksgiving goes, just think of all those grateful turkeys!

So what do you eat on a holiday that traditionally centers on meat? You have two options: leave out the ham or turkey completely and spice up your vegetarian dishes, or go for a meat substitute.

Here's a list of some of the vegetarian things found on my family's holiday dinner table:

- Salad

- Corn bread

- Muffins

- Rolls

- Soup

- Cooked vegetables

- Broccoli casserole

- Three-bean salad

- Cranberries

- Red grapes

- Sweet potatoes made with maple syrup, raisins, and walnuts

- Stuffing with celery and water chestnuts

Veggie Soup for the Soul

You'd think by the way some meat-eaters talk that the only thing they have for a holiday meal is the turkey or the ham. But plenty of other delicious—and mostly vegetarian—foods are traditionally served at a holiday meal. Think about the mashed potatoes, the cranberries, the sweet potatoes—the pie!

Here's a nice-looking vegetarian spread at one of my family's Thanksgiving dinners.

If you can't fill up with a mixture of these foods, you have a second option: use a meat substitute to replace your main meat, such as tofu turkey or imitation ham. Ask your health food store or specialty store what you might use as a roast beef substitute. I've never met anyone who felt the need for a meat substitute with all the other wonderful foods to fill up on, though!

Veggie Soup for the Soul

Real Food Daily, a pure vegan restaurant located in Santa Monica, California, uses not an ounce of animal flesh, oil, or refined sugar in any of its dishes. And on Thanksgiving, it offers a take-out meal that's out of this world! The meal includes a green salad and dressing, soup, tofu turkey, collard greens, sweet potatoes, stuffing, cranberries, and pumpkin pie with tofu whipped cream. Needless to say, this place is usually jam-packed with customers!

There are only so many ways to dress a turkey, so to speak, but as a vegetarian cook you get to experiment with a whole new variety of foods. After you get past not having a meat main course or even a meat substitute, you can enjoy a whole new range of dishes. You'll no longer see vegetables or salads as a garnish or a side dish, but as a delicious part of the main course. You'll get to mix tastes with a variety of textures. And instead of trying to force your vegetarian meat substitutes to look, taste, and smell like meat, you'll soon be putting your energy into tasting new things and enjoying the tastes of all types of plant foods.

Love Me, Love My Food

For most of us, food is part of our entertainment and social life, and there's nothing wrong with that. You "break bread" with friends, you share a nice romantic dinner with a lover, and you celebrate accomplishments by going out to dinner. Most holidays are celebrated with a large meal. The use of food as something to be enjoyed, shared, and celebrated is ingrained in all cultures.

So if food is a celebration, why not think gourmet vegetarian once in a while and make your meals *really* interesting? While a meatless burger and french fries count as a vegetarian meal, why not celebrate with your favorite vegetarian ethnic dish? Turn your typical vegetarian bean and rice–based Mexican feast into gourmet enchiladas with blue corn tortillas, goat cheese (or tofu cheese), pine nuts, and special cilantro cream sauce. You could even throw a "theme" holiday feast for Thanksgiving!

When you get the hang of it, you'll see that making interesting vegetarian dishes can open up a whole new world to you, not only in your kitchen, but in your mind. You might even discover that although you struggled to bake a turkey correctly and had a hard time poaching an egg, vegetable-based foods are much more versatile and easier to put together. You might discover that you make a very good vegetarian cook!

Meatless Holiday Hosting—No Ham, No Foul?

Holiday time is full of joy, but it also seems to be a time when families feud and tensions run high. Knowing this, if you plan to have a holiday dinner where no meat will be served, you should discuss this with your guests long before the scheduled event.

Give your guests the option of bringing their own meat dishes, to let them know you're not trying to control them or what they eat. It also might be a good idea to let everyone know beforehand that you respect their choice to eat meat, but that you simply won't be purchasing/preparing/serving it at your home. Having this mature conversation with your loved ones prior to the big day can ensure a more relaxed and enjoyable atmosphere because people know they can be themselves without worrying about offending you by their dietary choices.

And if, purely out of good spirit, some guests decided to go veg for the day, just to try it out, you can be especially grateful for the gesture—and the gift it is to animals!

Steer Clear

Keep in mind that some people look forward to having turkey for weeks before Thanksgiving, just like you might look forward to those mashed potatoes. Consider their feelings, like you'd want them to consider yours.

The Compassionate Chef

Hosting a holiday meal is a great opportunity to show all your family members how good vegetarian food can be! So make it a day to show off your cooking skills. If your nonveg family members can enjoy all the dishes you serve, they just might begin to think that going veg might not be all that bad and could be motivated to learn more on their own.

To make holiday meal cooking less stressful, you can prepare many casserole dishes the day before and keep them covered and stored in the refrigerator. My husband and I have done that with a few of the recipes at the end of the chapter. Just remember that chilled casseroles need a little more preparation time. Wait to prepare those items that are best served immediately—like mashed potatoes, tofu cutlets, hot biscuits, and vegan gravy.

Sprouts of Info

Say no to turkey with a vegetarian holiday meal. Soy-based Tofurky, Unturkey, and Tofu Turkey roasts are kind alternatives to the real thing. Tofu Cutlets are good, too, if I do say so myself (see the following recipe). For more information on having a vegetarian holiday, call 1-888-VEG-FOOD (1-888-834-3663).

Thanks, but No Thanksgiving

If you have a difficult family and sense resentment when notifying them that you won't be baking a turkey or ham for the holiday event, consider passing up having the holiday meal at your home that year to give family members some time to warm up to the idea (10, maybe 12 years?).

Sprouts of Info

Recognizing that free citizens have a choice in what they consume is a respectful and generous gesture, and promotes a great holiday atmosphere where people feel they can relax and be themselves.

And when you attend as a guest for holiday dinners at their homes, bring a few knock-your-socks-off vegetarian dishes to share. Eventually, you might be able to host a purely vegetarian holiday meal at your home with grateful dinner guests who have learned to enjoy your meatless dishes.

If you don't know where to start, try some of the recipes that follow. They're not just for holidays; several of them can be a standalone meal served simply with a side salad. Happy cooking and happy holidays!

The Least You Need to Know

◆ Tofu, tofu turkey, or ham substitutes can serve as your main protein source at holiday meals—if you even need it, with all the other veggie dishes you'll have!

◆ Preparing casserole dishes the night before a holiday meal is a great way to lessen the sometimes overwhelming task of cooking a variety of dishes the day of.

◆ Expecting nonvegetarians to give up meat at a holiday meal takes away from the kind, centered image that vegetarians who want to lead by example should have.

◆ Holiday meals naturally offer a variety of meatless foods.

◆ When hosting a vegetarian holiday meal, be sure to let your guests know about the meatless menu well in advance. Offer to let people bring their own meat, if they want.

Broccoli Cheese Bake

Pungent flavors of Gorgonzola blend with chunks of broccoli florets, scallions, and toasted pine nuts, and each bite contains a hint of spicy cayenne.

2 TB. butter

⅔ cup thinly sliced scallions

2½ cups broccoli florets, steamed, or 20 oz. packaged frozen broccoli, thawed, drained, and chopped

1½ cups cottage cheese

Egg replacer equal to 3 beaten eggs, premixed

2 oz. crumbled Gorgonzola cheese

¼ cup toasted pine nuts

¼ cup minced fresh parsley

2 TB. fresh slivered basil or 2 tsp. dried

3 TB. all-purpose flour

¼ tsp. cayenne

Freshly ground black pepper

2 TB. freshly grated Parmesan cheese

Serves: 4
Prep time: 20 minutes
Cook time: 30 to 35 minutes
Serving size: 1 cup

1. Preheat the oven to 350°F. Butter a 9-inch baking pan.

2. In a large skillet, melt butter over medium-high heat. When butter is hot and bubbly, reduce heat to medium. Add scallions and sauté until softened, about 3 minutes.

3. In a large bowl, mix together pine nuts, scallions, broccoli, cottage cheese, egg replacer, Gorgonzola cheese, parsley, basil, flour, and cayenne. Season with pepper.

4. Pour filling into the prepared baking pan. Top with Parmesan cheese, and bake 30 to 35 minutes or until puffed up and golden brown. Broil to brown top, about 3 to 4 minutes.

Variation: Blue cheese may be substituted for Gorgonzola.

Sprouts of Info

Gorgonzola cheese has a strong flavor, very similar to blue cheese. It can come in many textures, from creamy, to crumbled, to more firm. The length of time it is aged determines its consistency; the longer it is aged, the firmer it becomes.

Tofu Cutlets

In this dish, crunchy tofu strips are coated with seasoned crackers and spices and baked to be crispy on the outside and firm and moist on the inside.

Serves: 6 to 8
Prep time: 10 minutes
Cook time: 30 minutes
Serving size: 2 cutlets

2 lb. firm tofu

¼ cup tamari

1 cup cracker crumbs

1 cup unbleached white all-purpose flour

1 tsp. garlic powder

2 tsp. dried parsley flakes

½ tsp. turmeric

1. Preheat the oven to 400°F. Spray a cookie sheet with olive oil.

2. Cut tofu into rectangular shapes approximately 1 inch wide × 3 inches long × ¾ inch thick, and marinate in tamari.

3. In a separate bowl, mix together cracker crumbs, flour, garlic powder, parsley flakes, and turmeric. Dredge tofu rectangles through cracker mixture until coated on all sides.

4. Arrange tofu pieces on the prepared cookie sheet, leaving about ½ inch between each piece. Bake for 15 minutes on each side.

Sprouts of Info

Tofu makes an ideal low-fat, high-protein snack. About ½ cup raw, firm tofu packs about 100 calories, 11 grams protein, and 6 grams fat. Compare that to 4 ounces of regular cheddar cheese, with which you get about 440 calories, 28 grams protein, and about 36 grams fat!

Corn and Zucchini Dish

This delightful side dish or main casserole boasts sautéed corn kernels, zucchini slices, sweet green bell peppers, and onions, with three different cheeses mixed in. And for seasonings—a touch of hot cayenne, fresh cilantro, basil, and fresh ground black pepper.

3 TB. unsalted butter

1 medium red onion, diced

1 green bell pepper, seeds and ribs removed, and diced

1 lb. zucchini, sliced into ¼-inch rounds

2 cups frozen corn kernels, thawed

1 tsp. dried basil

1 tsp. cayenne

2 TB. minced fresh cilantro

Freshly ground black pepper

Egg replacer equal to 4 eggs, premixed

1½ cups cottage cheese

2 TB. cream

½ cup grated Monterey Jack cheese

2 TB. freshly grated Parmesan cheese

Serves: 4
Prep time: 20 minutes
Cook time: 30 to 40 minutes
Serving size: 1 cup

1. Preheat the oven to 350°F. Butter a 2-quart casserole dish.

2. In a large skillet, melt 3 tablespoons butter over medium-high heat. Add onion and bell pepper, and sauté until softened. Add zucchini and corn, and sauté a few more minutes. Add basil, cayenne, cilantro, and black pepper, and mix well. Remove the skillet from heat.

3. In a large bowl, mix egg replacer, cottage cheese, cream, and Monterey Jack cheese. Add vegetable mixture, and mix well.

4. Pour into the prepared casserole dish, top with Parmesan cheese, and bake 30 to 40 minutes or until top is golden and puffy.

Veggie Soup for the Soul

Cilantro contains properties that help your body detox from mercury, one of the most toxic metals known to man. Many health-conscious people go to dentists who do not use amalgam (silver and mercury mix) filling materials and choose to have any old fillings replaced with less-toxic composite (white) filling materials. Eating fresh cilantro as a garnish can help rid the body of the leftover mercury residue from old amalgam fillings.

Sag-Cappy on the Cusp Casserole (Broccoli, Walnut, and Tofu Casserole)

A filling casserole with firm tofu cubes, broccoli florets, walnuts, and water chestnuts in a thick, rich sour cream and sherry–based sauce, all layered on top of chewy, nutty wheat kernels and baked with cheeses until hot and bubbly.

Serves: 6
Prep time: 60 minutes
Cook time: 40 minutes
Serving size: 1½ cups

1 cup wheat kernels

1½ cups water

1 TB. olive oil

1 lb. firm tofu, cut into bite-size cubes

2 TB. butter

1 medium onion, diced

3 cups broccoli florets

1 (6-oz.) can sliced water chestnuts, drained

Freshly ground black pepper

1 TB. all-purpose flour

1½ cups sour cream

2 TB. tamari

2 tsp. Dijon mustard

2 TB. dry sherry

¼ cup minced fresh parsley

2 tsp. dried basil

1 cup raw walnuts, chopped into bite-size pieces

1 cup shredded sharp cheddar cheese

1 cup shredded Monterey Jack cheese

¼ tsp. cayenne

1. In a medium saucepan over high heat, bring wheat kernels and water to a rolling boil. Reduce heat to low, cover, and cook for 55 to 60 minutes.

2. Preheat the oven to 350°F. Butter a 9×13-inch baking dish, and add cooked wheat kernels to the bottom of the dish.

3. In a large skillet, heat olive oil over medium-high heat. Add tofu cubes, and sauté until browned. Remove and set aside.

4. Using the same skillet over medium-high heat, melt butter. Add onion and sauté until softened, about 3 minutes. Reduce heat to medium, and add broccoli, water chestnuts, and black pepper. Sauté until tender, about 5 to 7 minutes. Sprinkle with flour, mix, and sauté 2 more minutes. Add sautéed tofu, and stir well.

5. In a medium bowl, mix sour cream, tamari, Dijon mustard, sherry, parsley, basil, and walnuts. Stir sauce into vegetable and tofu mixture.

6. Add mixture to baking dish on top of wheat kernels, and cover with shredded cheddar and Monterey Jack cheeses. Sprinkle top with cayenne, and bake for 35 to 40 minutes or until cheese is hot and bubbly. Serve with dollop of sour cream.

Veggie Soup for the Soul

I named this casserole the Sag-Cappy on the Cusp because I created it using a recipe for stroganoff and a broccoli rice casserole dish I had in a restaurant. I blended my favorite things from both and came up with this. I was born on December 22—technically "on the cusp" of Sagittarius and Capricorn—so I thought the name was appropriate since it's a little bit of a blend of two very different things!

My Sag-Cappy on the Cusp Casserole includes tofu, broccoli, onions, wheat berries, walnuts, and sour cream, and makes a great dinner all on its own.

Pumpkin Casserole

Tender chunks of sweet, buttery pumpkin are seasoned with sweet cumin, thyme, brown sugar, and cream.

Serves: 8 to 10

Prep time: 35 minutes
Cook time: 1 hour
Serving size: 1½ cups

---

1 large onion, diced

4 TB. butter

1 tsp. ground cumin

1½ tsp. dried thyme

2 TB. brown sugar, firmly packed

1 small pumpkin (about 2 or 3 lb.), seeded, peeled, and cut into bite-size chunks

Freshly ground black pepper

½ cup heavy cream

Sprouts of Info

You don't have to use pumpkin in this recipe. Try this dish with a large butternut squash or any of the hard squashes. Just be sure to bake it long enough to make it mouth-melting tender.

---

1. Preheat the oven to 350°F.

2. In a large skillet over medium-high heat, sauté onion in 2 tablespoons butter until soft. Add cumin and cook for another minute.

3. Using a rubber spatula, scrape the contents of the skillet into a 12-inch baking dish. Sprinkle thyme and brown sugar over onion.

4. Melt remaining 2 tablespoons butter in the same skillet over medium-high heat. Divide pumpkin cubes in half, and brown in two batches, turning occasionally.

5. Sprinkle pumpkin with pepper, and scrape pumpkin and any remaining butter into the baking dish. Gently mix with onion mixture. Pour cream over the top.

6. Bake, uncovered, for 60 minutes or until pumpkin is melt-in-your-mouth tender. Allow to cool for 10 minutes before serving.

Chapter 26

Snacks and Party Foods

In This Chapter

- ◆ Easy vegetarian snacks
- ◆ Healthful sugar substitutes
- ◆ Cautions about potentially toxic sugar substitutes
- ◆ Party food recipes

When snack time hits, you just have to nosh. Good news! Most snacks such as nuts, crackers, seeds, soy cheese, apples, nut butters, and chopped veggies are meat free anyway. And if you're invited to a party and asked to bring a dish, I've included some great crowd pleasers to bring along. Even meat-eaters will enjoy these yummy party foods!

Snack Attack

Many processed snacks tend to be bad for you in one way or another, so for a healthful snack attack satisfier, try these instead:

- ◆ Smoothies
- ◆ Raw nuts and seeds
- ◆ Fruit, fresh or dried

- Rice cakes with jelly

- Granola, dry or with rice milk

- Carob-flavored soy milk (individually packaged)

- Soy yogurt

- Popcorn sprinkled with tamari and nutritional yeast flakes

- Whole-grain muffins

- Veggies, prewashed and chopped—carrots, celery, bell peppers, broccoli, and cauliflower

Sprouts of Info

Hitting the road? Many vegetarian snacks are great for packing for car trips, camping, hiking, or picnics. See Chapter 4 for some road-trip food kit ideas.

If you're not crazy about raw veggies, make them more enticing with a dip:

- Hummus

- Salsa

- Black bean dip

- Spinach and artichoke dip

And remember to keep prepared veggies in the refrigerator ready to eat. You'll be more likely to reach for them if you don't have to haul out the cutting board and take the time to peel, chop, dice, etc.

What's Wrong with Sugar?

No one says a vegetarian life can't be sweet! The good news is that, over time, the more you fill your diet with wholesome, natural, satisfying foods, the fewer cravings you'll have for refined sugar and refined sugar products. Your body actually evolves, and your tastes change in response to a cleaner diet. "But what's so wrong with sugar?" you ask. Let me tell you.

Steer Clear

Chocolate comes from the cocoa bean, which is actually very bitter. To make chocolate into the sweet, tasty treat we know and love, an abundant amount of sugar is added. Sugar not only lacks nutritional value, it also robs the body of nutrients.

Refined white sugar doesn't contain any nutritional value. If you were to eat a stalk of sugar cane from Hawaii or a sugar beet in its raw state, your body could process the sugar contained within it without much trouble because the other nutrients inherent in the whole food would keep all the elements contained in the food in balance.

However, sugar is a product that's refined to its purest form, and therefore is devoid of the nutrients that help the body break it down. When you consume sugar, your body must come up with its own nutrients, including the B vitamins and many minerals, to utilize the sugar. Eventually, the sugar depletes the body of its own nutrients. Over time, this may lead to many forms of illness and disease.

Don't Fake the Sweetener

"That's okay," you figure, "I'll just use a sugar substitute." Sorry, Charlie. I hate raining on anyone's parade, but I can show you a pile of studies I've collected on the harmful effects of sugar substitutes. (In fact, check my website for links that take you to much of my research information: www. HealingFeats.com/wakeup.htm.)

One popular sugar substitute is actually a petroleum by-product! Another, aspartame, has been shown in some studies to be damaging to the central nervous system, and many consider it a dangerous toxin. Sucralose goes by the brand name of Splenda and is controversial because of the toxic chlorine used in its processing. Some claim severe gastritis, or intestinal and stomach pains, with its use.

Steer Clear

Xylitol is a sugar substitute used in many sugar-free, natural health food products and is safe for diabetics because it doesn't spike blood sugar levels. However, *never* feed your pet anything made with xylitol. It's highly toxic to pets and can cause fatal liver failure.

Gooey Goods

Most of us like and crave sweets at one time or another, so what can we have in place of nutrient-robbing sugar or its potentially toxic substitutes? Here are some choices that not only are sweet to the taste, but contain nutritional properties as well:

◆ Of all *honey*, raw, unfiltered honey is the best because of its enzymes and nutritional value.

◆ *Blackstrap molasses* is an excellent and iron-rich food that's actually a by-product of sugar making and contains all the minerals that are extracted from refined sugar.

Steer Clear

Honey is a great option for vegetarians, but vegans will have to pass because bees work to make the honey.

- *Maple syrup* can be used as a sweetener on pancakes, in oatmeal, in coffee (if you're used to adding sugar to coffee), and in homemade soy or rice milk.

- *Brown rice syrup* is made from brown rice and contains some vitamins and minerals.

- *Barley malt* comes in powder or syrup form.

- *Raw, unprocessed sugar* (Sucanat), without the molasses removed, like refined sugar, at least contains many of the nutrients still found in the sugar cane.

Stevia: A Sweet, Healthful Choice

Speaking of sweet things, you might have heard about *stevia* (*Stevia rebaudiana*), an herb whose leaves are used to make a sweetener and flavoring agent. Unlike refined sugar, stevia contains nutrients and seems to increase people's energy. It has been used therapeutically to help alcoholics, diabetics, and those suffering from PMS, smoking withdrawal, stress, and hypoglycemia (low blood sugar). Its nutrients seem to help balance blood sugar levels rather than raising or lowering them; therefore, it's a favorite of both hypoglycemics and diabetics. And it's about 300 times sweeter than refined sugar, so 1 or 2 drops equal the taste of 1 teaspoon of white sugar.

Lettuce Explain

Stevia is an herb used as a sugar replacement and is even used by diabetics, although there's some controversy over its use. Stevia contains phosphorus, magnesium, potassium, selenium, silicon, sodium, manganese, and small amounts of calcium, iron, and zinc.

There's been a lot of controversy over the use of stevia as a sweetener in the United States, since 1991, when the FDA banned it as a sweetener for use in commercial foods and drinks. (Interestingly enough, this was around the same time that aspartame was introduced to the food supply.) The FDA now allows stevia for sale, but only as a nutritional supplement, and manufacturers are still not allowed to use it in their products. However, you can find this nutritional supplement in many forms, such as liquid, bulk powder, and even individual packets, for use in your own cooking and beverages. In other countries, stevia has been and is used as a regular sugar substitute in beverages and manufactured food items.

Before you decide on which sweetener you want to use, do some research on aspartame and on stevia, and come to your own conclusions. Keep in mind that some large corporations have a vested interest in the production of aspartame and other synthetic chemicals. And before you take the word of any study, find out who funded it.

Final Sweet Thoughts

Too much sugar or any one type of food in anyone's diet is unhealthful and can lead to problems. But that's the great thing about a vegetarian diet—there are so many foods to choose from. And all plant foods vary in their vitamin and mineral content, based on the type of mineral-rich soil a plant favors and where it grows. For instance, if you study herbology or botany, you become aware that certain plants favor certain soil conditions, and if left in the wild, these plants grow where the soil is favorable to them. Our farmers learn about which crops favor which type of soils and then use different chemicals, soils, and conditions to help their crops grow—all the more reason to go veggie!

But if you've got a sweet tooth and you're going to consume sweets occasionally, please stick to those that contain a natural form of sugar. And enjoy the sweet life!

The Least You Need to Know

- To make it easier for you and your family to snack healthfully, wash and chop vegetables and fruits before putting them in the fridge. Keep some dip on hand and have nut butters available, too.

- For a more healthful diet, limit nutrient-void refined sugar.

- Stevia is a sweet herb, contains no carbs, is rich in chromium, and makes a healthful sugar substitute.

- Research and make your own decisions about the side effects of commercial sugar substitutes.

Mexican Layer Dip

Spicy refried beans with layers of melted cheeses, fresh, ripe avocado, tangy salsa, and jalapeños make this Mexican layer dip a hit at any event! Serve with corn chips and/or crisp veggies.

Serves: 8 to 10
Prep time: 10 minutes
Cook time: 30 minutes
Serving size: 1 cup

2 (15-oz.) cans vegetarian refried beans

1 (6-oz.) can diced green chilies

½ cup vanilla yogurt

½ cup sour cream

2 TB. fresh lemon juice

2 ripe avocados, peeled, pitted, and chopped

½ cup medium or hot salsa

1 cup shredded cheddar cheese

1 cup shredded Monterey Jack cheese

4 whole scallions, chopped

1 (4-oz.) can sliced jalapeños, drained

1 bag tortilla chips

Sprouts of Info

Serve with an assortment of yellow, blue, and red corn chips for a more festive presentation.

1. Preheat the oven to 350°F.

2. Mix can of diced green chilies thoroughly with beans and spread in an even layer in a 9×10-inch baking dish.

3. In a small bowl, combine yogurt and sour cream. Spread mixture over bean dip.

4. Sprinkle lemon juice over avocados, and layer avocados over dip. Cover with salsa, and sprinkle with cheddar and Monterey Jack cheeses. Top with scallions and then jalapeños.

5. Bake uncovered for 30 minutes. Serve hot with tortilla chips.

Fruit Pizza

This fruit pizza, featuring sweet fresh raw fruits—kiwi, blackberries, blueberries, and strawberries—atop a sweet cream cheese layer on a baked sugar cookie–type crust is sure to be a sweet hit at any party, especially for summertime.

½ **cup butter, softened**

¾ **cup granulated sugar**

Egg replacer equal to 1 egg, premixed

1¼ **cups all-purpose flour**

1 **tsp. vanilla soy yogurt**

½ **tsp. baking soda**

¼ **tsp. salt**

1 **(8-oz.) tub whipped cream cheese**

2 **tsp. vanilla extract**

4 **ripe kiwis, peeled and sliced in rounds**

1 **or 2 cups frozen black cherries, thawed**

1 **or 2 cups fresh blueberries, washed**

1 **or 2 cups fresh strawberries, washed and sliced**

Serves: 12
Prep time: 25 minutes
Cook time: 10 minutes
Serving size: 1 slice

1. Preheat the oven to 350°F.

2. In a large bowl, *cream* together butter and sugar until smooth. Mix in egg replacer.

3. In a separate bowl, combine flour, yogurt, baking soda, and salt. Stir into creamed mixture until just blended.

4. Press dough into an ungreased cookie sheet, and bake for 8 to 10 minutes or until lightly browned. Cool.

5. In a large bowl, beat cream cheese with vanilla extract until mixed through. Spread on cooled crust.

6. Arrange kiwi, cherries, blueberries, and strawberries decoratively on top of filling. Chill pizza until ready to serve.

Lettuce Explain

To **cream** is to beat butter, margarine, or vegetable shortening, with or without sugar, until it's fluffy. The process traps in air bubbles, later used to create height in cakes and cookies.

Spinach and Artichoke Dip

Creamy, cold, and garlicky flavored puréed spinach and artichokes and blended with scallions, sweet cream cheese, Parmesan and ricotta.

Serves: 6
Prep time: 10 minutes
Serving size: ½ cup

1 (10-oz.) pkg. cut spinach, thawed and drained

½ cup artichoke hearts, drained

3 scallions, chopped

2 garlic cloves, peeled

1½ cups plain low-fat yogurt

1 cup low-fat ricotta cheese

3 TB. freshly grated Parmesan cheese

2 TB. cream cheese

Salt and freshly ground black pepper

1. Place spinach, artichoke hearts, scallions, garlic, yogurt, ricotta cheese, Parmesan cheese, and cream cheese in a food processor or in a blender, and process until smooth. Season with salt and pepper.

2. Chill dip overnight for best results and serve with fresh, raw veggies cut into bite-size chunks; crackers; or sourdough bread cut in small pieces.

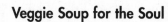 **Veggie Soup for the Soul** _____

This dip also makes a great sandwich spread.

Avocado Rolls

Fresh avocado chunks, sweet currants, refreshing cilantro, diced onion, and diced sweet red bell peppers are seasoned and baked inside crispy egg roll wrappers.

1 medium onion, chopped

1 large red bell pepper, seeds and ribs removed, and chopped

2 TB. chopped fresh cilantro

6 TB. dried currants

4 ripe avocados, peeled and cut in large chunks

12 egg roll wrappers

Serves: 10 to 12
Prep time: 15 to 20 minutes
Cook time: 40 minutes
Serving size: 1 or 2 rolls

1. Spray some olive oil in a skillet and heat to medium. Add onion and bell pepper, and sauté until tender.

2. Remove the pan from heat, let cool, and stir in cilantro, currants, and avocados.

3. Place 1 wrapper on a flat surface with a pointed edge toward you. Spoon a couple tablespoons filling in the center of wrapper, fold the point up and over filling, tuck underneath, roll the sides in toward the middle, and roll tightly to the opposite point. Moisten edges with water to seal.

4. Spray skillet with olive oil again, fry rolls until crispy, and serve hot!

Variation: You can also place the uncooked rolls on a cookie sheet and bake at 375°F for about 20 minutes on each side or until golden brown and crunchy.

Avocado rolls are a crowd-pleasing appetizer.

Baked Garlic and Brie

Hot, gooey, pungent Brie, spread thickly onto crunchy baked baguette slices with mild, semisweet baked garlic, makes for a great intimate date snack.

Serves: 2 to 4	
Prep time: 7 minutes	
Cook time: 30 minutes	
Serving size: 3 (6-ounce) slices	

2 to 4 large garlic heads	**2 to 4 tsp. olive oil**
1 crunchy French baguette	**1 (8-oz.) wheel Brie**

1. Preheat the oven to 350°F.

2. Slice the top off garlic with a sharp knife, and place garlic heads on separate small sheets of aluminum foil. Drizzle approximately 1 teaspoon olive oil over each head, and seal each head in foil. Bake for approximately 20 to 30 minutes or until soft.

3. Slice an X across the top of the Brie wheel, cutting through the skin. Place Brie on a cookie sheet, and add to oven approximately 15 minutes prior to garlic being done.

4. Slice baguette into 1½-inch-thick slices, drizzle olive oil between each slice (or spread with butter), and wrap in aluminum foil. Add to oven approximately 8 minutes prior to garlic being done.

5. When all is done cooking, serve bread and garlic and brie on a serving tray with a knife for each participant. Gently break off a clove of garlic, and squish the contents out of the skin onto a piece of bread. Use a butter knife to apply some melted Brie on top of bread and enjoy!

Sprouts of Info

Baked Brie and garlic can make for a perfect food for an intimate party. Serve with red wine. Follow with breath mints.

Sweet and Sour Lean Balls

This vegetarian version of sweet and sour meatballs contains browned, soy-based balls, seasoned with garlic, green bell pepper, cayenne, and scallions, and brushed with a pineapple and vinegar sweet and sour sauce.

1 pkg. ground beef substitute (Boca, Lightlife, Morningstar Farms, etc.)

½ green bell pepper, seeds and ribs removed, and finely chopped

5 whole scallions, finely chopped

2 garlic cloves, minced

1 slice sourdough bread, chopped finely

Egg replacer equal to 2 eggs, premixed

¼ tsp. freshly ground black pepper

¼ tsp. cayenne

Vegetable oil

1 cup unsweetened pineapple juice

6 TB. apple cider vinegar

4 TB. stevia

2 TB. tamari

1½ TB. arrowroot powder

¼ tsp. garlic powder

Serves: 5
Prep time: 20 minutes
Cook time: 10 minutes
Serving size: 4 balls

1. In a large mixing bowl, combine ground beef substitute, green bell pepper, scallions, garlic, bread, egg replacer, pepper, and cayenne, and mix well. Form into 20 (1-inch) balls.

2. In a large skillet, heat oil until hot. Add balls to the skillet, and fry until browned and cooked through.

3. In a saucepan over medium heat, combine pineapple juice, vinegar, stevia, tamari, arrowroot powder, and garlic powder. Whisk until smooth, and cook, stirring constantly, until thickened.

4. When meatballs are done, cover them in sweet and sour sauce. Arrange on a serving dish, and add toothpicks to each for self-serve snacking.

Sprouts of Info

Fresh pineapple juice contains an enzyme called bromelain, good for breaking down protein. Significant evidence suggests that bromelain has anti-inflammatory properties in the body as well.

Veggie Vocabulary

al dente   An Italian term used to describe pasta or rice that's cooked firm, but not hard or too soft. It's the ideal form of cooked pasta.

autointoxication   A condition caused by a constipated bowel in which the blood stream harbors and circulates bowel toxins throughout the rest of the body.

beans   Plants with edible pods and seeds eaten cooked as a vegetable.

bioflavonoids   Nutrients found mainly in the rinds of citrus fruits and in the edible skins of most fruits, such as grapes and apples. They play a role in strengthening capillary fragility and permeability and serve as antioxidants.

bob veal   Infant calf meat, slaughtered at about 2 to 3 days old. Regular veal is the anemic meat from a calf about 14 to 16 weeks old. Bob veal is cheap meat usually sold for processed foods such as TV dinners.

breatharianism   The philosophy that teaches that when a person reaches a perfect state of health and a natural state of being, he or she will be in perfect harmony with the Creator and require no food or water. Because of this, the aging process will be slowed dramatically.

carob (also called **locust bean**)   A tree used for its bittersweet leathery beans. The tree is native to the Mediterranean area and other warm climates. Carob is frequently used as a chocolate substitute.

casein (also **caseinate** or **sodium caseinate**) A milk protein used as an additive in some "nondairy" replacers. Read labels if you're eliminating all animal products from your diet.

ciguatera poisoning A toxin occurring mostly in reef-dwelling fish from tropical and subtropical climates; the toxin becomes more concentrated as it moves up the food chain. Commercially harvested red snapper and barracuda have been found to contain this toxin, but hundreds of other species have been implicated. Symptoms of ciguatera poisoning include diarrhea, vomiting, burning sensations in your mouth and throat, and numbness. It can affect the nervous system, heart, and respiratory system.

circulatory system The body system that pertains to your entire blood transportation system and consists of the heart, veins, arteries, capillaries, and blood vessels.

complete protein Contains all essential amino acids and is found in animal products and in some plant foods such as soybeans.

concentrated foods Most starchy and heavy protein foods such as animal products, baked potatoes, grains, nuts, and seeds. Concentrated foods are, for the most part, devoid of water content. When food combining, eat only one concentrated food per meal.

cream To beat butter, margarine, or vegetable shortening, with or without sugar, until it's fluffy. The process traps in air bubbles, later used to create height in cakes and cookies.

cruciferous vegetables Vegetables from a huge family called *Cruciferae* or *Brassicaceae,* or the mustard or cabbage family. Cruciferous vegetables include broccoli, Brussels sprouts, cauliflower, cabbage, kale, rutabaga, seakale, turnips, radishes, kohlrabi, rapeseed (canola), mustard, horseradish, wasabi, and watercress.

cruelty free or **manufactured with compassion** Terms that describe any product, such as household cleaners, solvents, dish detergents, cosmetics, toothpastes, beauty aids, mouthwash, and so on, that have not been tested on animals or made with animal derivatives.

curry A pungent mixture containing up to 20 spices, herbs, and seeds, turmeric chief among them. Other ingredients can include sesame seeds, cloves, cardamom, fennel, nutmeg, red pepper, black pepper, coriander, saffron, and pimento. Curry is generally found in powder form, but pastes and liquids are also available. Curry originated in India and is used to flavor many Asian foods.

cyanocobalamin   The usable part of the B_{12} vitamin. Other forms of B_{12} are called analogs, and scientists believe that the analogs could interfere with the useful cyanocobalamin, leading to a deficiency.

dairy   Any milk-based product such as cheese, milk, yogurt, and butter.

dendrites   Branched extensions of nerve cells that receive electrical signals from other neurons and act as conductors for signals to the cell body. Any new, repeated behavior creates new dendrites, making pathways for the new behavior.

diverticulitis   A condition in which abnormal protrusions of the lining of the colon become inflamed, causing severe abdominal pain, often accompanied by fever and constipation.

essential amino acids   Amino acids that cannot be manufactured by the body and that need to be supplied in the diet. These eight amino acids are lysine, isolecine, leucine, methionine, phenylalanine, thereonine, tryptophan, and valine.

essential fatty acids   Fatty acids that are not manufactured by the body but that are essential to proper functioning of the body. Essential fatty acids are the building blocks for hormones, cell membranes, and other chemical messengers.

ethics   A system of moral standards or principles.

eye teeth (also referred to as the **canines**)   In adults, these are teeth numbers 11, 6, 22, and 27 on dental charts, and C, H, M, and R in children.

farrow   To give birth; the term used to describe the birthing process for a female pig (sow).

feedlot   A place where cattle and other livestock are kept to be fed grain and soy products, and often to be injected with hormones and antibiotics as well. These feedlots exist to fatten animals before slaughter.

foie gras   A food made from duck or goose livers swollen by the force-feeding of corn. When the birds are slaughtered, their livers are removed, ground up, and sold as pâté, a fancy party spread for nonvegetarians.

free radicals   Unstable and destructive oxygen atoms. They are created by the body's natural processes, so everyone lives with an undisruptive amount at all times. However, when excess free radicals are created by exposure to toxins in the air, water, and diet, or by constipation and stress, the damage they do increases and can cause cancer, premature aging, and other degenerative conditions.

gelatin   The boiled bones and hooves of animals, often used to make capsules for supplements.

genetically modified organisms (GMOs)   Organisms that have been genetically altered using genetic engineering methods.

halitosis   Bad breath. Can be caused by constipation, which can result from eating animal flesh and dairy products.

haustras   The bulbous pouches that make up the large intestine. The haustras work by peristaltic action to move food material back and forth inside the intestinal walls for final processing before elimination.

healing crisis   A positive, natural detoxification process that the body performs when given the opportunity to release toxins. Symptoms are similar to illness and vary per individual, but usually are involved with the body's elimination channels. Symptoms of a healing crisis can include fever, diarrhea, nausea, headaches, boils, and foul or mucus discharges via the skin, bowels, respiratory system, and urinary system.

holistic   Emphasizing the whole and the interdependence of its parts, as a philosophy and way of practice as in natural medicine.

hominy   A type of corn sometimes referred to as *posole*, especially in the southwest. Ground up hominy makes the traditional southern hot breakfast dish known as grits. It can be further processed and ground into a powder to make cornstarch.

hybrid   The offspring of two plants of different breeds, varieties, species, or genera, produced through human manipulation and sometimes naturally, for specific genetic characteristics.

hypoglycemia   An abnormally low level of sugar (glucose) in the blood. Symptoms may include headache, shakiness, sweating, fatigue, intense hunger, and spacyness. Prolonged and/or severe drops in blood sugar cause brain damage.

incomplete protein   A protein that lacks one or more of the essential amino acids. Most incomplete proteins are found in plants, but eating a variety of foods ensures an adequate consumption of complete proteins.

irradiation   The process of showering foods with powerful radiation after the foods are placed in an irradiation chamber. The purpose of irradiation is to burst the DNA molecules of food-borne bacteria that might be in the foods and cause food poisoning. Irradiated foods must be clearly marked in markets, but no regulations are in place for restaurants or hospitals.

kosher   A Hebrew term for "proper" or "fit." The term is used especially for foods Orthodox Jews are allowed to eat according to Jewish law.

lacto ovo vegetarian   A person who eats no animal flesh but who does eat eggs and dairy.

lacto vegetarian   A person who eats no animal flesh or eggs but who does eat dairy.

legumes   Plants that have pods as fruits and roots that contain nitrogen-fixing bacteria. The word *legume* comes from French *légume* and from Latin *legumen,* which means "bean of unknown origin."

lemon zest   The concentrated, essential oils from the lemon peel.

lipemia   A condition in which dietary fat is accumulated in the blood. This condition lasts for about 4 hours after you consume fat as the liver attempts to break it down and eliminate it from the body.

listeria monocytogenes   A bacteria that can be found in and on dairy products, poultry, and eggs. Listeria poisoning is termed listeriosis; symptoms include headache, nausea, fever, and vomiting. It can be potentially deadly to those with weak immune systems such as the elderly, people with immune system diseases, and young children.

macrobiotic diet   Based on an Asian philosophy of yin and yang—both life force energies. Different foods are categorized as more yin or more yang, as are different conditions of the body. The idea is that you can help your body back to balance by feeding it more yin- or more yang-type foods. When the body is harmonized, it is free of disease.

mad cow disease, bovine spongiform encephalopathy (BSE), or **Creutzfeldt-Jakob (CJD)**   A fatal affliction of the nervous system. The disease is contracted by consuming the meat or other products of an animal afflicted with BSE.

meat   The term used throughout this book to define foods made from the flesh of animals.

metabolism   The ongoing interrelated chemical processes taking place in your body that provide the energy and nutrients to sustain life. Your metabolism is controlled by glandular activities in your thyroid, adrenals, and pituitary glands, and can be slowed or sped up depending on how your glands perceive the needs of the body. A slow metabolism can be linked to weight gain.

Murphy bag   A container of food snacks you can put together and use while traveling to supplement your meal or serve as a backup when you're stuck somewhere without vegetarian food.

net carbs   The amount of carbohydrate a given food has per serving, minus the amount of fiber it has per serving.

nut   The fruit of a plant that usually has a hard shell.

nutrient   Any substance that provides nourishment—for example, the minerals a plant takes from the soil or the constituents in food that keep a human body healthy and help it grow, maintain, and rebuild tissue.

ovo vegetarian   A person who eats no animal flesh or dairy but who does eat eggs.

peristalsis or **peristaltic action**   The wavelike contractions of the intestinal tract that move partially digested food through the digestive tract.

pescatarian or **pesco vegetarian**   A person who eats a primarily plant-based diet but who also eats fish or sea life. *Pesco* is Spanish for "fish."

pinch   A term used in cooking as an approximate measurement for dried spices, usually equivalent to about ⅛ teaspoon, or the amount of a dried spice you can pinch between your thumb and forefinger.

prostaglandins   Hormonelike substances that are made by fatty acids and have functions that include controlling smooth muscle contractions and regulating body temperature and inflammatory responses. They also play a role in blood pressure control, blood clotting, and water retention. Their balance is important in preventing PMS.

pyruvate   A naturally occurring substance in the human body that also is found in apples, red wine, and cheese.

quinoa   A tall crop plant, *Chenopodium quinoa*, of the goosefoot family. Native to Peru and Chile. It is known for its small, ivory-colored seed, which is used as a food staple.

radura   International, green, flowerlike symbol that's required by law to be posted where irradiated foods are sold, either nearby or directly on the foods themselves. This symbol is not required in places where these foods are served, however, such as in hospitals or restaurants.

refined grains   Grains considered less nutritious than grains in their whole state because of the grinding and high heating process. Examples of refined grain products are rolled oats and flours.

rendering   The process of separating fat from meat and other animal remains by the process of slow heating.

ruminants   Hooved animals that chew their cud, including cattle, sheep, goats, deer, and elk.

salmonella   A bacteria commonly found in and on eggs, and in and on poultry products such as chicken. Three types exist. The two common strains cause food poisoning called salmonella gastroenteritis, which creates acute symptoms such as diarrhea, cramps, fever, and vomiting and can be fatal for immunosuppressed individuals. A third type is responsible for typhoid fever.

scombroid poisoning   Occurs from eating fish that has not been properly refrigerated and has had the chance to begin decomposing. Proper cooking of fish does not eliminate this toxin. Symptoms of scombroid poisoning include allergic-type reactions, headache, diarrhea, dizziness, irregular heartbeat, itching, shortness of breath, flushing, muscle weakness, and a peppery taste in the mouth.

seafood   The term used in this book to refer to fish and other animal life from the sea.

seeds   Pods that contain the embryo of a new plant. You can think of them as the eggs of the plant kingdom.

seitan   A brown, slick-textured, high-protein, low-fat form of wheat gluten found in health food stores, generally near the tofu. It is made from whole-wheat flour and is used in sandwiches and stir-fries and as a meat substitute.

soya flour   Flour made from soybeans.

stevia   An herb used as a replacement for sugar that's suitable for use even by diabetics, although there's much political debate over its use. Stevia contains phosphorus, magnesium, potassium, selenium, silicon, sodium, and manganese, as well as small amounts of calcium, iron, and zinc.

stomach teeth   Molars. In adults, these teeth are numbers 3, 2, 14, 15, 30, 31, 18, 19, and 1, 16, 17, and 32 (the wisdom teeth, which may or may not come in). In children these teeth are letters S, L, I, and B, which usually come in first, indicating that the child is able to chew and digest solid foods. They are followed by A, J, T, and K.

tamari   A less-salty version of soy sauce; a dark, salty liquid made from fermented soybeans, used as a flavoring agent, especially in Asian foods.

tempeh   A fermented soybean, meat substitute product with a chewy texture.

testa   The protective coating on the outside of a seed that keeps it from germinating until conditions are right. The testa serves as an enzyme inhibitor, which can inhibit our digestion as well. Therefore, it's best to eat seeds that are well ground or chewed thoroughly.

textured vegetable protein (TVP)   Textured soy protein used as a meat substitute.

thickening agents (or **thickeners**)   Substances, usually starchy powders, that add body and thickness to foods like soups, stews, chowders, puddings, and gravies.

vegetarian   A plant-based diet of vegetables and fruits, nuts, seeds, and grains, and the people who follow this diet. Vegetarians do not eat meat.

waddling   A type of identification marking used in addition to or in place of branding. It is a procedure that entails cutting chunks out of the animal's hide in the area under the neck, making it large enough so ranchers can identify cattle from a distance.

whole foods   Foods that are created by nature and eaten in their unaltered, unprocessed state, such as raw fruits and vegetables.

whole grains   The most nutritious grains. They contain many vitamins and minerals, and when cooked correctly, can provide natural enzymes. A whole grain is in its unprocessed state.

More Vegetarian Cookbooks

With a few vegetarian recipes under your belt now, I'm sure you'll want to try more. Check out the following vegetarian cookbooks for more vegetarian recipe ideas. I hope you'll find more vegetarian recipes in them you can add to your list of favorites.

Cooking with Meat Substitutes

Cooking with Seitan: The Complete Vegetarian "Wheat-Meat" Cookbook by Leonard Jacobs and Barbara Jacobs (185 pages). This cookbook is a must for anyone new to or wanting to try seitan.

Fabulous Beans by Barb Bloomfield (143 pages). Beans have many benefits; they are a great source of protein, fiber, vitamins, and minerals—not to mention being extremely affordable! Use them often in place of meat—this cookbook gives you more than 100 vegan recipes to show you how!

Soyfoods Cookery by Louise Hagler (112 pages). This book focuses on all soy foods, their benefits, and easy ways to add soy to your diet.

The Tempeh Cookbook by Dorothy R. Bates (96 pages). Don't get stuck in a rut using tempeh only as a burger replacement or in stir-fries. With this cookbook, you can learn fun, easy, and healthful ways to cook delicious tempeh.

Tofu Cookery by Louise Hagler (160 pages). This beautifully photographed cookbook entices you with glossy 8×10 photos of the finished product and then shows you how to turn tofu into almost any dish, including main courses, appetizers, condiments, and even dessert. (One of my personal favorites for tofu creativity.)

Tofu Quick and Easy by Louise Hagler (96 pages). Filled with quick and easy menu tips for preparing more than 120 delicious tofu dishes.

The TVP Cookbook: Using the Quick-Cooking Meat Substitute by Dorothy R. Bates (96 pages). This book is fun and easy to understand as you learn to make TVP work for you as a meat substitute in a variety of dishes.

Low-Fat/Low-Cholesterol Vegetarian

Most vegetarian (especially vegan) diets are low fat anyway, but for those of you giving up meat for heart health, try these great cookbooks.

The Almost No-Fat Cookbook: Everyday Vegetarian Recipes by Bryanna Clark Grogan (192 pages). Grogan is wise in understanding how what we eat is deeply engrained in our psyche. Her recipes are for comfort foods such as low-fat chocolate cake, low-fat homemade ice cream, and even low-fat fries. All are dairy-free and healthful but still able to feed the psychological need.

Fat-Free and Easy: Great Meals in Minutes! by Jennifer Raymond (152 pages). Inspired by the requirements of Dr. Dean Ornish's "Open Your Heart Program," the author, a nutrition specialist and guest chef with Dr. Ornish, supplies quick, easy vegan meals sure to delight you and keep your heart healthy.

Lighten Up! Tasty, Low-Fat, Low-Calorie Vegetarian Cuisine by Louise Hagler (160 pages). In this cookbook, Louise shares her delicious and filling recipes that help you trim the fat, calories, and cholesterol from your diet while adding fiber. More than 130 easy recipes are featured.

The Vegetarian No-Cholesterol Family-Style Cookbook by Kate Schumann and Virginia Messina, M.P.H., R.D. (147 pages). Wonderfully creative and delicious recipes geared toward home-style cooking but with a new twist—and all low in fat!

Meatless Cooking

The American Vegetarian Cookbook from the Fit for Life Kitchen by Marilyn Diamond (422 pages). A fantastic potentially life-changing cookbook that helps you prepare vegetarian meals with proper food combining. Learn to eat well and stay fit with inside information about what occurs in your body when you eat various foods. Inside you'll find interesting and empowering information.

Classic Vegetarian Recipes by Sue Ashworth, Carole Handslip, Kathryn Hawkins, Cara Hobday, Jenny Stacey, Rosemary Wadey, and Pamela Westland (256 brightly photographed pages). This book is absolutely packed with close-up photographs of beautiful veggie dishes, along with the recipes, of course—I like to have the photos to see what looks good to cook. So far, everything made from this one has tasted as good as it looks!

Cooking Vegetarian: Healthy, Delicious, and Easy Vegetarian Cuisine by Vesanto Melina, R.D., and Joseph Forest (239 pages). This cookbook not only serves up a rich variety of vegetarian dishes, but includes nutrient analysis, shopping and simplifying tips, and information for creating full-flavored vegetarian meals.

Diet for a Small Planet by Frances Moore Lappé (479 pages). The first half of this book makes a strong political case for not eating meat; the last half contains recipes for a variety of meatless meals. Well researched.

GardenCuisine by Paul Wenner (386 pages). Wenner is the creator of the famous Gardenburger and GardenVegan, and not only shares more than 150 delicious recipes, but also tells how to heal yourself and the planet through meatless eating. Inspirational and motivational reading and cooking.

Meatless Meals for Working People by Debra Wasserman and Charles Stahler (96 pages). A great book for busy or hectic lifestyles; great tips for where and how to eat as a non-meat-eater. Also includes nutritional information.

Moosewood Restaurant Cooks at Home: Fast and Easy Recipes for Any Day by The Moosewood Collective (416 pages). Contains a huge variety, sure to please all tastes, along with low-fat vegan kids' foods and time-saving tips.

The Higher Taste: A Guide to Gourmet Vegetarian Cooking and a Karma-Free Diet by The International Society for Krishna Conciousness (161 pages). This book contains some of my favorite recipes for Indian, Mexican, Italian, Asian, and a variety of other delicious meatless dishes. It also explains why we can all be vegetarian and instructs you on how to make your own ghee and curd. The book contains a complete list of Govinda's restaurants (vegetarian Krishna restaurants) around the world. (This book might not be available in book stores. You can get a copy through ITV, 3764 Watseka Avenue, Los Angeles, CA 90034, 213-559-7670.)

Vegetarian Cooking for Everyone by Deborah Madison (742 pages). Described as the most comprehensive primer for vegetarian cooking ever published, this beautiful volume features 1,400 diverse gourmet recipes from the founding chef of the Greens restaurant in San Francisco. (The majority of the recipes are vegan.)

Vegan Cookbooks

Cooking with PETA: Great Vegan Recipes for a Compassionate Kitchen by the staff at PETA (223 pages). This fun book includes 200 favorite compassionate—animal-free—recipes and explains the sources of many vegan ingredients.

The Millennium Cookbook: Extraordinary Vegetarian Cuisine by Eric Tucker and John Westerdahl (258 pages). The Millennium Restaurant in the heart of San Francisco has been praised for its fabulous and innovative approach to vegetarian cuisine. This cookbook provides gourmet vegan recipes that are delicious and beautiful, and have an international flair.

Nonna's Italian Kitchen by Bryanna Clark Grogan (255 pages). So you can't figure out how to make cheesy-tasting Italian dishes without the cheese? This author makes vegan Italian look and taste *delicióso!* And she should know—*nonna* is Italian for "grandma."

The Single Vegan by Leah Leneman (127 pages). So many of my single friends tell me, "I'd eat better, maybe even vegetarian, if I wasn't cooking for just myself." This book is the answer. It features great ideas for recipes and even shopping lists and vegan staples to have on hand to make it easy.

Table for Two: Meat-and-Dairy-Free Recipes for Two by Joanne Stepaniak (192 pages). This is a much-needed vegan cookbook for couples. The author helps you create simple, tasty recipes for two requiring less than 30 minutes to prepare.

The Uncheese Cookbook: Creating Amazing Dairy-Free Cheese Substitutes and Classic "Uncheese" Dishes by Joanne Stepaniak (192 pages). This book is a hit with cheese lovers who want (or need) to go vegan. Turn nuts and other nondairy foods into your own dairyless Brie or un-cheesecake!

Vegan Vittles: Recipes Inspired by the Critters of Farm Sanctuary by Joanne Stepaniak and Suzanne Havala (contributor) (176 pages). Cited by readers as the best of the best vegan cookbooks, here's more proof if you need it: some turn from vegetarian to vegan after making these delicious mouthwatering recipes. You can't pass this one up!

Special-Needs Cooking

150 Easy Meatless Vegetarian Times Low-Fat and Fast Recipes by the editors of *Vegetarian Times* magazine (288 pages). Includes 175 tempting recipes using a variety of grains, such as quinoa, couscous, pastas, Asian noodles, and fresh vegetables.

American Heart Association Kids' Cookbook by the American Heart Association, edited by Mary Winston, Ed.D., R.D., with additions by James H. Moller, M.D. (127 pages). A cookbook for kids, the 34 recipes included in this book are mostly vegetarian, and 9 are vegan. Older kids can use this on their own, while younger ones will need some supervision.

Better Than Peanut Butter and Jelly: Quick Vegetarian Meals Your Kids Will Love! by Wendy Muldawer and Marty Mattare (176 pages). The title tells all! This cookbook includes 150 low-fat, low-sugar, kid-tested recipes.

CalciYum! Calcium-Rich, Dairy-Free Vegetarian Recipes by David and Rachelle Bronfman (192 pages). Worried about getting your calcium when you give up dairy? Worry no more. The 120 delicious dairy-free, calcium-rich recipes in this book show you how to get calcium from breakfast to dessert. These recipes are great for helping you build better structural system health.

Eat Right, Live Longer by Neal D. Barnard, M.D. (336 pages). Want to eat not only for longer life, but to live healthy longer? Find out how foods can slow and reverse some aspects of aging and play a role in weight, menopause, hypertension, diabetes, arthritis, and a host of other age-related illnesses. Healthful vegetarian recipes by Jennifer Raymond are included.

The Schwarzbein Principle Vegetarian Cookbook by Dr. Diana Schwarzbein (340 pages). This cookbook contains 371 high-protein lacto ovo vegetarian recipes. Dr. Schwarzbein specializes in hormone replacement therapy and reversing type II diabetes through her groundbreaking nutritional and lifestyle program. Her practice specializes in studying endocrinology, metabolism, diabetes, osteoporosis, menopause, and thyroid conditions.

Vegetarian Cooking for People with Allergies by Raphael Rettner, D.C. (128 pages). Includes many vegan recipes that are free of common allergy-causing foods—a great way for the allergy sufferer to go veg.

Vegetarian Cooking for People with Diabetes by Patricia Le Shane (144 pages). More than 100 low-fat vegetarian recipes are featured in this book that can help you manage diabetes while still enjoying tasty food.

Veggie-Related Videos and Instructional Posters

Cooking with Kurma: Gourmet Vegetarian (video). Kurma presents a vegetarian cookery video that has exciting, tasty recipes, many for great Indian-style foods. For those who like to follow along with a video instead of reading, what a fun way to learn to cook tasty veg!

A Diet for All Reasons by Michael Klaper, M.D. (video). In this presentation of the reasons for going vegetarian, Dr. Klaper shows surgical footage of a hard string of cholesterol being removed from a heavy meat-eater's artery—if that's not a great visual for giving up animal products for heart health, I don't know what is! Overall, this video is a very informative and entertaining presentation. Order by contacting Paulette Eisen Nutritional Services, 4900 Overland Avenue, #234, Culver City, CA 90230; 310-289-4173.

Healthy, Wealthy, and Wise (video). Based on the book *The Higher Taste*, which is based on the teachings of His Divine Grace A.C. Bhaktivedanta Swami Prabhupda. You'll find this video where you find *The Higher Taste*.

The New Four Food Groups Posters, the Choose Health! versions from Physician's Committee for Responsible Medicine. These 22×17-inch posters for kids as well as for adults use brilliant color photos along with serving recommendations for getting your nutrition without cholesterol or fat. Purchase via PCRM's website (www.pcrm.org) or at online bookstores.

Index

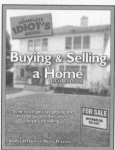
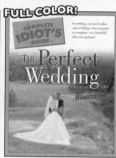
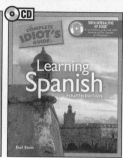

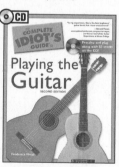